TRESNA, GATE OF LOVE

CHRONICLES OF A BALINESE PRIESTESS

FRANCES TSE ARDIKA

TRESNA
Gate of Love
Memoir One
Chronicles of a Balinese Priestess
Frances Tse Ardika

Editor: Tenyia Lee
Cover: Xavier Comos, Cover Kitchen

First Edition published October 10th, 2021
Copyright 2021 Frances Tse Ardika

ISBN hardcover 979-8-9850079-2-3
ISBN paperback 979-8-9850079-1-6

For more information, contact Frances@francestseardika.com

For Mom who brought me to life and to my soulmate, Adi.

1

BALI, OCTOBER 2000

*"This is your place, Frances. Bali has your name written all over it.
You gotta get here fast. 1,000,000 FAPs collected. —Cam"*

My business school friend, Cam, had scrawled but a few short lines on the back of a postcard I'd just received. Little did I know at the time how significant those two lines would be. I flipped it over. On the front of the postcard was an exotic Balinese dancer perched on a cliff with a temple rising from the ocean behind her. Being an architect's daughter, I wondered, *How did they build that temple?*

I'd received this postcard in October 1994 and, unbeknownst to me then, the idea of Bali had covertly burrowed into my subconscious. It would be six more years before I made the trip there

Cam and I had this ongoing competition to see who could collect the most Frequent Adventure Points or FAPs. We were constantly trying to out-do each other on who could rack up the most exciting life experiences. We were both twenty-four years young. Unlike the painfully slow accrual of airline points or trying to get to nine coffee stamps just to get one free, you get to enjoy your FAPs immediately.

The more adventures you had, the more points you earned – instant gratification!

Some examples:

- Leaving work early for a stroll in the park and diving into a pile of crimson, burnt orange and gold autumn leaves – 100 FAPs (minimum level).
- Savouring the last morsel of butter-poached lobster on my plate at an indulgent celebratory dinner at Canoe with my sales team – 800 FAPs.
- Visiting Bali in 1994, when the small Indonesian island was still little known to the rest of the world's jet-setting crowd – 1,000,000 FAPs indeed.

We started our FAPs competition when Cam moved to Hangzhou, China, to run his father's silk garment factory. Cam had an unfair advantage having taken the road less travelled while I had continued to toil away in our hometown of Toronto.

Collecting FAPs had helped to cure my broken heart and to start living again. Seven years earlier, I'd been unceremoniously dumped, over the phone no less, by my boyfriend Vern who had promised to marry me. I'd buried myself in my work and uprooted to San Francisco to escape all reminders of his existence. It was my friendship with Cam that had led me to Asia and, eventually, here to Bali.

October 6th, 2000, four days before my 31st birthday, I finally set foot onto Balinese soil. I've always been one to remember numbers and dates, sort of like how you always know when and where you heard a piece of important news. I didn't know it at the time, but the next few days would be etched in my mind for always.

Coming from Hong Kong where Cam and I had ventured into the world of Internet start-ups ten months earlier, I was overtaken by the sudden and inescapable rush of heat and humidity the second I exited the artificially cooled comfort of the plane. I wore my usual black "plane outfit" of comfy yoga pants and a long sleeve tee – perfect for the arctic levels of air conditioning in the airplane but utterly unsuitable for the sweltering tropical climate of Bali.

My mom should have been travelling with me. She'd flown to Hong Kong, intending to unwind with me for a week in Bali before we flew to Singapore for one of my best friends' weddings, but she'd been denied boarding in Hong Kong that Friday morning. She hadn't realized that Indonesia immigration required visitors to hold a passport that expired beyond six months of the date of entry.

Mom waved me onwards and said, "Go, go and relax. You travel all over the world by yourself. You'll be fine. Anyways, you'll be busy golfing every day. I'll get my passport renewed at the Canadian Embassy on Monday. I promise to get to Bali before your birthday."

So here I was in Bali, waiting for my golf clubs at the oversized baggage carousel, alone.

Ever the optimist, I decided this unfortunate setback might work in both our favours. I had harboured doubts that she would enjoy four days at a golf resort. Her idea of fun was shopping, shopping, and more shopping. I would also be saved from her constant nagging of, "Why do you always have to be in the sun so much?" Trying to explain to her that I was in fact golfing, not trying to be in the sun, would have been an exercise in frustration. I understood that she was constantly worried about me, my skin, and my happiness. However, she didn't quite appreciate that golf contributed significantly to my happiness. Golf provided a sanctuary from my stressful career, a way to hide from reality for a few hours. In fact, a game of golf earned me 3,000 FAPs. If it involved an ocean view, 2,000 bonus points!

As I walked out of the baggage area, about fifty men were waving handwritten signs with names like "Mr. Jeff" and "Mrs. Smith." My eyebrows drew together in confusion as I noticed the lack of surnames in some cases and first names in others. How were we expected to find our driver? I navigated my cart slowly through the sea of signs and leaned closer to read each one, looking for my name. Eventually I saw: "Miss Frances Tse" typed neatly on cream paper and pasted to a wooden placard with "Le Meridien Nirwana, Golf and Spa Resort" etched in gold. I steered toward the man with a huge sigh of relief.

The mustached man lowered the sign and introduced himself as Komang, then relieved me of my baggage cart. He led me to the waiting car and the driver hopped out to help with my suitcases. I climbed into the back seat of the dark green Toyota Kijang, and we were off.

I was mesmerized by my first glimpses of Bali. I half-listened to Komang saying something about entering Kuta as I thought to myself, how is it that the beach is right beside the airport? I turned my head to the left as we drove up a long white stretch of sand. The sun was still high. The azure water looked incredibly inviting. Despite the car's air conditioning, I sweated uncomfortably in my black city uniform.

Something felt different here. Slowly, I became aware of the spaciousness. There were no skyscrapers closing in around me; in fact, there were no buildings above two stories high.

I'd travelled to more than thirty-two countries including some smaller beach islands, and I'd never seen anything like this before; there weren't any highways despite the resort being 26 kilometres away from the airport.

We turned northwards from the beach onto a narrow two-lane road lined with little shops and cafés. Motorbikes and chickens scooted out of the way. We seemed to be one of only a handful of cars on the road. As we drove on, the shops disappeared. Emerald green rice fields came into focus on both sides of the road, and then a village emerged; hundreds of terracotta-shingled rooftops hovered above low walls hiding clusters of little black shrines. As our car bounced along the undulating road, the view became lush paddies again, these ones terraced.

At last, we reached a signpost with the resort name etched into white stone. Turning into the Le Meridien, we wound through a pristine landscape with the golf course laid out on either side of the asphalt. On my right, I saw the ocean at the end of the manicured fairway. This was my definition of paradise.

I was so excited; I practically jumped out of the car. I've always had a child-like spirit; my emotions always leapt forward whether it was appropriate or not. But I think anyone arriving to a hotel to be greeted by a ring of fragrant white flowers being draped over her head would have been just as ebullient. I tipped my nose into the abundance of flowers and inhaled the intoxicating scent of frangipani.

As if in a dream, I floated through the marble-clad lobby to the edge of the carved teak-wood balcony. I shook my head in disbelief. Right in front of me was a temple in the ocean with the sun setting behind it – the exact temple from Cam's postcard.

2

$\mathcal{I}$ trudged through the muddy rice fields of Nirwana Golf Course searching for my ball on the first hole. By the second hole, my Balinese lady caddy recommended the precise club to strike and showed me where to hit it. Her efforts were for naught. Her well-meaning advice might have worked for Tiger Woods, but it was lost on me.

My brilliant caddy chauffeured us towards the seventh hole, which could be named "Seventh Heaven."

This hole was a straight shot directly towards Tanah Lot Temple. Looking across the sparkling sea, I slowly released a deep breath I didn't know I was holding. The mystical temple seemed to float upon the ocean. Waves crashed against the rocky base of the temple, blessing the tall shrines with droplets of seawater. Snapping out of my reverie, I realized that my ball needed to launch over an unforgiving expanse of ocean to get to the tiny green. I peered over the cliff and thought, *How many white dimpled balls has the Indian Ocean swallowed?*

Back then, golf was my most fervent obsession.

Toronto's golf season ran from April to October. In my first year playing, I'd racked up fifty-four rounds, playing in the snow if need be. How? I was in advertising sales, and my friend Fred was a member of Clublinks, Canada's premier group of private courses.

Every Monday morning, I would start my calls. Sales calls? No, golf calls.

I'd run through my list of golfing clients until I'd filled at least two "client relationship-building" days on the fairways. Fred and I would follow up with one or two additional rounds on the weekend.

Golf was how I dealt with the systemic unfairness I faced at the 100-year-old newspaper giant, *The Toronto Star*, where I had been an anomaly in management, a 28-year-old Chinese woman.

There wasn't any overt prejudice to speak of, instead there was deeply entrenched male chauvinism.

In my first summer as a manager, I'd walk down the line of management offices and hear little else besides my own footsteps; I was usually one of the very few there. The majority of management – all older white men – made cameo appearances at our Monday briefings to report their sliding numbers. Meanwhile, my technology advertising sales team drove revenue higher month after month.

Fury motivated me to create women's golf clinics where I'd cement relationships with top female clients while we honed our skills in the real game of business – golf.

My golf obsession had me meticulously marking each one of my strokes, good or bad, on my scorecard. I even jotted down which club I'd chosen and my approximate yardage. I rarely got frustrated; instead, when I teed up, I'd whisper to myself, "Smile at the ball, and the ball will smile back."

Not many of my friends or clients had the time or inclination to play at my pace, so I embarked on a "Solo Amateur Tour" in the summer of 1998. I'd walk on as a single, paired with three men. Initially, it was intimidating. However, there were only two rules of golf: keep pace, which I could, and practice proper golf etiquette, which I did.

At the end of that epic summer, I'd hit my ball onto a green at Nicklaus North in Whistler with the guys shouting, "Whoa, look at that!" I looked up, thinking I'd hit a hole in one. Instead, a bear had walked onto the green as if he was going to mark my ball for me. Nicklaus North was my best score ever.

My golf tour expanded into the States when I moved to San Francisco in early 1999. I scored an eleven-dollar round as a local resident at Torrey Pines in San Diego. My old mentor from the newspaper, Drew, gifted me a game at Pebble Beach when I left Toronto for San Francisco. I'd waited for my Canadian golf buddies to visit me in California, but I'd already moved on to Hong Kong before they ever came. (I still have those gift certificates, which, thankfully, never expire.) My last golf adventure was the trio: Bay,

Village and Plantation courses at Kapalua, Maui. I'd stubbornly hobbled around even though I could hardly walk after finishing the Honolulu Marathon just days earlier. With all these courses under my belt, I'd smugly believed that I'd experienced the pinnacles of golf.

Nirwana reminded me that the golf frontier was endless. And that my life wasn't.

By October 2000, I'd been away from the fairways for ten months. I spent most days and too many nights hunched over a laptop.

Back in January, Cam had lured me to Hong Kong to join his Internet start-up, which we branded HungryForWords.com and called Hungry for short. Cam gave me a co-founder title, a pile of stock options and a promise of unlimited FAPs. Cam had invented the e-Flashcard, an innovative email tool for the voracious English learners in China and Japan. We planned to take the first-mover position in Asia, mimicking successful tactics from Silicon Valley. Our aggressive development plan would have me back in the States in six months to head our American operations. But six months turned into ten and returning to America turned into exile in Japan.

During my first four months at Hungry, I basked in the camaraderie and early success; I sold our first ad campaign to IBM Japan, proving we were a real business, not just a "business model."

On the verge of securing our Series A funding of ten million dollars from Morgan Stanley in May 2000, the Internet boom went bust.

My plans to move back to San Francisco evaporated overnight. Instead, I manned our shoebox of a Tokyo office and pitched to ad agencies with my sole Japanese sales manager in tow. By October, we were running on fumes. Morale was non-existent.

Desperate to leave, I hadn't figured out how to break it to Cam, who was not only my business partner but also one of my best friends. My stomach turned even thinking about it. *Never mind*, I thought, *I just need a massage, and then I'll figure it all out.*

I'd chosen Le Meridien Golf and Spa Resort in Bali because its name screamed, "This is your place, Frances!" 5-star, check. Golfing, check. A spa, check.

With unlimited expense accounts in my sales jobs, I'd led a well-pampered career wooing clients. Sleek city spas in Toronto greeted me weekly. San Francisco offered new forays into this hedonistic world of full-body massages, exfoliating scrubs and cocooning wraps. Whether it was wine-themed spa retreats in Napa Valley or hot stone massages in Japantown, I was an eager recipient. In Hong Kong, a Filipino freelance masseuse visited our shared company penthouse every Saturday to tackle the stubborn knots of me and my colleagues.

I'd learned to temper my expectations for resort spas. The diminutive spa therapist was stunningly beautiful, but I was dubious about her strength. Sadly, my skepticism was warranted. She tortured me for ninety minutes as her small and meek hands hesitantly squeezed and prodded. It was like being petted by someone afraid of animals. I still cringe thinking back on that experience.

After a soothing shower in the luxurious changing room, I marched up to the spa receptionist. I leaned over the counter and said, as calmly as I could, "That was the worst massage I've ever had. It's not her fault, but my masseuse, Puji, is definitely not in the right job. Don't worry, I don't want my money back or anything like that. Heck, I even gave her a tip. That girl needs retraining. Or maybe, she should move to another department. Anyways, I'm coming back tomorrow. Please make sure that I get your very best massage therapist. I came here to destress, not be stressed. Understand?"

This was Bali of the year 2000, not the polished hospitality mecca of today. The receptionist peered at me with her wide, frightened eyes, nodded nervously and whispered, "Certainly, Ms. Frances. We'll arrange the best for you tomorrow."

I huffed, "Good." And then, I giggled apologetically in a failed attempt to lighten the mood.

A young man had been quietly observing this exchange from the other side of the reception area. Little did I know that he was thinking the same thing: "That guest is right; Puji's massages are really bad."

3

My aching ankles yearned for relief as I limped off the 18th hole. Despite having a cart and caddy, I detested having to zip back and forth to the golf cart. Approaching my golf ball on foot not only gave me a better sense of each hole but also primed my state of mind for the next shot. I relished the feeling of bouncing along the springiness of the fairway grass, but I hadn't accounted for the heat exhaustion from playing golf eight degrees south of the equator. After four hours in the oppressive humidity and my unyielding spiked golf shoes, my throbbing feet screamed for mercy, and my body cried out for some much-needed TLC.

Thankfully, I had a three-hour spa session booked right afterward.

The same timid receptionist introduced me to the small Balinese man who'd been in the spa reception the day prior. His name was Adi. He had a genuine smile and the biggest biceps I'd ever seen. *Hmmm, he'll do.* I nodded to myself.

Automated booking systems didn't exist in the Bali of 2000. The booking chart was a hand-drawn list, times down one side and names of the spa therapists across the top. I later learned that my name had jumped around the chart all morning, pencilled in, and erased possibly fifty times. Most of the spa therapists were women. They'd heard about me — "The Complainer" – from the receptionist. None of them wanted to deal with a demanding "problem" guest, but they didn't want to forgo the big tip that I'd given to Puji.

My name finally landed on Adi's spot.

Once I'd changed into a robe, Adi led me away from the main spa area and down the stairs, explaining that more rooms were outside. He watched me carefully as I stepped onto slippery stones that wound a path towards one of the hotel wings.

I settled onto a sofa in the living room of a suite while Adi lowered himself onto a stool across from me. A terra-cotta basin filled with warm water and floating flowers sat between us.

"You already try foot reflexology before, Miss Frances?"

"No. I read in the spa brochure that it's a good technique to relieve pain."

"The pain depend on your body. Try to relax. Tell me if it hurt too much."

I prayed that the reflexology would ease my abused feet, forcibly reacquainted with the stiff leather golf shoes after ten months away.

Having my feet washed in warm fragrant water by this man's capable hands, I thought, *this is what babies must feel like when they get bathed.* Every motion was gentle and caring; he swirled soothing water around my toes, cleansed my soles with fragrant soap and exfoliated them with a coconut scrub. All the while, I had nothing better to do than stare down at the therapist as he pampered my feet.

This is how I came to watch Adi's every move.

With Adi bent over my feet, my eyes were directed to the top of his head. He straightened up and caught me staring at his dark curly hair. I quickly glanced away as I was now looking into his big brown eyes. I hadn't meant to stare, but there was nothing else for me to focus on. Adi smiled shyly and laid a towel on his thigh. He gently pulled my foot towards him to dry it before placing it back into my slipper. Next he did the same with the other foot and then removed the washbasin.

Adi held my left foot, examined the scar on my ankle and asked if he could massage it.

"Yes, it's fine. It's an old injury."

His touch was very soothing. If he looked up, he would've seen a silly grin on my face as my body relaxed. A minute later, the grin vanished as he hit a point on my foot that sent shooting pain into my shoulder. I pulled back and grimaced.

He looked up, "Your right shoulder is painful, yes?"

I chewed my lip and nodded.

"Let's check this point too." He dug his thumb into the bottom of my foot. I scrunched over from what felt like a jab into my lower back, even though he was nowhere near my back.

"Ouch," I squeaked.

"Ah, I see. You spend too much time on computer."

I nodded again, wondering how he could hit different points of my body just by touching my feet.

After another forty minutes of this torture, my feet were finally released. Adi led me into the bedroom which had been converted into a spa room. I disrobed and lay face down on the massage bed while he expertly draped sheets to cover me.

Adi explained he was going to give me a *lulur* scrub. I'd read about this traditional scrub that all Balinese brides have before their wedding day. It was a mix of rice powder, turmeric, ginger and essential oils. Adi's deft hands rubbed the mixture all over my back, and then he asked me to flip over. He carefully maneuvered the sheet to hide my private areas and then applied the scrub to my front. I felt like a well-marinated ham ready for the oven.

I lay face up while the scrub dried. The bedroom opened up to the bathroom through an indoor window framed with wooden shutters. From the massage bed, I watched as he filled a massive bathtub.

He returned and rubbed the dried scrub from my body, releasing all the dead skin with it. He wrapped me back into the sarong and led me to the shower. I stood there wondering what was next.

He said, "Yogurt polish."

"Ah, of course, yogurt polish."

I tried to sound nonchalant, but I was really thinking, *But I'm naked. I never wear the paper spa underpants, especially in Asia where double XL equates to a size 8. Whatever, I'd studied Fine Arts where we drew nudes. This was not the time to be demure.*

I shrugged off the batik sarong and stepped inside the oversized marble shower. Adi worked from behind, lathering my body in the cool yogurt starting from my neck and working his way down. My skin tingled after the warm spice scrub. As he bent in front of me, his hands ran up and down my legs. This was such a strange turn-on. I couldn't believe that I was standing here naked with this stranger rubbing yogurt all over me.

Adi avoided looking at me as he said, "Okay, shower and relax in the flower bath. I'll wait in the living room. Take your time to enjoy."

The sweet scent of frangipani rose from the hot steam as I sank into the oversized bathtub. I prayed internally that I could stay here forever. As the water cooled, I sighed, finally drying off and wrapping myself into the fluffy bathrobe that hung on the hook. Gosh, this guy thought of everything!

He led me back to the massage table for the finale – frangipani body lotion. He tapped some of the pale mint-coloured moisturizer onto his hands and smoothed the cool cream onto my dewy skin, trapping in the goodness of my three-hour pampering session.

Stepping into the living room, my body radiated wellness as I reclaimed my position on the sofa. Adi presented me with an aromatic cup of ginger tea.

Blowing on my tea to cool it, I blathered, "You've worked wonders. All the knots in my neck are gone. Usually, my shoulder hurts so much that it's hard to sleep. And sometimes, I get these weird pains right here." I pointed to my lower right stomach and giggled.

Adi just stared back at me.

"Sorry, am I talking too fast?" I asked, punctuating my question with another giggle and thought, *What is with this guy? It's like he can see right through me.*

"If you have pain, why you laugh?" asked Adi with his hands clasped together.

I chortled and said, "Right, my laugh. You know the funny thing? I laugh without realizing it. It's just a habit since I was young." Hesitating for a minute, I came back from my thoughts and said, "I don't have any pain now because the stomach pain comes and goes. Anyways, do you know what's wrong with my body?"

He looked down, seemingly embarrassed, and quietly said, "Yes."

Eager to learn more, I pushed on. "Tell me, it's okay. There's nothing to worry about."

Adi stared at a point above my head and then said slowly, "Well, yes. You have problem with your neck, shoulder and lower back because too much work on computer."

I nodded, "Yes, I work quite a lot."

"Your left ankle hurts when you walk too much. I don't sense problem with your stomach, but maybe because it don't hurt now?"

"You know all that just by touching my feet?"

"Some because of your feet. Some because of what you told me. Each point in your foot connects to a part of your body."

My body felt light, relaxed and somehow, healed. Adi had quite literally lifted the weight off my shoulders and released the tension in my lower back. That night, I slept like a baby.

An international smorgasbord was laid out every morning at the resort breakfast buffet: nasi goreng (fried rice) or mie goreng (fried noodles), an assortment of dishes such as babi guling (Balinese roast pork), pepes ikan (fish in banana leaves) and a whole Japanese section with sushi, miso soup and tempura. Cooks manned made-to-order egg and waffle stations too. I'd spend at least ten minutes walking around inspecting the buffet stations to plan the best line of attack.

Being in Bali, I gobbled down the Indonesian options, made even more delicious with spicy sambal sauce. A freshly made waffle topped with strawberries and maple syrup completed my breakfast. (Yes, dessert at breakfast!)

To recover from the food coma, I'd read by the multilayer rockpool under fragrant frangipani trees. The sweet tropical scent of the flowers mixed with the salty sea air lulled me into a dreamy state. The lush green leaves thrived, happy and healthy. I pondered if I could be happier and healthier too, living in a natural paradise instead of the concrete jungle of Hong Kong.

A pool boy gave me the time and I hurried down the stone steps to an open-air spa pavilion. My one-week vacation in Bali was halfway through. I had one final massage with Adi before leaving the resort for the last four days up in Ubud. Perched high above the Indian Ocean, facing Tanah Lot Temple, I thought I'd stepped onto a movie set. Adi crossed the expansive gardens, balancing a tropical concoction on a tray.

He handed me a colourful cocktail that held a pineapple fan on the edge and proudly said, "I prepared this welcome drink for you."

I thought, *Wow, he made me a special drink! This guy is so nice. Not like those players back in Hong Kong.*

I tucked 200,000 rupiah inside the letter and sealed the envelope. I hesitated. I wanted another one of his massages which were, by far, the best I'd ever had. Should I really do this? Would Adi think I was coming on to him? It was weird, but Adi felt like someone I already knew. This would be my last chance to see him. I shook my doubts away and gave the note to the spa receptionist to pass to Adi.

> *Dear Adi,*
>
> *Thank you so much for your amazing spa massages. You're the best massage therapist I've ever had (and believe me, I've had many massages).*
>
> *If you have time, I would like you to come to Ubud to Waka Di Ume tomorrow, Tuesday, October 10th at 10:00 a.m. to give me another massage. I don't want to risk getting another bad massage in Bali. I'll pay you the rates listed on the hotel spa menu and any transportation costs.*
>
> *Please leave me a message in my room #358 if you're able to come to Ubud tomorrow.*
>
> *Thank you,*
>
> *Frances*

Later, Adi told me that when I had tipped Puji 50,000 rupiah (equivalent to 300,000 rupiah today) and him 100,000 rupiah for my first massage, 200,000 rupiah for my second, and then, 700,000 rupiah for the third massage in Ubud, it equaled half a month's regular pay for him.

October 10th, 2000 was my thirty-first birthday.

Mustached Komang and his driver, Robert, were escorting me north to Ubud. I was moving to Waka Di Ume, a boutique designer hotel that was splashed all over the architecture and travel magazines I collected. We bumped along the two-lane road, past verdant rice terraces shimmering from gold to emerald green. We passed no other cars on the road, only an occasional scooter.

My tiny automatic camera couldn't capture Bali's stunning natural treasures. My eyes tried to soak it all in, but I kept turning my head trying to look in all directions at once – the scenery was so expansive. The pure vividness was beyond imagining. Massive mountains rose from undulating rice fields. On the other side, the rice fields raced down to the sea, azure ocean merging with the cerulean sky.

We drove under a canopy of tall trees that lined both sides of the road. At one intersection stood a massive Banyan tree. As we passed, Robert the driver honked his horn twice.

"Why did you honk your horn? There's nobody else around here," I asked.

Robert said, "I'm asking permission from the tree spirits to pass."

Komang pointed out the sacred Banyan tree and told me how Balinese revere these trees and would never chop one down. The tree's distinctive tangle of roots, branches and trunk emerged from the earth, dominated the landscape and dwarfed all the other surrounding trees. Pura Dalem, one of the three main village temples, and the village cemetery are found in close proximity to Banyan trees. The Balinese believe that powerful spirits live in these trees.

Robert piped up again and elaborated, "We might disturb the spirits when we pass the tree, so we ask that they excuse us." This explanation made me smile. How polite!

I fell in love with Ubud the second we entered the quaint little village. At the bottom of the main road, aptly named Monkey Forest Road, jumping monkeys greeted us. More reserved monkeys sat further away on stone walls, protecting their babies and grooming each other. Monkey Forest Road was a one-way street heading north, lined with a hodgepodge of tiny, open-air shops with a few cafés dotted here and there.

Astonishingly, everything for sale was displayed openly; there were no walls, no doors, and no windows to the shops. We passed brightly patterned sarongs flapping in the wind, a rainbow of glittering beads separated into woven baskets, sparkly sexy sandals, coffee-coloured wood statues of giraffes, ducks . . . and a penis? – I looked over my shoulder to double-check – indeed, a row of erect phalluses lined one shelf! And in front of every shop on the floor were these little square saucers filled with vibrant flower petals. I wondered, *what are those?* This was one big open shopping mall!

I made a mental note of which shops to explore on foot when Mom arrived from Hong Kong later that evening.

The car headed north out of town and Komang pointed out the Royal Palace – ancient low buildings hiding behind an ornately carved gate of stone. A few kilometres further, Robert turned the car into Waka Di Ume. This designer haven was a collection of thatched cottages with modern aesthetics. The understated terrazzo tiles and linens in hues of cream, grey and black were a massive departure from traditional Balinese design, which tended towards the ornate.

I navigated the uneven stones set into the grass as the bellboy led me to my "Sunset" cottage.

The welcome drink of lemongrass, pineapple and orange danced on my tongue as I sat at my little terrace, facing a view of uninterrupted rice fields.

A small thought fluttered into my head: *A massage with Adi is definitely a gratifying way to celebrate my birthday.*

My stomach had sudden butterflies as I glimpsed Adi walking tentatively towards me. He was half an hour early. The morning sun highlighted the angles on his face as he drew closer. His smooth mocha skin broke into laugh lines as he grinned widely in greeting. Was this what my rebound guy looked like? My friends had spent seven years trying to get me to move on. I'd always been one step ahead: dodging passes, declining blind dates, and cementing another layer over my protective wall. Before I could fully analyze these strange stirrings, I leapt out of my chair and asked Adi to sit down, offering him the other welcome drink.

I stepped into the cottage and looked at the bed, draped in wispy, romantic mosquito net. Quickly, I stowed the pillows and bed runner in the wicker linen closet in the open-air bathroom. With the volcanic stone tub and tropical foliage cascading down the walls, it was a bathroom straight out of a magazine. Slipping out of my camisole, strapless bra, flouncy skirt, and underwear, I donned a light cotton kimono.

A warm feeling spread through my body as I invited Adi into the room.

Shifting from one foot to the other, he asked, "May I use the bathroom?"

"Of course. Go ahead. Take your time."

I glanced at the bed and wondered, *Why does this feel awkward?* It was just a massage. A voice at the back of my mind whispered, *Really?*

While Adi held up my sarong for privacy, I clambered onto the bed, shrugging off the kimono, and laid face down.

Adi draped the sarong over my body and asked, "Are you comfortable, Miss Frances?"

I nodded and then realized he couldn't tell with my head laying on its side, so I mumbled, "Yes, very comfortable."

Adi reached for a small bottle of massage oil on the bedside table. He unraveled the twine covering, popped out the lid and held the bottle under my nose. I breathed in the uplifting scents of cinnamon, citrus and peppermint. Adi showed me the bottle, labelled "Energizing," saying this was the same oil that I'd chosen at the spa. This guy is incredibly thoughtful. He had remembered which massage oil I liked.

He asked me to relax while he adjusted my sarong. Starting with my right leg, he took long strokes, which became stronger and more rhythmic as he moved up and down my leg. I exhaled softly as his firm touch sent shivers up my spine. I could barely hold in my gasp of surprise as his fingers eased the tension in my body, which somehow released the tightness in my heart.

Rays of sunlight seeped through the thatched roof, making abstract, slanted patterns across the speckled terrazzo floors. The whirl of the ceiling fan did little to cool my burning body. I sighed involuntarily in pleasure as Adi moved to my other leg. How did such a small man exude so much power?

Adi spread the healing massage oil onto my back, moving slowly from the top of my buttocks, then tracing up my spine and over my shoulders. I felt like purring; my body surrendered. Despite Adi being nearly a stranger, I felt protected instead of vulnerable.

I must have dozed off. The next thing I remembered was Adi gently shaking me awake, smiling at me shyly.

"Sorry to wake you. Please turn over," he said, holding the sarong up for my privacy.

"Oh. Okay." I slurred as I slowly rolled over and quickly wiped the dribble of drool from the side of my mouth.

How does he not break into laughter? I studied his serious face while he rearranged the sarong around the front of my body. His movements were quick yet precise.

Adi rubbed more massage oil between his hands while he observed me. He picked up my right leg, bent it at the knee, leaned in towards me and held my foot at his stomach, massaging the sole of my feet. I inhaled as he stretched me deeper. He ran his coffee-coloured hands up and down my leg in a rhythmic motion. I was transfixed. I couldn't stop staring into his intense dark brown eyes. I wanted to reach out and touch his long curly eyelashes, so soft and inviting.

Overcome with the headiness of my own cinnamon-orange-peppermint scented body mixed with the jasmine flowers on the bedside table, I pulled my eyes away from Adi as he held up my left leg. I focused instead on the drapes, thin muslin cotton swaying in the whirling of the ceiling fan, that shielded us from the noontime glare. He stroked my ankle slowly, working deeper into my calf and inched up my inner thigh. I bit my lip and held my breath, pushing down an unbidden moan of pleasure. Adi let the sarong fall back over my legs and moved over to my arm. I exhaled.

Adi stood beside me as he massaged my right arm. He was so close that I felt him shudder slightly as he moved up my shoulder and gently brushed my hair to the side. I drew the sarong around my body when he asked me to sit cross-legged on the bed. Adi climbed onto the bed and knelt behind me. He bent my head to the left and pressed down on the side of my neck, trailing his fingers down my shoulder. He switched to the other side. My eyes closed in pleasure, not wanting him to stop.

When I opened them again, Adi was kneeling beside me and said, "I hope you enjoyed the massage, Miss Frances."

Without a second thought, I reached over and kissed him as my sarong fell away from my body.

4

"Frances, are you listening to me?" Mom peered into my face. "You look a little flushed. Do you have a fever?"

"No, Mom. I'm fine. It's just hot here in Bali."

I snapped out of my daydream. My morning with Adi was beyond out of character. *What is up with me?*

After my massage, Komang and Robert had returned with the car to escort me down to the airport to pick up my mom. Stroking his moustache with eyes glinting, Komang promised us the best barbequed seafood down at Jimbaran Beach while he directed Robert towards the fish market. Popping out of the narrow laneways, we found ourselves in a parking lot facing the cobalt ocean and blindingly white sand beach. Komang led us through the dimly lit café, past tanks of fresh seafood out to the beachside where wooden tables and chairs were dotted along the beach. I plopped down on the table closest to the water and kicked off my sandals while Mom sat down hesitantly beside me.

"It's too hot here. This is no good for your skin. You're already too dark from all the golfing and swimming," Mom admonished as she pulled her massive hat over her face, already half-covered behind her fancy designer sunglasses. Rummaging in her bag for sunscreen, she passed me the tube and indicated with her chin that I should slather it on my face.

"Mom, just relax. It'll be sunset soon, so it'll cool down. Look how beautiful it is. Can you believe you're finally in Bali?" I asked as I dabbed on a bit of sunscreen to avoid further commentary.

"What's good here?" Mom asked, flipping through the plastic-laminated menu.

"Umm, seafood? Let's go check it out."

We walked back inside the café to handpick our seafood. Being avid cooks and Chinese, we'd never trust the restaurant to willingly part with their freshest inventory. We assumed that they'd dump their old stock on tourists. I peeked inside one of the Styrofoam bins. The prawns glistened in their firm skins as I scrutinized them, one by one, and tossed a select few onto the metal scale.

Live lobsters and snappy crabs held pride of place in the glass tanks. Unsure of which crustacean to choose but knowing Mom preferred crab, I vacillated.

Mom interrupted my deliberation. "It's your birthday so we're getting lobster. Don't get one too big or the meat will be tough," she said, pointing to a medium-sized one.

Laughing, I wheedled the price down until the owner wailed, "You bankrupt me!"

I pointed to two young coconuts still attached to their siblings on a big branch. A cook hauled one onto a massive slab of wood and cracked it open with an old-fashioned cleaver. He then reached for the other.

Mom smiled as the waiter settled the mammoth coconuts on our table along with frosted glasses of ice and slices of lime.

She wedged off the top of the pale, green coconut, inspected the inside, and sipped at the straw warily, "Hmm, this is sweet and refreshing, but it needs to be cold."

"Add some ice," I said.

"No, no ice cubes. Dirty. Don't ever eat ice in places like this, Frances."

Holding my tongue, I sipped my own lukewarm coconut and drank in the sunset as the sky ignited in varying shades of deep cherry, cotton candy pink, plum purple, and tangerine, reminiscent of a Turner painting.

Platters of smoky seafood arrived. Everything had been butterflied, slathered with spicy tomato sambal and grilled over coconut husks. We tucked into my birthday feast. Mom noisily sucked the juice from the lobster legs, one at a time. She had far more patience than me.

❋

With Mom having only one full day in Bali, I'd instructed Komang that we wanted to go where locals go, eat the food that locals eat.

He smiled widely and said, "Yah, yah."

I'd later learn that "Yah, yah" means "Yah, whatever lady, I'm going to do exactly as I please, not what you want."

For example, if you're confirming an order and ask, "Will this be ready on Tuesday?" You'll get back a "Yah, yah," meaning, "Not a chance. In fact, my shop will be closed for ceremonies, but I'm not going to mention that to you now."

I mapped out a plan catered to our two shared interests: shopping and eating. We'd start at the artisan villages, lunch at a local warung, shop at the Ubud handicrafts market and dine at Café Wayan, an outdoor café renowned for Rijstaffel, a Dutch-Indonesian feast.

Two massive oil paintings by the same Balinese artist caught my eye; one portrayed a traditional fruit market under a Banyan tree and the other depicted the terraced rice fields with Mount Agung in the backdrop. The gallery rolled up the canvases. I had no idea where these paintings would finally be displayed, as they were huge and I still had no fixed address. No matter, they'd have a home when I found one.

Mom was less impressed with the silver shops as she preferred "real jewelry." I bought delicate filigree dragonflies and butterflies for various friends in Hong Kong, Tokyo, and Toronto.

Komang insisted that we had to visit the volcano for lunch.

"No, we're really not interested in volcanos. We want the best local place for lunch."

"Yah, yah, there is a good restaurant at the volcano."

"Really? A local place? One you would eat at with your family?" I asked as my eyebrows scrunched up in doubt.

"Yah, yah! Let's go."

Mom looked at me and said in Cantonese, "Let's not argue. He's local. Maybe the restaurant is good?"

I was skeptical, but I got into the car and sat back as we drove an hour north to see the famous volcano.

Mount Batur and the surrounding Kintamani area were underwhelming. The volcano was a large grey mass of rock without the lushness of Ubud or any rice terraces.

The 23rd mile of my one and only marathon had been at Diamond

Head, a volcano in Honolulu. Had Diamond Head been as unremarkable? I hadn't noticed at the time, focused as I was on dragging my feet one in front of the other in my attempt to finish the grueling marathon. The peanut butter sandwiches at the finish line had tasted like heaven. At this volcano in Bali, I craved succulent satay, rich curries, maybe some more smoky barbeque seafood.

Robert pulled the car into a nearby tourist restaurant with "All You Can Eat" buffet signs. My eyebrows went up. "This is the place?"

"Yah, yah," responded Komang as he held the door open for Mom.

I followed them inside and saw a lackluster buffet area on one side with tables and chairs facing the aforementioned grey mountain. I opened the first metal buffet pan, revealing over-fried greasy noodles. The next tray held dry-looking beef satay sticks that had likely been sitting there for hours. I was livid.

I turned around and hissed, "We're not eating here. This place is for tourists. It's not local food."

Mom tugged my arm and said in Cantonese, "*M say faan, sik siew siew.*" *Don't make a big deal, let's just eat a little bit.*

I shook my head in stubbornness. This is not what I wanted to show my mom. She did not travel all the way from Toronto to eat some substandard fare that could give her a bad case of Bali Belly.

"Let's go, Mom." I marched back into the car with my mother in tow.

Fuming and through clenched teeth, I glared at Komang and stated, "We want real local food. Stuff that you'd eat."

Robert turned from the driver's seat and bravely spoke up, "You want to eat what we eat?" He was looking a bit astonished. Remember, this was Bali in 2000, when packaged holidays were the norm and Anthony Bourdain wouldn't arrive for another decade. "Umm, I can take you to my mother's market in Gianyar."

"A local market. Yes, that sounds great. Let's go." I turned to Mom. "Wait Mom, I'll get authentic local food for you soon."

My mom shook her head and smiled at her relentless daughter.

Half an hour later, we wove our way through a crowded street market, following Robert's lead. We'd left our "Yah, yah" tour guide Komang back in the car. Balinese women wearing colourful sarongs and T-shirts balanced huge woven baskets perched on their heads as they bartered and joked. Robert stopped in front of a rickety satay stall. The sizzling chicken satay was dripping hot oil into the burning coconut coals. The smoky, salty, sweet aroma was mind-boggling.

I asked, "How much?"

The weathered old man said, "One dollar."

I said, "One dollar each? I'll take ten."

Both Mom and Robert burst out laughing. They understood that ten satay sold for $1.

I would've happily paid the man ten dollars as I bit into the most succulent and spicy satay.

Robert raised his eyebrow at me, "Is the local food you've been looking for?"

"Yah, yah! I mean, YES!" I laughed back.

Standing in the middle of that bustling market with chicken juices dripping from my chin, this moment would become one of my happiest memories with my mom in Bali. As I tucked my change back into my wallet, Adi's business card slipped out. I picked it up and quickly shoved his card behind my HungryForWords.com name cards in my Muji aluminium card holder. That was safer – I didn't want to lose the only proof that Adi actually existed.

5

The gleaming skyscrapers sparkled in such contrast to the swaying coconut trees of Bali. We'd only flown two and half hours, but we could've been in another world.

Our taxi pulled into the enormous entrance of the Conrad Centennial Singapore Hotel where Nate, one of my best friends from university, was hosting a second reception for his bride's family. Last month in Toronto, Nate had married Rachel, a former Singaporean airline stewardess, in a proper church wedding followed by the requisite Four Seasons dinner reception. This was part two of their epic wedding.

Land of shopping malls and hawker stalls, Singapore suited my mom. The bellboys rushed to collect our baggage and whisked us to our modern suite. I stepped across the plush carpet to the floor-to-ceiling windows that faced two other shiny towers. Everything was efficient. Sterile.

It was still early, but Nate insisted on bringing us to the food court for breakfast. Food court for breakfast? Nate introduced us to his Singaporean favourites – fish ball noodles, a sizzling plate of *chow kwei tau*, and finally, a massive pile of shaved ice with fluorescent green jelly noodles, coconut milk and palm sugar syrup. Mom swooned with delight.

Nate said, "Auntie Bessie, why don't you go back to rest. I'll take Frances to get a foot reflexology massage."

I stopped in my tracks. "Did you say foot reflexology?" I asked, as my mind flew back to Adi.

"Yes, there's a massive spa right here inside the mall – the Singaporeans have perfected every aspect of shopping," said Nate.

"Um, okay, let's go. Never argue with the groom, right?"

Rows and rows of high-tech massage chairs lined the glass walls facing out to the mall. Nate slumped into a chair beside mine. The massage chairs had built-in washbasins. The therapists washed our feet, covered the washbasin and stretched out my legs to work on my clean feet.

Unlike Adi, this masseuse poked my feet with a sharp wooden peg and it hurt like hell. I asked, "Nate, you're enjoying this?"

"The more pain, the better, Fran."

"I tried reflexology in Bali, but there wasn't this painful stick." I grimaced as the woman jabbed my foot again.

Nate pressed his two fingers to his right temple and said, "I have mixed feelings about Bali. I love the island, but my last trip there, years ago, was with Pam and well, it was rather… awkward."

"I had no idea that you guys had met up again," I said. Pam was Nate's ex. Nate and Pam had had an intense romance during and after university, and ending the relationship wasn't easy. "What happened?" I asked cautiously.

"After years of waiting for her, she suddenly wanted to get back together. But I'd just met Rachel," Nate mumbled, looking straight ahead.

I sympathized with Nate's past heartache, but I pushed away the sadness and asked, "Talk about bad timing. If Rachel wasn't in the picture, would you have gotten back together with her?"

Nate paused before replying. After a moment of deliberation, he said, "That's a moot point because I was already with Rachel. Regardless, I'd already moved on."

"You certainly did," I said, pointing to his wedding ring. "I'm happy for you, Nate. Now it's my turn to find my forever guy with the 4Cs."

Nate tilted his head to the side and said, "Car, Cash, Career and Condo? Really, Fran? You've changed, living in Asia. I'd never figured you for one of those women."

I broke out laughing, "I've never heard that definition! I'm talking about Curiosity, Consideration, Communication and Compassion."

"That's the 4Cs? Not here in Singapore. Girls only want the guys with the goods."

Wrinkling my noise, I said, "That's so shallow. Remember that biz school trip to Harvard? When we each made a list of our top qualities we wanted in our future spouse?"

"I wasn't at that lunch. Jason told me about it though, he said he wanted a glamourous lady like Jackie Onassis. And he got it when he married Suzie."

"Well, seems like everyone but me has found their ideal mate. Keitha and Tom, Crystal and Ted, Ian and Cathy, and you and your Singaporean airline stewardess – every boy's dream!" I nudged him in the shoulder, "You know, I'm just teasing right? I'm so happy that you finally found 'The One.'"

Nate fell quiet. After a moment, he ventured, "Has there been anyone since Vern?"

I winced and looked down at the masseuse stabbing the torturous stick into my sole. That pain paled to the hurt of hearing Vern's name said out loud.

"No, no one. Vern was my 4Cs. I don't know how to come back from that."

Mom zipped up my dress, turned me around, inspecting me from head to toe and sighed happily. You'd think I was the bride, the way she was acting!

The saying "Something old, something new, something borrowed, something blue" jumped into my head as I gazed in the full-length mirror. An unrecognizable girl looked apprehensively back at me.

I'd had this slip of a dress cut from an ancient piece of powder blue silk covered in delicate patterns of sequined embroidery. My sparkly toenails peeked out from the strappy new sandals. Kai Ma, my godmother, had given me a taffeta shawl in ethereal shades of shimmering blues to cover my bare shoulders.

At work, I wore tailored Armani, preferably black, or less extravagant Banana Republic suits paired with a bit of softness like a silk bodysuit. I was not used to looking like a fairy princess. Seeing my reflection dressed like this, I thought, *Maybe I have a chance to fit in with this Singaporean set.*

Loud chattering and gaiety streamed forth from the bridal suite. Pushing the door open tentatively, I glanced around for Nate while Mom took up rank among the infamous posse of aunties. The cloying and clashing scents of expensive perfumes combined with the flamboyant outfits made my head spin.

Rachel crossed the suite, grabbed my hand and squealed, "You're the blue girl. Look! Even your nails are blue, la!"

On the surface, it sounded like a compliment. But did I detect a mocking edge? I couldn't place my finger on it. Perhaps I just wasn't used to the Singaporean "la" at the end of every sentence.

I stood at the edge of the room to observe the tea ceremony.

Rachel, ensconced in a red silk cheongsam, bowed, poured tea, and offered the cups to her parents one at a time. In return, each parent gave their only daughter a red envelope and little silk pouches filled with family heirlooms which Rachel placed on the ornate tray. Nate did the same for his in-laws. After the newlyweds poured tea for Nate's parents, each aunt and uncle followed, in order of birth. The staggering pile of jewellery and cash teetered precariously on the tray, but Rachel stashed everything safely away before anything precious tumbled down.

Later that night at the dinner reception, course after course of overly rich but bland Cantonese banquet food went mostly untouched; I much preferred the aromatic spices of Mom's simple, home-cooked Shanghainese dishes. Looking down at my bowl of gelatinous shark's fin soup, I wished I could magically replace it with Mom's hearty pork and spinach wontons. I looked over and saw her looking as bored as I felt. We didn't know a soul at our table, set at the edge of the ballroom.

I smiled down at my bare feet under the tablecloth when the last course was finally served. At least there was one saving grace of a Chinese banquet: No dancing.

6

was back in Hong Kong where friends had lined up a series of belated birthday celebrations for me. I appreciated their gesture, but thinking back to Bali, I felt like I'd already commemorated the special day with Adi.

"Audrey, you've outdone yourself!" I said, gazing at the overflowing vases of flowers, low candles, and sparkly baubles that adorned the long table, a birthday bash of blues and purples.

Hailing from New York and Taipei, Audrey had triumphed in her interview with Cam, nailing the ninth position at HungryForWords and instantly capturing Cam's heart. The two had been dating ever since.

My smile faltered as I took in those seated at the table: Mom, my best friend Grace, Kayo, and some colleagues who'd been hired when I was mostly in Tokyo. Other than Kayo, a university friend whom I'd recruited to Hungry in our early days, the faces smiling back at me were strangers. Cam and Jake, the other two co-founders at Hungry, were visibly absent.

Only a few months earlier, our team had been inseparable. Start-up life was intense; we took it to another level of closeness. Being ensconced in our open office where we could follow the sound of each other typing for twelve hours a day wasn't enough. Kayo and I also lived in Jake's penthouse. On the rare Sunday off, we'd gather for high tea at The Library; journey to Macau for Portuguese seafood; or simply huddle on the couch to play cribbage.

Jake and I had been circling each other for months; flirting across our open office or networking at dotcom launches. He'd slowly drawn me out of my shell. Audrey had predicted that Jake would be making a move soon – perhaps at his birthday cruise. My heart sunk and with it my hopes, when he boarded the Chinese junk, with his arms draped proudly around his ex-girlfriend.

Audrey later told me that Cam had whispered, "I don't know what he's doing."

Perched on a hard wooden bench at the end of the creaky boat in Hong Kong harbour, as far away from the canoodling couple as possible, I shivered despite the sultry night. After enduring the party with no way to escape, I was the first to disembark at midnight. Audrey came home with me to dissect the last six months of Jake's actions.

The following morning, Jake shook me gently awake. "Hey sweetie, what are you doing in my bed?"

"Oh, Audrey slept over so I gave her my room and I slept here. You said that you weren't coming home."

"Actually, Lizzie misplaced her keys so we came back here last night, or maybe you can say earlier this morning."

I blanched. "Lizzie's here?"

"No, she went home. We slept on the rooftop."

Imagined scenes of them having sex under the stars invaded my thoughts, and tears leaked from my eyes.

Jake took my hand and peered into my face, "Why are you crying?"

"I… I think I really like you." I hiccupped. "I thought you felt the same way. All those times we were together. You even slept with me that night with your arms around me." *Yeah, the heater was broken that night, and it was freezing, but we kissed...almost...*

"Oh, honey…" Jake raised his eyebrows, pausing like he needed a moment to find the right words. "You're like a sister to me. I'm not worthy of you. You're too good for me."

I flinched as his words hit me. He might as well have said, "It's not you, it's me." I fumbled out of his bed feeling mortified. Jake reached out and pulled me into a hug. I froze. I was such a fool.

After that, I kept my eyes downcast at the office, not wanting to see the pity in Audrey's face or the questions left unasked from the rest of the team. Gone were the days of joking and camaraderie. The only blessing was that Jake spent every night at his girlfriend's place.

Jake's absence from my birthday made sense, but where was Cam?

Tucking into the fiery dishes of hot and sour soup, fish fragrant eggplant, and sizzling General Tso prawns, Grace looked up and asked, "Hey, what's wrong? Don't tell me the food's too spicy?!"

We were at her favourite Szechwan restaurant, ChongQing, a narrow shoebox of a place on Elgin Street in SoHo to continue my birthday celebrations.

I slapped on a smile and said, "No, no. I can actually handle this spice level after trying all the spicy sambals in Bali. I'm just not that hungry."

"Oh YUM! Jonathan and I had the best BBQ seafood on the beach. It was smokey and coconutty and it was slathered with this killer sambal sauce! Sooo…are you gonna tell me about your time in Bali? You haven't said anything about it. It's not like you. Are you okay?" asked Grace, tilting her head and studying me more closely in the dim light.

"Going away to Bali kinda woke me up to the nightmare of my life at Hungry. I've never felt so alone." I looked down at my hands, struggling to hold on to how I'd felt just the week previously, wrapped in Adi's arms.

Grace grew still and put her chopsticks down, "But you're such a tight-knit team…"

Shaking my head, I said, "Not anymore, things have changed. The team's now twenty-one people, not nine. It's splintered into little cliques. When I'm in the Hong Kong office, I don't fit in anymore. Ever since the Jake thing."

"Ugh, Jake! PLEASE tell me you are not still hung up on that loser?"

"Definitely not," I said a little too quickly, "He's an arrogant jerk. Today when I put on my Sarah McLachlan CD, he looked up from his desk and asked if I was sad."

"Why would he ask that?"

"That's what I said to him. He said that I always play Sarah when I'm feeling down."

"Well, that is kinda true." Grace knew me well.

"I hate that he picks up on my feelings. Like he even cares about me."

"Well, I'm sure he does care about you. Maybe not in the way you want. I think he just doesn't know how to be around you anymore."

I smiled at my beautiful friend. "You're right, I'm just being nostalgic about the early Hungry days. You know how stubbornly I hold on to the past. I need to move on."

"Speaking of moving on…" Grace said as she picked up a succulent prawn and plopped it on my plate. "Eat! It's your birthday!"

Grace had been my most fervent ally since I was two years old. She was six at the time and thought I was a real-life doll to play with. The Chinese community in Toronto back in the early '70s was tight-knit. Our parents played mah-jong together every weekend, carting our families from one Chinese home to the next. Our dads were architects, engineers, or owned construction companies – all entrepreneurs. I'd expected us to see each other often when I'd moved to Hong Kong where Grace lived with her Kiwi husband and her daughter, my goddaughter, Ashlyn. Sadly, we rarely hung out because of my unrelenting start-up schedule those past ten months.

As we walked back towards the parked car, Grace suddenly stopped. "We're here!" she announced.

I looked up and saw a little shop lit up in bright lights, with easels lining the narrow room. "I thought we were heading home. Where are we?"

"This is my birthday gift to you! We're going to paint together!" she exclaimed, clapping her hands together before opening the door for me to step through.

I was too drained and tired for this. After that fantastic meal, all I wanted to do was sleep. But of course, I couldn't refuse such a generous and thoughtful gift.

Grace and I were born artists. Creating was in our blood, whether it was bookbinding, sketching or clay sculpture. Grace graduated from design college and curated at the Art Gallery of Ontario before becoming an interiors architect. She created exceptional living spaces.

Dad dreamed that I would become an architect like him. He'd preach, "Building houses and skyscrapers is how you leave your footprints on the world. Few people have both artistic and math skills – but you… you were BORN to be an architect!"

Since I was young, Dad would wrap my fingers around a pencil while he guided my hand across the paper to sketch wherever I was. If we were at a neighbourhood restaurant with paper tablecloths, the entire table would be covered in designs by the time we finished our meal. Dad taught me how to quickly scan a room or slowly draw out the details. I learned that if you could conceive an idea, put it down on paper, come up with a plan, you could succeed in anything. Dad taught me that anything was possible if you imagined it.

Grace and I sat down, side by side, in front of our easels. I'd chosen my favourite colours: burnt sienna, cobalt blue, titanium white. I didn't have a clue what to paint. I was tempted to tell her about my Bali tryst, but I could hardly acknowledge Adi's existence to myself. So I stayed silent as I pushed the paints around on my palate, mixing the colour of my still-tanned hand, lacking any other inspiration. The shape of my face appeared on the canvas. I peeked over at Grace's canvas which was already awash with vibrant reds, oranges and amber. I added haunted eyes to my achingly sad face, depicting how I felt. Hollow. Depleted. I drew a baby on the forehead, wishing I could start over. Start the painting over. Start life over. I was deeply dissatisfied with the image that stared back at me, but time was up. We left our paintings at the art studio to dry.

A few months later, Grace drove by the art studio and saw my painting displayed in the window. Sixteen years later, in Queenstown, New Zealand, Grace would give me a published art book with my painting in it.

7

My mind fixated on the dire situation at HungryForWords. We were at the end of October and had payroll to complete. I wasn't sure how Cam was going to do it. He'd hinted that morning that I shouldn't put a deposit on any apartment, but Mom was only in Hong Kong for a few more weeks. And she was an apartment expert.

My apartment search put Mom in a conundrum. She much preferred that I move back to San Francisco – a five-hour flight from Toronto, versus eighteen to Hong Kong, and it was where both my brothers lived, my younger brother Ken and my older half-brother Andrew.

Houses ran in my blood. Dad, the architect, designed and built them, and Mom, the real estate agent, sold them.

Dad lived in an older part of Hong Kong called Tin Hau with his second wife, Fong Fong. Dad's place was typical for local Hong Kongers, a three-bedroom apartment of 500 square feet.

Since I moved to Hong Kong in early-2000, I seldom saw Dad because of my work and my wariness of our tenuous relationship. Once, so that we could depart early to golf at Sha Tin, I'd stayed in his spare room (read closet) on a narrow 60-centimetre-wide hard cot, bending my knees to fit.

Walking to the MRT station, we had breakfast at the local dim sum house – mouth-watering aromas of tea and steamed dumplings wafted out onto the sidewalk, stopping anyone in their tracks. I'd peep into the bamboo steamers and choose a selection to share: Dad's favourite *cha siu bao* (BBQ pork buns), *pai kwuat* (garlicky spareribs in black bean sauce) and, my favourite, *siu mai* (pork and shrimp dumplings). Elderly men sat on stools in front of little metal tables, reading their newspapers, sipping their jasmine tea and ordering their one basket of dim sum.

Eating dim sum this way was a novelty to me. Dim sum usually meant squashing myself at a big round table, surrounded by family or my team at HungryForWords. We'd order baskets by the dozens to ensure that everyone could get a morsel of each. Here, one wandered in, ordered just one basket of their favourite dim sum without having to share, and discussed the news of the day with their neighbours over fragrant tea. This would have been my ideal morning, but Tin Hau was too far away from our office on Lyndhurst Terrace.

I'd been spoiled staying in the penthouse with Jake and Kayo. We had massive amounts of space and sweeping views of Hong Kong Harbour – by day, the concrete jungle set against the blue skies and by night the entire city lit up like a giant amusement park for adults. Plus, the Central–Mid-Levels escalator was ten steps away. This free outdoor escalator was ingenious. You could jump on and hitch a ride from the financial and shopping centre of Hong Kong up through the Mid-Levels, saving you from having to walk up winding hills steep enough to rival anything in San Francisco. In the mornings, from 6 am until 10 am, the elevator would convey pedestrians downhill towards Central and the CBD, and then it would switch to the "up" mode bringing people to hip eateries along the Mid-Levels or carrying weary workers home until midnight. You'd be out of luck if you stayed too late in the Lan Kwai Fong bars.

Mom found an ideal studio apartment for me right off the Central–Mid-Levels escalator. The building was a blush-pink cement – refreshingly feminine amongst the grey buildings towering around her. Being an older building, the rent was within my budget. Quaint cafés and shops were only one level down from the escalator – easily walkable in the improbable event that I stayed out past midnight.

"This place is perfect," I said.

Mom glared at me, subtly shaking her head. "Not so fast. We have to check the plumbing," Mom said loudly in Cantonese, trying to mitigate the harm I'd done to our negotiating powers. Turning to me, she whispered in English, "Don't look so enthusiastic. I'm trying to bargain the deposit down."

✳

I slid into the leather seat facing Cam, wondering why he'd asked to meet at The Mandarin for afternoon tea.

"I think I found the perfect apartment, it's just off the escalator."

"You'll need to hold off. That's why I wanted to meet you outside of the office. Things aren't looking good." He hesitated and then said, "I'll have to start laying off some of the team."

"Oh no. I thought you and Jake had some potential prospects for funding, maybe dipping back to the angel investors."

"The meltdown in Silicon Valley makes it almost impossible for us to get funding. We need revenue," Cam said as he opened and closed his hands. "I'll need you to spend more time in Tokyo."

"Are you going to come too? I hate being alone there."

"You have Kubota-san. And I need to deal with the layoffs. Believe me, I'd rather be in Tokyo."

"Yeah, I guess my problem of eating alone pales in comparison."

"You have a problem with eating by yourself?" Cam looked baffled.

"Maybe it's because you're a guy. When you're a woman alone, especially in Tokyo, there's no way to be inconspicuous. I feel like everyone's staring at me."

"Bring a book?" Cam suggested.

"Very funny. Seriously, life in Tokyo without you and Kayo is far from fun."

"There's something else I wanted to talk about." Cam's mouth became grim as soon as he changed the subject. "Your emotions really affect the rest of the team. When you're excited, you motivate everyone around you. But when you're depressed, you bring everyone down."

"What?" I pulled back in my chair, holding in words while I processed what Cam said.

"It's just I need you to be on an even keel. The team looks up to you for leadership."

I studied his face while I thought about how unhinged I'd felt for months and conceded, "Okay, I see what you mean. I'm sorry."

"No need to be sorry. I just want you to be aware."

"I guess the good thing is that the team won't be seeing me much anyways. I'll spend November and early December in Tokyo. This might be for nothing. Advertising budgets have been slashed. Internet spends are the first to be cut. It's a long shot for us," I said as I rubbed the crease between my eyebrows.

"I understand. Just work your magic," Cam said as he passed me the tray of scones and finger sandwiches.

8

I descended deeper and deeper into depression as my time in Tokyo wore on. I dragged my feet along as Kubota-san, my Japanese sales manager, sought the address of yet another advertising agency for us to pitch HungryForWords.com to. I'd sold to ad agencies in Toronto, San Francisco, Los Angeles, Portland, and Seattle with consistent success. Tokyo alluded me.

Every grey building was the same: thick smoky hallways, stale overheated offices. A lot of bowing.

Being November, I peeled off the layers so I could breathe. Our presentations were on auto-pilot. Kubota-san ran through the PowerPoint of our e-Flashcard. Unlike my usual animated and energetic self, I sat restrained and silent, a painted smile on lips that lacked Japanese language skills.

After a particularly forgettable meeting, an elderly man caught my eye as we passed on the sidewalk. He was slicing into a glistening slab of tuna as if he manned Nobu's sushi bar. Plastic stools scattered around a makeshift table made of a sheet of steel on top of upturned paint buckets. I smiled. This was my kind of sidewalk café.

Kubota-san shook his head vehemently when I insisted that we sit down for lunch, but he relented as even he could not resist the live version of Iron Chef Japan playing out in from of our eyes.

I sighed in appreciation as I slid a thick slice of sashimi into my mouth. The miso soup hid baby clams at the bottom of the melamine bowls. Cam and I had dropped some serious cash at the buzziest places in Roppongi and a centuries-old sushi establishment in Ginza, but this serendipitous experience earned me 10,000 FAPs.

At our Monday briefing, Kubota-san confessed that he'd taken his family back to the same sidewalk sushi bar so they could indulge in the freshest fish in Tokyo – and all for the price of a few yen.

Looking back to February, I could now see how I had landed IBM as our first client for Hungry. I'd sold directly to an American expat working at Ogilvy and Mather – no bowing, no translators, no endless meetings going nowhere. I'd had the advantage of knowing their marketing goals intimately, as IBM had been my number one client at *The Toronto Star*. My client at Ogilvy had been a spark of colour in this sea of grey, introducing me to funky, out-of-the-way restaurants and showing me where to collect the handmade ceramics that graced the tables.

My Japanese team had been shocked when I'd ventured on my own to Kappabashi, the remote restaurant supplier district in Tokyo on the hunt for the aforementioned ceramics. And they were even more shocked when I'd dragged Jake to Tsukiji Fish Market for a succulent sushi breakfast at 5:00 a.m. Jake had actually groaned as he devoured piece after piece.

Now in mid-November, I felt like I was in a different city altogether. Nothing excited or surprised me. It was the same old grey buildings one after another. The neon lights of Shibuya or Shinjuku were the Tokyo of tourists. Living here alone in a shoebox of a hotel room, eating out of plastic takeaway boxes from Takashimaya, wasn't my idea of the jet-set expat life.

Flying back and forth between Hong Kong and Tokyo always wasted a whole day. I'd spent far too long in Toyko this time. I was looking forward to my trip back to Hong Kong. I'd arrive there in the evening, just in time for a girls' catch-up with Audrey. She was a little firecracker of fun, pulling me into little boutiques and making me buy the most outrageous outfits. Audrey was the little sister I'd never had.

We met at Ritz Carlton's coffee shop. Audrey looked white as a ghost.

"What's wrong?" I asked as I plunked down beside her on the sofa. We were tucked into a hall-like area of the café, totally hidden between the tall sides of the high-backed sofa.

"Let's look at the menu and order first," she said, pushing her stylish glasses further up her nose as she peered at the menu.

"Okay." I shrugged in agreement. "Hmmm, I'm going to have the Russian borscht followed by the cod. I need something soupy with lots of veg."

"I'm not that hungry. I'll get the cream of mushroom soup."

"Okay, so what's up? Are you and Cam okay?"

"Not really, we got into a big fight last night."

"Oh no, I'm sorry. What happened?"

"It was actually about you."

"What? What did I do?" My eyebrows scrunched in confusion.

"Nothing, nothing. Just listen. While you've been out of Hong Kong, Jake and Donald came over to my apartment at night to talk to Cam. They told him that you're not doing anything in Tokyo."

"What? That's bullshit! Every time I call Cam, the boys are downstairs playing foosball. I've never even see them in the office. That's crazy. It's Jake's job to get funding. Where's that at? His only investment lead is through my Japanese friend, Yosh. What a load of crap... Wait, does Cam believe these assholes?" My forehead pinched together as I processed these lies.

"Yeah, that's why we've been arguing. He spends all his time with them. They play basketball together, they eat all their meals together, it's like they've brainwashed him. You're his buddy from business school and like a sister to him, but he believes them."

I leaned back and closed my eyes, "What am I doing here? You know how miserable I am in Tokyo. I have absolutely no life except working for Hungry. Cam himself has been to meeting after meeting with Yahoo Japan. The Japanese take years to develop relationships before making any agreements, especially with a foreign company like us. I don't even know what Jake and Donald do! I don't see any value in either of them except as insecure gossips."

"I just wanted to warn you, Frances. You're a good person, and I don't want to see you hurt," said Audrey. She wrung her hands, looking like a messenger about to get shot.

"Thanks, Audrey. I don't want this creating a problem between you and Cam either. Seriously, this is crap. It's crazy that Cam actually believes them. I know he's totally stressed, but he should know deep in his heart who's in his corner."

"I'm sure he does, but he can't see clearly right now," Audrey said.

"You know Yosh, my friend from San Francisco? He's connecting us with his ex-colleague who now works at Softbank Japan. I can't believe Jake is talking shit behind my back." I felt my face become flushed.

The more I spoke, the more betrayed I felt. If I hadn't been in one of Hong Kong's poshest cafés, I would have flipped the table in rage.

"I can't stomach this. Or any food for that matter. Can you cancel my order for me? I'm sorry, Audrey. Please don't tell Cam that I know they're all scheming against me, okay? I need to think this through and protect myself from now on."

I got up, fists balled up and shook my head. Audrey grabbed me for a tight hug, tears trickling down her face.

"Don't cry, Audrey. Just be careful. I don't know what Cam is thinking, but he's obviously not himself right now. I won't do anything drastic. I care about Hungry and the team that's still left."

"I'll be okay, Frances. I'm so sorry to tell you this…I've been dying for you to come back from Tokyo so I could warn you. I'm here for you. Know that. You're not alone."

I don't think Audrey knew how wrong she was, and neither did I when I walked out of the café that day. But I know it now. I was alone. I had only myself to depend on. Audrey would side with Cam in the end. And I didn't blame her. She loved him.

Minus 1,000,000 FAPs, I thought as I walked towards the escalator, back to the penthouse that I still shared with Jake.

9

"What do you mean that my credit card won't go through?" I asked the perfectly attired saleswoman behind the counter at Holt Renfrew – "Holts" as Torontonians called this luxury fashion mecca, held center stage on swanky Bloor Street, Toronto's version of Fifth Avenue.

I rarely bought anything here. It was enough to walk through the glass doors, held open by the elderly doorman, and take in the enchanting scents of Chloe mixed with Chanel No. 5. But while observing the somewhat excessive Christmas decorations, my eye caught a soft sky blue peeping out from a sea of dark grey, navy and black. The last thing I needed was another coat, but I couldn't help but stroke the sumptuously soft shearling on this elegant yet sporty jacket. It was waist length, feather-light, and pure luxury. It wouldn't hurt to just try it on, right?

The saleswoman called my bank. They'd placed a hold on my credit card because it showed recent purchases in Hong Kong, Tokyo, Hong Kong again, Seattle and now Toronto. The bank reasoned that I couldn't be in all those places within a few days of each other.

Impatiently tapping my foot, I grabbed the phone and said, "That's my life. I travel like that for my company. I'm exhausted and need some relief. Please give me a smidgen of joy by putting the charge through."

✳

I carefully hung up the blue coat in the guest room closet at my mom's condo. I planned to debut the shearling at the upcoming Christmas parties with my old friends.

It'd been over two years since I'd moved away from Toronto. Being back at Mom's place was comforting. Mom still lived in the building where my younger brother Ken and I grew up. Even though she now lived in a smaller unit, sub-penthouse, the guest room felt like my room. I'd left remnants of my childhood there when I moved to San Francisco back in 1998. I never imagined that I would move even further away to Asia.

Mom's kitchen wafted mouth-watering scents of deliciousness. I stole a peek. Homemade chicken stock simmered away while a fresh batch of her Christmas butter cookies cooled on wire racks. I popped two of the cookies into my mouth, risking the burn and scolding from Mom. They were warm, buttery, and a bit crumbly – the aromas and tastes of my childhood.

I lay on the bed to inventory my life. Most of my belongings, including my car, still resided in San Francisco. Hong Kong was supposed to be for 6 months, not a whole year. I'd crammed the few bedroom items from the Hong Kong penthouse into a small room in Cam's apartment where two of our techies from the Philippines lived – a halfway house for newly hired Hungry staff. Mom joked that I was a person "with no fixed address." I'd never felt less settled; I was completely unmoored. The thought was exhausting... *I'll close my eyes for just a moment...*

Three days later, Mom shook me awake. "Oh, thank God. I was about to call 911 to get an ambulance."

"What? What happened? Oh, my body is so sore."

"You've been sleeping for three days! I couldn't wake you up. I kept checking that you were still breathing. I called the doctor. He said that it was probably exhaustion."

"What? What day is it?"

"It's Boxing Day."

"What?! I missed Christmas? I was supposed to go to Kelly's party. Oh no. This is awful. I'm so sorry, Mom. I've ruined your Christmas too."

"I'm so relieved you're awake. Frances, you must stop working so hard. I called your dad in Hong Kong. He said that he never sees you even though you can walk to his office from yours in ten minutes! We think you need to stop working in Hong Kong."

"No, Mom. I'm totally fine."

"You're not 'fine,'" Mom said, making quotes in the air. "You didn't wake up for three days."

I laughed and imitated her air quotes. "Mom, you're being 'dramatic.' It was all the travel. Flying from Hong Kong to Tokyo, back to Hong Kong, to Seattle and then home was too much. I just needed to sleep it off. See, I'm fine now," I reassured her by getting up and stretching.

"You missed Christmas! You missed your friends. Kelly called worried when you didn't show up. You never do that. Your friends mean everything to you. Frances, you need to stop and think about what's best for your health and your life."

"Okay, Mom, I will. Right now, Cam still depends on me. Jake and Donald already quit. They have their last day on January 10th. I can't suddenly bail too."

At our last staff meeting, Cam announced that Jake and Donald were "sacrificing" themselves for the good of the company. My mouth flew open but nothing came out. Those two scoundrels were clearly saving their own skins by jumping ship.

Later that day, I nibbled at a plate of leftover turkey in Mom's kitchen while I pondered my next steps.

Although I hadn't shown my fears to Mom, sleeping for three days solid was definitely worrisome. A month prior in Hong Kong, I'd had a severe allergic reaction after a sushi meal at Tokyo Go Go in Lang Kwa Fong. In the middle of the night, an itchy rash woke me. When I looked in the mirror, I was bright red with giant hives all over my face. Not wanting to wake Jake or Kayo, I took the elevator down thirty-one floors, hailed a taxi and asked the driver to take me to the nearest hospital. The emergency nurse gave me a shot in the arm and said that it was likely fish that had gone off from my dinner. My body had never reacted this way despite me eating street food from suspect places. What was wrong with my immune system?

I quickly drafted an email to Cam telling him that I needed to take care of my health and step back from the company. However, I wouldn't leave him in a lurch. I'd stay until Cam could replace me and hopefully help secure funding before I left. Before I changed my mind, I pressed "send."

10

*C*am's eyes flew open when I walked into the office in Hong Kong. Cool as a cat, he got up and led me back out, "Let's get some coffee."

We walked down Lyndhurst Terrace to a coffee shop that I'd never tried, as I was actually a hardcore tea drinker.

As we stood by the window looking out onto the street, nursing our cappuccinos, Cam quietly said, "I didn't expect you to come back."

I was taken aback. "That's not what I wrote. I said that I'd try to replace myself and continue dealing with Softbank until I left."

"Hmmm, lost in translation?" Cam peered at me with a smirk.

In that second, I remembered why I'd come back. "So do you want me to stay? The Softbank meeting is confirmed. Kubota-san and Kayo can deliver a strong pitch. There's a chance that we can secure some funds to pull us through."

Cam looked at me, a bit dazed. I couldn't tell if he could see the hurt that lay behind my encouraging face.

I held back from punching him in the arm and blurting out, "Who's still standing here beside you? Are Jake and Donald here? No. They bailed on you after bad-mouthing me, your one true friend at Hungry." Instead, I bit my lip and waited.

"Okay, let's do this. There's nothing to lose."

A week later, we sat around a rectangular table in a sterile meeting room, setting up our presentation for Softbank Japan.

My stomach was in knots thinking about the long road that Cam and I had travelled to get to this point. We'd done the impossible, surviving when so many well-funded Internet companies went under last year. Kayo looked pretty and professional in her pale lilac suit – her favourite colour that she wore almost daily. Kubota-san fiddled with the laptop, checking that the presentation was properly projected onto the screen. I breathed in, saying a little prayer, as Yosh's former colleague Taka slipped into the meeting room and sat down.

The pitch, created by our whole team, was presented in Japanese by Kayo and Kubota-san. We asked for two and a half million dollars. This would save our company and grow our Hungry e-Flashcard membership to accelerate ad sales. Even though Cam and I had done this presentation multiple times in English to investment banks in Hong Kong, I still beamed proudly as we went through each slide. Our e-Flashcard solved many problems both for the English learner in Asia as well as for astute advertisers. In addition to our big win with the IBM campaign, Kubota-san had had some success selling to local Japanese advertisers, proving that our e-Flashcard was viable. Now we just needed to persuade Softbank to invest in our vision too.

After the meeting, I insisted that we celebrate at my favourite sushi restaurant, Sushi No Midori, at Mark City in Shibuya.

In our earlier days in Tokyo, I'd skipped a meeting in the office tower above, asking Cam, Jake and Kayo to deal with the potential partner. I had a much more important goal – to be the first in line to get a table at Sushi No Midori, notorious for hour-long waits. My team thought I was nuts until they sank their teeth into their first morsel of *chutoro* (medium fatty tuna).

Jake had grinned and said, "From now on, your job is to line up for lunch."

Their sushi assortment was exhaustive; not only did they have different cuts of tuna: *maguro*, *chutoro* and *otoro*, but also different ages and types of yellowtail: *kampachi*, *hamachi* and *buri* depending on the season. Each delectable slice stretched out to about 15 centimetres, not like the bite-sized pieces of fish you find everywhere else. It wasn't just the size either; the fish was so impeccably fresh it practically swam off our plates. I remembered how much we'd laughed and eaten that day.

Today, we were sombre after the Softbank meeting. We knew this was the end of the line. If we didn't secure this funding, we'd have to shut down Hungry.

It was January 2001, a year since we launched Hungry. Kayo invited me to a special New Year's event at her aunt's tea ceremony school, located in Kayo's hometown, a quaint suburb just outside Tokyo that resembled an old French town, named Jiyogaoka – cobblestone lanes, tiny cafés serving chestnut filled pastries, and a famous shop selling accessories made from vintage kimono trimmings. I was honoured and hopeful; maybe an auspicious tea ritual would inject new life into me and our flailing company.

What should I wear? How should I behave? I'd never been to a *chanoyu* (a Japanese tea ceremony) before. Even more intimidating, I was attending the first tea ceremony of the new year called *hatsugama*.

I settled on my green embroidered Shanghai Tang jacket. Everyone else would don their most elaborate silk kimonos. It didn't really matter what I wore since I would stick out like a sore thumb regardless. *Stop second-guessing yourself and relish this once-in-a-lifetime experience.* Previously, I would have been eager and elated to have a chance to collect FAPs in Japan, not dreading other people's reaction to my outfit.

When Kayo opened the little wooden gate to let me in, I stepped back to see her full kimono and smiled wide in approval. "Kayo-san, you look like a Japanese princess!"

Kayo wore a stunning burgundy red silk kimono painted with beautiful black brushstrokes. Kayo turned around to show me the elaborately tied obi. She resembled a geisha who'd stepped out of time.

With her feet in white toed socks and traditional wooden clogs, Kayo delicately tread over the flat stones of the garden pathway leading into the teahouse. I followed silently behind her, reminding myself to be graceful and push away any impulses to giggle as I often did when nervous. Both of us being tall for Asian women, we had to duck underneath the wooden lintel leading into the room where the other women were gathered in a loose circle on their tatami floor mat, sitting on their knees in full kimono. I panicked a bit as I realized that I couldn't sit on my ankles the way these lovely Japanese ladies were. Kayo pulled me down to sit beside her. I leaned over and asked if it was okay for me to sit cross-legged. Thankfully, she smiled and nodded.

The tea ceremony moved at a dream-like pace. The older Japanese ladies were enchanting to watch. Each, in turn, scooped a bit of matcha into a teacup, poured the perfect temperature water from a height, skillfully swirled the tea with a bamboo whisk and presented it to their neighbour to drink. When it came to my turn, Kayo patiently took me step by step through the ritual that included a complicated rotating motion. Sinking back down on my cushion, feeling relieved after mixing the matcha properly, I sighed inwardly as I nibbled on the little Japanese cake – matched for the tea and the season.

To my surprise, I won the prize of the New Year's ceremony, an ornate tea ceremony cup. I turned the cup in my hands to admire the characters drawn on a ceramic bowl, glazed a sunny yellow. As I walked back to the Jiyugaoka train station that afternoon with my gift securely tucked away, I wondered if this was a sign of brighter days to come.

It was. We'd succeeded in securing the funding from Softbank, and Cam and Kubota-san were actively recruiting for my replacement. I was free to leave Hungry.

By February, Cam had scaled down our office at Lyndhurst Terrace.

When we'd rented the entire 21st floor of The Workstation a year earlier, the building manager had asked us what colour cubicles we wanted and how to set up the partitions.

Without discussion, Cam and I both blurted out, "No cubicles."

We gave each other high-fives as we laughed. It was only the two of us that day, but we could envision the growth of our company. We designed our office in keeping with the culture of inclusion and creativity that we wanted to create.

The new office on the seventeenth floor was the standard set-up with closed cubicles. It would house the remaining essential employees of Hungry. My heart sank seeing how our big dreams had shrivelled. I would not miss this. I hated cubicles. I'd hated the grey smog that floated by each evening at 5:00 p.m. like clockwork. You could literally see pieces of pollution drift past the glass windows. I had no idea where I was going next, but I wanted clean air and to be able to breathe freely again.

1 1

Stepping gingerly down the worn slippery stone steps of market lane, I balanced the takeaway from Tsui Wah, my favourite greasy *cha chaan teng* (Chinese tea shop). I flagged the correct *siu bah* (little bus) that would take me to Grace's place in Pokfulam on Hong Kong's east coast. None of the other expat staff dared to get into one of these, as you had to have at least a rudimentary knowledge of Cantonese, which I practiced with the local fruit hawkers right outside our office.

I relished riding on that little bus, listening to elderly Chinese grandmas chat about how expensive the *choi sum* was that day or that lychees were finally in season. In my suit, I didn't exactly fit in. I didn't care. I wanted to experience the real Hong Kong, not the polished bits created to make expats feel at home.

Grace was cradling my goddaughter, Ashlyn, in her arms as she opened the door, "Oooh, I'm starving! Thanks so much for bringing my fave!"

She traded her daughter for the iced coffees and curry boxes. I cuddled Ashlyn close and took a deep sniff of baby. I loved how she smelled. I reluctantly relinquished Ashlyn to her nanny so she could put her down for her nap. I peeked into the most perfect nursery I'd ever seen – soft blues and greens evoked a nautical feel which merged with the wide-open ocean views of their apartment. Grace had outdone herself with this labour of love.

We tiptoed into the den; Grace closed the sliding doors so Ashlyn could sleep.

"Oh my God, this is sooooo good!"

"I think this is the only reason we have been best friends for decades – food!"

"It's certainly not for your humour." She nudged me and grinned. "So, your last day at Hungry, how are you feeling?"

"I'm relieved that I'm finally free, but I'm sad that it had to end this way. Cam really let me down," I sighed.

"Yeh, I'm so sorry Fran. Funny, Vern never did like that guy."

"That's the understatement of the century. He hated Cam with a passion."

"So, what are you going to do now?"

"I don't know. I don't really want to go back to Toronto or San Francisco. You know, I'm considering moving to Venice to be a sculptor. It is especially romantic in the winter, and I can ski in Cortina."

"Fran, I love you and your crazy ideas! I don't doubt that you can do that, but is that really what you want? Honestly?"

"Well, there's one more idea. I'd like to go back to Bali."

"Oo-kay… Why….?"

"I haven't told anyone this, but I met a guy there."

"Whaaaaat??" squealed Grace, who lived for romance. "Who? When? How? And WHAT??"

"Well, remember when I went to Bali on the way to Nate's wedding last October? I met him then. Never mind, it's really nothing."

"Nothing?!!!! Frances, hello!! How many men have you even talked about post-Vern?!! I mean how long has it been?!!! Like seven years?!!! This is something! Not nothing! So…. he was another tourist?"

"No, actually, he's local. A Balinese guy."

"SHUT UP!!!"

"Shhhhh, you'll wake Ashlyn."

"Okay, this is crazy! Who are you and what have you done with my friend?!! Ok, spill… Did you… y'know…"

"Grace, I do not kiss and tell."

Growing up with Grace, I'd always been her third wheel; she was always with a guy, trying to get rid of one or juggling a few at once. She taught me everything about love.

I never did things in halves. It was always all or nothing of me. For instance, I'd been the shortest at my all-girls school for years; seemingly overnight, I shot up to 168 cm and was moved to the back for school photos. It was the same story with love. I'd never dated, never even been kissed. When I turned twenty-one, Vern became my first love, and I became his. It was an all-encompassing, passionate love.

He was without equal in my mom's eyes: Chinese, check. Tall, dark, and handsome, check. Med-School, check. In truth, Vern was the least Chinese person I knew. Born outside of Toronto, bred at a prestigious boarding school, and not understanding one Chinese character, he was just Vern. The guy that I would marry.

Vern detested Cam. I'd wanted to ask Vern to our business school ball, but he was in Toronto in his first year at medical school. Instead, I'd asked Cam, as a friend, but he already had a date. So I asked Vern if he could come up from Toronto. That was the weekend when we got together. In Vern's mind, if Cam hadn't been occupied, he might have been the one. I spent three years trying to prove how much I loved Vern…to Vern.

Vern broke up with me over the phone and flew halfway across the country for a ski week the very next day to escape the aftermath of ripping my heart to shreds. My girlfriends rallied around me, taking me to Keitha's farm to heal from the shock. But something inside me broke. I grasped at any chance to be with him as we bounced back and forth, unable to be apart but also not back together. I was THAT girl, the crazy ex-girlfriend. Often, after sitting outside Vern's condo in my car for hours, I'd find my way to Grace's door at 3 am, not sleeping, not eating. She'd always let me in.

At the lowest point of my depression, Dad had taken me out to lunch. It was highly unusual when he started the conversation by telling me how worried he was about me. Many friends had tried to reach me, tried to console me, but I was inconsolable.

I didn't want to show Dad my pain even though one of my best friends had told me that grief was etched all over my face. I didn't want Dad to see me heartbroken, even though I knew I was like a ghost – not really living but not dead either.

Dad had talked slowly, unravelling for me the secret of everlasting love.

"Wah-Wah," he said, calling me by my childhood name, "there are many kinds of love. Sometimes love is like a firecracker, an explosion of passion that is all-consuming. Sometimes love is like a candle; the flame may not burn as hot or bright as firecrackers, but it burns slow and long. You'll experience both in your life, but a candle is what you need for a good marriage."

I looked at Dad in shock. I was twenty-three at the time, and he'd never, ever given me advice about relationships, and certainly not about love.

As the words sunk in, tears started rolling down my face, "But Dad, Vern was my firecracker and my candle. He was my everything."

"No, Wah-Wah, he wasn't. Take time to heal. Try to stay busy with your friends. Go out and meet new people. You'll find your candle one day. Just be patient."

It took another year and me flying in the other direction to Europe to piece myself back together. I rediscovered myself among thirty strangers on a tour bus that travelled through eleven countries in twenty-eight days. I remembered that I sought adventure. I remembered that I was brave. I remembered how to laugh. That's also when Cam stepped back into my life as a friend and we started our FAPs competition.

Breaking me out of my reverie, Grace slapped me on the arm. "Whoaaaa...I've known you since you were two and you have never, *ever* done anything like this. I mean, it was Vern or nothing, right?"

"Vern. God, I really need to move on; it's been...seven years! What's wrong with me?"

"Nothing, sweetie. Yours was a deep, deep first love. You know how hard it was for me to get over Rick."

"Yeah, but you got on with it! I can't even count how many hearts you've left in your wake."

"Errr– let's focus on the matter at hand! Have you kept in touch with this Balinese guy?"

My stomach fluttered when I said, "No, no, it's nothing like that. It was just a passing thing. You're right. This is crazy. I don't know why I'm even considering this. My parents would kill me."

"Yeah, that's for sure, from 'perfect Dr. Vern' to some island boy in Bali. Come on, give me the details. What's his name? What happened?"

"I guess it all started with the worst massage ever, like that one that you got at Elemis Spa but about a thousand times worse. Me being me, I pretty much demanded that they get me their very best masseuse for the next day. That's when Adi showed up."

"Ah, Adi. I see. He seduced you with his fingers," Grace teased.

"Well, no, it was a foot reflexology massage where I sat across from him.

I don't know, but I felt right at home. Like I already knew him. He's like the total opposite of all the players here in Hong Kong. Nothing slimy or gross. Just a really sweet, gentle guy," I said, with this weird, dreamy look on my face.

"Hello? Frances? Earth to Frances! Looks like you've got it bad. What happened next? Wait, what about your mom? How did you hook up with a guy with her around?"

"We didn't 'hook up!'" I looked at Grace, mortified and thinking to myself, *Is that what they call it now? God, I'm so clueless.* "I mean, it was an utterly romantic experience. Nothing as lurid as your dirty thoughts... Now get your mind out of the gutter."

"Yeah, whatever, Fran. Come on, I'm married with a baby in tow. Let me live vicariously through you for just a second. Like, was he good?"

"Grace!" as my face turned red, "Okay, okay. If inquiring minds need to know. Yes, of course, he's the resort's top masseuse! So let your imagination run wild."

"So, is there some way for you to get in touch with him?"

I opened and closed my mouth without saying anything. I slowly replied, "Well...yes. I have his business card."

"Where is it?"

"Never mind, this won't go anywhere. He's in Bali," I said as I diverted my eyes.

"Fran, just tell me – where is the card already?" coaxed Grace.

"Fine...it's in my purse." I mumbled reluctantly.

"What!? You've been carrying his business card around with you for six months?" asked Grace as she got up, snatched my bag and started digging around. "Where is it?"

I tried grabbing my bag back, but Grace held fast.

"Ah, here we go," Grace said. She had found it tucked inside my business card holder, hidden behind my own name cards.

I put my hand to my forehead, "I really hate that you know me inside and out."

She read out his name, "I.M. Adi Ardika. What does I.M. stand for?"

Shaking my head, I shrugged, "How should I know? I hardly even know this guy."

Grace picked up the portable phone and started punching in the number. "Thankfully, I know the country code for Indonesia is +62. Jonathan does business in Jakarta."

"What are you doing? Stop it!" I hissed as I tried to grab the business card back.

Grace pushed the phone into my hand, "Take it. Now."

"Hello?" answered Adi.

Before I could think, I answered back automatically, "Oh, hi Adi. This is Frances. Remember me? The Canadian living in Hong Kong?"

"Yes, of course. So, when are you coming back to Bali?"

12

BALI, MARCH 2001

A week later, I was stepping off a plane in Bali. It was March 7th, 2001. Almost exactly six months to the day from when I'd arrived in Bali the first time.

Robert, the driver who had taken me to his mom's local market for the best satay, waved me over with his hand-written sign. A friend in the sea of faces. I'd ditched the slimy tour guide Komang, who'd only been interested in my wallet.

Robert opened the back door for me, but I hesitated and said, "I'll sit in the front with you, Robert."

Taken aback, Robert asked, "Are you sure? Guests always sit at the back. It's more comfortable."

"No, I've met your mother. I've eaten satay in the market with you. You're my first friend in Bali, not my chauffeur."

He grinned and opened the front door, "Umm, okay. How are you? You're back so soon. Do you have business here?"

"No, no business at all." I could hardly believe that I was saying those words.

I had no business, no work, no plans, no idea really what I was doing here in Bali. I couldn't wait for life to begin again. I felt free. I leaned back, shoulders relaxed, and smiled. I sat back up when I noticed a little square filled with colourful flowers on Robert's dashboard with a little wisp of smoke spinning up from an incense stick.

"Hey, what's that? I saw one on the counter of the customs desk too, and on the floor outside. I almost stepped on it," I said.

"That is a *canang*. It's an offering. For God," answered Robert. "My mom give me to protect me when I drive."

"Wow, that's so beautiful. I love the beliefs here."

Robert navigated the road up to Ubud, travelling north and east past the sleepy village of Sanur as my finger followed the map in my guidebook, *The Rough Guide to Bali and Lombok*. I'd spent the four-and-a-half-hour plane ride devouring the food section as well as highlighting the temples and villages that I planned to explore.

Jobless, I needed to be frugal. Five-star resorts were no longer an option. I had a limited budget of thirty dollars a day. Affordable beach towns such as Kuta and Legian weren't safe for a single woman travelling alone, especially in 2001 when solo travel was pretty much unheard of. I'd researched where to stay and booked my first week in a quaint little guesthouse called Pringga Juwita in the heart of Ubud, where I'd be able to walk around on my own safely. Bali lacked public transportation so the village of Ubud was my only long-term stay option to be able to find places to eat on foot.

The only other time I'd ever scrimped and saved for long-term travel was when I was seventeen living in London with plans of backpacking through Europe. I could imagine my mom now, tutting to herself, thinking that I wasn't much further in life than I was at seventeen. She'd freaked out when I said that I was spending a few months travelling around Bali and Australia.

She asked, "Are you burnt out? You're only 31. You should come home, rest and settle down."

Behind her words, I could almost hear her real unspoken concern. *What good is a top business degree if you're on a beach?* I shook my mom's voice out of my head.

My business degree gave me this – the freedom to choose, to not get boxed into a conventional life where I would indeed burn out. Maybe not in the flaming, explosive way as I'd done in Hong Kong, but in an even worse, slow death of my spirit.

Robert pulled into a narrow lane full of potholes. I looked up at the crooked street sign: *Jalan Bisma*.

"Hmmm, this doesn't look promising, does it?" I said, rubbing my head which had bumped the ceiling when we suddenly dropped into a huge hole.

"Don't worry, Ms. Frances. My van can handle this road," Robert said reassuringly.

He drove very slowly for another 500 metres, passing squares of emerald green rice fields on both the right and left, then pulled into a cobblestone driveway with a *Pringga Juwita Cottages* sign hanging over the stone gate. I jumped down to help with the bags, but Robert waved me off.

Ducking under the wooden gate, I almost tripped over a wooden ledge. Why would they put a ledge in a walkway? I'd passed unscathed into the tropical oasis that had distracted me. Lush green leaves protruded everywhere, and tall coconut trees swayed above blooming fuchsia and tangerine-coloured bougainvillea. The sound of a waterfall soothed any remaining tension.

I'd booked one of the two-level cottages for a week to start, figuring that I'd sort out the rest of my stay later. This was unusual behaviour for me; I typically preferred to map out every minute of my travels in a neat little itinerary. For the first time ever, I had no plan and no responsibilities.

The friendly bellboy gestured for me to follow him through the hopscotch game of flat stones set into the grass. I stepped gingerly, minding my weak ankle. We reached the first of three straw-roofed cottages. It looked like somewhere Snow White and the dwarves would live. Wayan, as stated on his name tag, pushed open the narrow wooden doors, ornately carved and painted in shades of robin's egg blue, moss, and dusty rose, to reveal a terracotta and stone rain shower. The tropical jungle crept right into the open-air bathroom. My forehead crinkled in worry. While I found this absolutely gorgeous now, I'm not sure I'd feel the same at night in a sleepy unguarded state.

I climbed carefully up the wooden ladder behind Wayan, who'd scurried up nimble as a monkey, hoisting my heavy suitcase on his narrow shoulder. There was a lovely balcony with a daybed piled with bright cushions overlooking the jungle-like gardens. Thin wooden sliding doors led into the bedroom.

Perched at this height, I smiled. I'd left behind a penthouse in the concrete jungle of Hong Kong for a real-life fairy tale treehouse in Bali.

13

*N*othing beat washing off the grime of the plane in an open-air rain shower. To my dismay, there are drawbacks of having the bathroom accessed by a wooden ladder – it's impossible to climb up or down wrapped in only a towel. I'd have to remember to bring a fresh set of clothing with me to the bathroom.

I slipped on a swishy black skort with a delicate pattern of tiny white flowers and my favourite charcoal-coloured cotton camisole.

I was ready. Okay, maybe not exactly ready. More like totally freaking out inside, but I thought: *You're here. Take one step at a time. Nothing is set in stone.*

Adi was seated on one of the low bamboo sofas in the open-air lobby. My heart ticked a bit faster when he looked up at me and smiled.

"Hi, Frances, welcome back to Bali. I'm glad you came back." Adi's gentle demeanour put me immediately at ease.

"Hi, Adi, good to see you again. Ummm, let's go get some dinner," I said, holding out my travel guide as I pointed to the place I'd highlighted in the book.

"That sounds good. Are you okay to ride on my motorbike?" Adi asked.

I shuffled my feet as I glanced at his red scooter. "Sure, why not. First time for everything, right?" I said, ending in a high-pitched laugh.

"You've never been on a motorbike?" Adi asked in his slow, soft voice.

I shook my head slightly, "No, never. I'll be fine as long as I can hold onto you."

"Yes, you sit behind me and hold on tight."

Adi maneuvered around the potholes laid out in front of us like an obstacle course. We flew the rest of the journey. A light breeze lifted my hair as we sped along, and before I knew it, we were in front of Kafe Batan Waru. The warm glow of the lights above the open-air bar invited us in. Large, rectangular tables with bench-like seats faced the street with smaller round tables tucked in between.

I bounced over to an intimate table for two and sat down. The waitress hovered with menus in hand. Adi's eyes glowed as he sat down beside me and smiled.

I pushed a menu over to him. I flipped through the menu while Adi studied it quietly. Everything sounded exotic and delicious. I wanted to order a few dishes to share, but I wasn't sure how Adi felt about sharing.

"What are you getting?" I asked.

"*Nasi goreng*. Fried rice."

I ordered the *ayam rica rica*, which I'd never seen on any other menu in my life. The waitress also recommended the ginger fizz, which was chalked on the blackboard as their specialty drink.

The waitress walked away with our orders, and then it was just me and Adi. I was at a loss for words. I really didn't know what to say. I'm usually one of the most talkative people in the world. I looked around everywhere except at Adi.

I finally settled on, "What does Batan Waru mean?"

Adi leaned a little closer as he responded, "You see the tree at the front of the restaurant? That's a Waru tree. Batan Waru means under the Waru tree."

"Oh, how interesting." I was stumped for anything else to say.

Thankfully, our drinks arrived. I bent over mine, sipping slowly on the refreshingly zingy ginger concoction. There wasn't much I could ask Adi about his, as he was having a Coke.

"So, how long are you staying here?"

"I'll be here for one month and then to Melbourne, Australia for a month. I'll come back through Bali on my way back to Hong Kong."

"What are you doing here?"

I looked at him and thought, *I don't really know. I just wanted to see you and see what happens.* But of course, I wasn't going to tell him that.

What I said aloud was, "Hmmm, I just need a break from life. My job was really stressful. Remember when you massaged my feet and found all the problems with my body?" I giggled nervously.

"Yes, I remember. You work a lot on computer." He said as he observed my bare shoulders.

I shivered a bit, even though the night air was still warm.

I was saved from having to say anything as the waitress placed my dish of ayam rica rica and Adi's nasi goreng down. She opened a woven basket and offered steaming white rice to accompany the spicy chicken. I inhaled the delicious scent of the fiery chili sauce full of garlic, onions, and tomatoes. Automatically, I offered Adi some first. He smiled and took a tiny morsel of chicken with the white rice.

"Hmmm, it's pretty good. Not very spicy, though."

I looked down at the grilled pieces of chicken smothered in chili oil and thought, *This isn't spicy?* I tried a bite and started coughing, "This is quite spicy. Is Balinese food usually spicier than this?"

"Yes, a lot spicier. I think they make it like this for tourists. Balinese eat at home. We don't eat in restaurants."

"Oh, I didn't know that. Are you okay to be here?"

"Yes. I'm used to handling guests."

"You consider me a guest?"

Adi remained silent for a moment before he answered, "Yes, we call you 'tamu,' which means guest. We're responsible for taking care of you while you're here on our island."

"That's really sweet. I feel safer knowing that I'm your guest and not just a tourist," I said, smiling back at him.

"This nasi goreng isn't bad. Everyone knows how to make it. I figure that if it's good here, the rest of the food should be okay too."

"That's smart, but I like to try new things all the time, like this ayam rica rica. I'm guessing that 'ayam' means chicken? What does 'rica rica' mean?"

"In Bahasa Indonesia, we say 'richa richa,' not 'rika rika.' A 'c' followed by a vowel is pronounced 'ch.' Rica rica is the sauce. It's not Balinese. It's from another island, maybe Sulawesi."

"Good to know. I need to learn more of your language," I said.

"Bahasa is easy to learn. Not complicated like English or Japanese," Adi said.

"You can speak Japanese too?" My eyes widened.

"Yes, we have many Japanese guests. The hotel gives us lessons in English and Japanese."

I scooped up another yummy bite as I peered at Adi's long eyelashes. "So you've never tasted ayam rica rica before either? It's the first time for both of us."

"Yes, the first time." He stared back at me and suddenly reached up with his napkin to wipe the sauce from the side of my mouth. That simple gesture broke down any barriers that I'd put up.

I laughed, "I'm always so messy."

"I think you're cute."

"Thanks," I said, smiling back. "Do you want dessert or coffee?"

"Do you?"

"I'm really full, and I don't drink coffee."

"So…are you ready to go?" Adi asked, his eyes saying so much more.

"Okay, let's go," I said.

I tilted my head thinking how laughing with him had eased my nervousness. I grabbed his hand as we got up. I felt like I'd come home.

14

*A*di and I fell into a dream-like existence. He'd kiss me awake and gently rouse me out of my slumber. He'd drawn me out with soulful stares mixed with a lot of laughter.

I revealed myself bit by bit through my favorite songs: "By Your Side" by Sade, "I'm Like a Bird" by Nelly Furtado and "Don't Know Why" by Norah Jones. Connected via the earbuds we shared, me using the left bud and him wearing the right one, we listened to one CD after another on my Sony Discman.

I learned that in order to see me Adi suffered a punishing routine – forty-five minutes on his little red scooter to Le Meridien, nine hours of exhausting work, a quick visit home to see his parents before riding another hour up to Ubud. Most Balinese remain within the confines of their village, commuting only a few minutes to work. His colleagues and family thought he'd lost his mind. I asked if the travel was too difficult, but Adi said that he preferred for me to stay in Ubud, away from the prying eyes of his village where everyone knew everyone, and there weren't any tourists for miles.

For the first time in my life, I had eleven hours a day all to myself.

Leaving Pringga Juwita, I turned left and walked north to the main road of Ubud. Jalan Bisma was difficult to navigate even on foot, but the scenery made up for the lack of walkability. Swaying coconut trees framed my favourite patch of rice field that stuck out as an anomaly between rows of guesthouses. Directly across from the lush green, a Balinese stone gate was a window revealing a shimmering swimming pool in the shade of frangipani trees. Walking around Bali was akin to exploring a living art museum, each masterpiece more exquisite than the last.

In the afternoons, children wearing dark burgundy uniforms with crisp white shirts spilled out from the elementary school at the end of the road. The little girls wore braids tied with coloured ribbons, some days a bright blue, another day sunshine yellow. Past the school, I inched down the steep hill, tucking myself into the hillside to avoid the scooters revving up to make it to the top. At the hillside café, a waitress placed frangipani flowers on each step, transforming an ordinary stoop into a romantic and enchanting path.

The cost of freedom in Ubud was a dollar a day for my rented bicycle. I zoomed down Jalan Hanoman to relieve my aching limbs at Bodyworks and Nur Spa. These inexpensive local spas exuded a whimsical, hippy atmosphere; marigolds decorated every surface including the massive terrazzo bathtubs.

Adi spoilt me for all other masseuses. So much so that I'd soon stop going to spas so "The Complainer" in me would lay dormant. Instead, I monopolized Adi's capable hands every night.

Most lunches, I spent time with my trusty guidebook, highlighting in different colours where I'd already visited and writing little notes in the margins. Jotting down my thoughts felt like chatting with a friend as I sat sipping young coconut juice. Wanting to keep it as a sort of journal of my time with Adi, I took great care in turning the pages so as not to break the spine.

I ate almost exclusively at Batan Waru or Ary's Warung. Ubud had only a handful of cafés and a few local warung serving uninspired Indonesian staples such as nasi goreng or mie goreng that'd been spiced down for tourists' tastes. Worse were the inedible versions of Western favourites such as spaghetti Bolognese or reminders of Dutch colonization – croquettes and rissoles, and various other deep-fried snacks.

Riding the bicycle up Campuhan Hill quickly drained my energy; I had to jump down and walk the last few metres. Eager to learn more about Indonesian painters and artists, I strolled through the vast galleries of Neka Museum, but the musty, old museum was uninspiring.

I found a treasure across the street; spectacular paintings of Balinese women in glittery gold mesmerized me as I peered through the glass window. Their faces spoke directly to me. I ventured in and asked if the artist would consider a custom commission. For once in my life, I had time to sit for a portrait. If not now, when would I ever do this?

Later that afternoon, the gallery owner and a middle-aged Indonesian man named Mohammed with a greying beard, showed up in the lobby of my guesthouse. Adi arrived just as we sat down.

"What's going on, honey?" he asked, assessing the men with narrowed eyes.

"This is Mohammed, a fabulous painter. I'm thinking of getting him to paint me," I said, excitedly.

"Paint you? Oh, okay," Adi said and then opened a bag of mangosteen, my favourite fruit. "I got these from my aunt. She has a fruit stall in the market."

He was so thoughtful. I squeezed his hand as he offered them to the others.

Mohammed studied my face and said, "Yes, yes, I can paint you."

"That's great. How much would it cost for a painting like the one in his gallery?" I asked, pointing my chin to the gallery owner.

"Four hundred dollars. No frame," Mohammed answered quickly.

"That's reasonable. When can you start? How long will it take?"

"Well, you'd need to come to East Java for the sittings."

My eyes flew open. "Java? You mean another island? Can't I give you a photo?"

"No, no. I don't work from photo."

Adi held me closer as I sat up straighter, "Well, I'm not sure about that."

"Don't worry, you stay at my house. I have many wives. They will take care of you."

"Wives?"

Adi's eyebrows went up, and he gave me a slight shake of his head. I really wanted a portrait by this talented artist, but even I had to admit that going to East Java with this man would likely mean a massive drop in my FAPs collection when I became one of his harem. Mohammed grew to become one of the top painters in Bali. And I have yet to have a portrait painted.

❋

One day, I went out the door and turned right to see what the other side of Jalan Bisma offered.

I discovered another guesthouse called Stardust Cottages, 100 metres away on the other side of the road. Through the stone gate, I passed a few older-looking cottages before reaching the reception desk near a grand two-story house. A friendly girl named Suryani showed me around. Room #6 oozed romance. A mosquito net draped over a four-poster bed covered in crisp, clean, white linens edged with navy blue. I sat down at the little desk and opened the little guestbook that described the owners, Brenda (an Australian), Gede (her Balinese husband) and their six kids. *Wow, this is interesting*, I thought, *an Australian lives here. In Bali. And they own a guesthouse and two restaurants. Living in Bali is possible.*

When Adi came home that evening, I told him the exciting news that we were going to move across the street in a few days. Funnily, we hadn't even tried the swimming pool at Pringga Juwita yet as Adi didn't have any swimming shorts.

He explained, "Most Balinese don't know how to swim. Swimming pools are for tourists."

I was taken aback, "You live on an island. Don't you go to the beach?"

"We do, but we don't go far. We walk in with our clothes on. We don't actually swim. The sea is dangerous. One day...my friend drowned beside me in the ocean," Adi said as he cast his eyes down.

I reached out to squeeze his large bicep, "Oh, I'm so sorry, Adi. Well, if you get a swimsuit, I'd like to teach you to swim. For me it's not just about having fun, it's about safety too."

On our last day at Pringga Juwita, Adi showed up with a brand-new swimsuit, a skin-tight, black, boxer-type suit with a colourful abstract design. I wasn't crazy about it, but it did suit his compact body.

We made our way to the pool, protected by high stone walls, vibrant, tropical flowers and giant coconut trees. The pool was entirely shaded by the foliage. The minute we got in, we both started shivering uncontrollably. Adi yelped and jumped back out. In the freezing water, I persisted and urged my body to swim laps to warm up.

I stretched out and floated, looking up at the glorious blue sky framed by the leaves of the coconut trees.

"Come in, darling, you'll get used to it," I said encouragingly.

Adi held back but eventually eased himself into the water. He lay on his back, but his body was so lean and dense that he immediately sank down into the water. I stood up to hold his legs up, but then his shoulders and head sank beneath the water, making him cough and sputter. He kept sinking over and over again, no matter what we tried.

"Maybe floating is a learned skill?" I pondered more to myself than to Adi. I'd taken swimming lessons since I was a young child, so I'd assumed everyone floated.

"I'm…so…cold," said Adi, his lips a weird shade of blue.

"Oh, darling, I'm sorry," I said as I got out and bundled Adi up in the thick pool towel. "You know, not knowing how to swim, it isn't safe. We just have to practice more. I'm going to help you."

I'd rarely been one to teach an athletic skill, but Adi was open-minded and curious to learn. Other men might have been scared to get into a pool with their new girlfriend, but Adi had this quiet confidence that drew me to him more and more every day.

1 5

I didn't want my old life infringing on this new one. My Tokyo-based friend Yosh emailed that he would come to Bali with his girlfriend and one of their friends for a few days. Knowing that I was an avid golfer, Yosh asked me to arrange a golf tour for the four of us in Bali.

How was I going to weave this part of my life into the tapestry I'd so carefully spun over three decades without tearing apart the fabric? I still hadn't told anyone about Adi. When I was with him, I was in this perfect, happy bubble. I didn't want anyone from my previous life to come barging in and risk them bursting that bubble.

Adi, being Adi, helped me arrange my golf dates despite being hesitant when I'd told him that my friends from Tokyo were coming for a golf tour and that I'd be sharing a room with one of them.

"Who are sharing the room with?" Adi had asked softly.

"Yosh's friend Yoko. I've never met her before."

"Is it normal in your country to sleep beside people you don't know?"

I looked up at his inquisitive eyes and could see how odd this would be to him, sharing an intimate space with a stranger. Adi knew everyone in his village, from the newest newborn to the most elderly grandparent. Balinese men lived their whole lives in the family compound where they were born. The women didn't go far either, often marrying into the closest neighbour's compound.

I tried to reassure him, "It'll be fine. Back at university, nine of us once slept in one tiny hotel room. We'd driven to Montreal at the spur of the moment. Being students, we didn't have any money, so the girls all slept lined up on our sides like a tin of sardines on the bed and the guys all slept on the floor."

Eyes wide in mild shock, looking even more uncomfortable than before, Adi shrugged and mumbled, "Sardines? I don't understand, but I trust you and your judgement."

My analogy was definitely lost in translation. I'd only unnerved Adi more by describing my unpredictable behaviour as a nineteen-year-old student.

Checking into The Ritz Carlton Bali felt like coming home. The only other time I'd stayed at a Ritz was in Maui after completing my first and only marathon in Honolulu, right before I'd moved to Hong Kong to start HungryForWords. Oddly, or amazingly, this resort had almost the same layout as the one in Maui. I'd later learn that Bali was the first resort property for The Ritz Carlton Group. They'd been a city-based hotel chain before embarking on the luxury resort sector. The Ritz Carlton Bali was a successful partnership of the two founding owners, one Indonesian and the other Japanese. This resort was the model resort for the designs of all future Ritz Carlton resorts.

I'd just checked into my room and started unpacking the few things I'd brought when there was a knock at the door. I opened it to a slim and pretty Japanese girl a few years older than me with a ponytail tucked under a baseball cap.

"You must be Frances! I'm glad that we have an expert guide to show us around Bali." The girl smiled brightly as she moved aside to let the bellboy bring in her luggage and golf bag.

"Well, I'm not exactly an expert, but I can't wait for you to play Nirwana. It's a stunning golf course."

"I can't wait to jump into the pool. I'm going to change into my bikini now. Let's go meet up with Yosh and Marie."

"Ready when you are." I smiled back, hoping she wouldn't notice the hesitancy in my voice.

Walking past fuchsia and peach-coloured bougainvillea and my favourite white frangipani trees that smelled just heavenly, we both stopped in our tracks at the sight of the blue infinity pool that stretched towards the ocean. The water had no end and no beginning. The effect was mesmerizing. Yosh was waving us over to where he'd already staked out four sunbeds around the massive pool. He introduced me to Marie, who was just as gorgeous as Yoko, if not even more so, tall and graceful with a slight European accent to her English.

I sucked in my stomach a bit more as I sat on the edge of one sunbed trying not to look frumpy in my tankini, while Yoko and Marie sat so lithe and relaxed in their posh bikinis. I breathed in. Relax already. These are super polite people who aren't here to judge you. They're here to golf and enjoy Bali, not question why you're not wearing a bikini too.

I needn't have worried. Everyone was too busy staring at the waiter who had walked into the pool, fully dressed, carrying a tray of sliced pineapple and watermelon. I had to shake my head and look again, but yes, the waiter was now offering the fruit to the guests swimming in the pool. Well, that's it; I wasn't going to waste another second fretting about my thighs when I could be in an infinity pool overlooking the Indian Ocean, being served little satay sticks of tropical fruit. This was hospitality at a totally different level.

"No wonder we lost you to Bali," Yosh said as he grabbed another skewer of pineapple. "When I tell Cam about this, I think he'll understand why you left Hungry."

"I wish. This is my first time in a 5-star since I got here. I've been staying at little guesthouses, about thirty dollars a night."

"What have you been doing? Or should I say…who?" Yosh asked, fishing around for real answers.

"That's disgusting, Yosh, I'm not even going to answer that," I scoffed, trying hard not to blush the same colour as the watermelon I was holding. "Let's talk about the golf tour I've set up. We'll be golfing Nirwana twice – beginning and ending there – with Handara and Bali National sandwiched in between."

"Ah, avoiding the topic. Nice, but I'll get it out of you before we leave Bali," Yosh said, throwing his head back and laughing as I swam off.

Robert was always on time. So were we. We piled into his white van while he arranged our four golf bags in the back so they'd stay in place as we sped along the bumpy road past rice fields to Nirwana Golf Club.

I introduced everyone to Lui, one of the golfers I'd been paired up with on my first trip to Bali in October 2000. I'd been amazed by how well he knew every hole until he explained that he was a member there. A member of Nirwana Golf Club – that was like my Holy Grail! My overflowing enthusiasm for the course had compelled him to offer his business card and kindly offered to sign me in as a guest whenever I wanted to play a round. Lui was just as friendly when I called him to ask if my three other friends could join too.

As expected, Yosh, Marie and Yoko were blown away by Nirwana. I realized how much more fun golf was when surrounded by like-minded friends instead of random strangers. I wondered how Adi could ever fit into this part of my life. The only Balinese out here were the women caddies who could tell you exactly how, where and what to shoot with on every hole while telling me that they had never, not once, played themselves. The course was reserved for tourists who could afford daily fees that amounted to one month's salary for a local.

"Ms. Frances, it's your turn," said the caddie, bringing me back from my thoughts of why I wasn't brave enough to tell Yosh about Adi.

Was I somehow ashamed of my relationship with him? I looked over at Yosh, who'd gone back to investment banking after the whole Internet boom went bust. Marie was a successful executive flying back and forth between Europe and Tokyo, while Yoko was also a banker. During our meals together, they all complained about different aspects of their job and wished they could do what I did. But did they really think that? Would they ever be okay to stay in a thirty-dollar-a-night guesthouse instead of The Ritz? In their eyes, was I flourishing or floundering? Yes, I seemed to be living a life of freedom and travel, but was there a feasible future for me in Bali or was my time here just a fleeting sojourn?

If I told them about Adi, would they think I'd completely lost my mind? They were Japanese, a culture that abided by traditions and status even more than the Chinese. I wished the words would just come out. I'd never been afraid to speak my mind, yet now I was clamming up every time Yosh teased me about any potential beach boys. How bad could it be if I told them and possibly even introduced them to Adi? Then, I thought how quickly this news would travel to my mom. Somehow we were all connected, and it would only take seconds (even without social media) for my whole world to know.

After playing uneventful rounds at Handara and Bali National, we found ourselves back for our final round at Nirwana. I was missing Adi so much that in a split-second decision, I suddenly said that I wasn't going to golf that day and instead, I preferred to spend the day at the spa. Yosh, Marie and Yoko were all surprised that I'd suddenly changed my plans and would forego playing my favourite course for a massage, but they went off with Lui, who would now join them in their foursome.

I walked from the pro shop back down to the spa, where I knew Adi was working. He happened to be at the reception when I arrived. His massive grin confirmed that I'd made the best decision. He quickly signed me in for a three-hour pampering treatment, and we spent the rest of the afternoon in bliss.

Yosh looked at me as I got back into the van. "The spa must have been amazing. You're absolutely glowing."

"Yes, it was perfect. Exactly what I needed."

*N*yepi Day, Bali's New Year, crept up on me at breakneck speed and before I knew it, I had only a week left in Bali before flying to Australia.

Bali runs on three different and rather complicated calendars. The first calendar that hangs in every Balinese compound is called *Pawukan* consisting of thirty weeks with one cycle totaling 210 days. The second calendar is the Balinese lunar calendar that follows the moon phases and determines *Nyepi* (Balinese New Year). This year, Nyepi fell on April 4th, 2001 on the third calendar, the Gregorian one, but according to the Balinese lunar calendar the Balinese year was 1923.

Nyepi is also called Silent Day. On this day, the entire island goes completely quiet – no work, no pleasure, no fire and no movement. Even the airport is closed! No planes in or out.

Adi apologized to me that he'd be too busy to visit me in Ubud for the period leading up to Nyepi, as he had to practice *gamelan* every night in the *Bale Banjar*. Adi's fingers were constantly tapping on the back of my hand whenever we were sitting together. Music was in his blood.

He explained that gamelan was a traditional Balinese orchestra made up of thirty instruments, mostly made of metal. Boys learned gamelan from a young age in the village and at school, while girls mastered the eye movements and intricate Balinese dances that went along with the rhythmic, often mesmerizing music. I'd seen one of these gamelan groups practicing every day at the *wantilan*, a square pavilion hall across from the royal palace at the main intersection of Ubud village. Gamelan did not discriminate – young men sat beside elderly grandpas on the floor in front of their instruments. No matter their age, nimble fingers flew across different Balinese percussion instruments such as *pemade* or *kantil*, striking the metal with little hammers while simultaneously dampening the note. Using only their bare hands, others banged away on *kendang*, drums made from jackfruit wood and cowhide that were played horizontally while sitting down on the floor.

Three days prior to Nyepi, all Balinese participated in an island-wide cleansing ceremony called *Melasti*. Every village would carry their gods and goddesses to the ocean, river, or lake to be symbolically cleansed for the new year. Adi was extra busy, as his gamelan was practicing songs for a special "walking gamelan" that accompanied the chariots carrying the gods and goddesses for the entire 7 kilometres to the water and back.

Robert, my trusted driver and now friend, invited me to join him and his family for Melasti in his village, Gianyar, which was about twenty minutes east of Ubud. Robert proudly let me know that he was the head of the "young generation" group in his Banjar.

A Banjar is a subset of the village, usually your closest neighbours, and often connected through family lines. The Banjar were the married men, and the "PKK" were the wives of these men. The "young generation" were the children of the Banjar. A man joined his Banjar once he married. In Bali, being a patriarchal society, women followed the men. A woman marries into a man's family compound and village. There were exceptions when a family only had daughters, but this was uncommon as most Balinese families at the time had four children, and sometimes as many as ten.

Robert led me into his family's compound where his sister and mother helped me dress appropriately for the ceremony at the beach. They took a cotton sarong, wrapped it tightly around me, and knotted it above my right hip. They also gave me a lace *kebaya*, which I wore on top of my camisole, and finally, they tied a sash around my waist, which they called *selendang*.

"*Cantik sekali*, Princess!" announced Robert's mother.

She said I looked very pretty and pronounced my name "Princess," which many did, as the Balinese and Indonesian languages did not have the "Fr" sound. Her approval was the signal that we were ready to go.

Unlike the thousands of villagers walking towards the ocean, Robert was taking me by car. As the car slowly made its way through the throngs of people, I felt painfully conspicuous as all the faces looked up towards the car. However, I was put at ease as each person smiled up at me and waved. I really did feel like a princess.

Robert helped me down from his car because I wasn't used to being tightly bound in a sarong down to my ankles. I stepped onto the black sand that became wet as we got closer to the ocean. As far as I could see on both sides, thousands of Balinese gathered on the beach, all dressed in beautiful attire, some in all white and many in yellow and white. Dotted along the beach were elaborately carved red and gold chariots with long flags protruding from the front, waving in the wind. It was a magnificent sight! I had never been anywhere like this before. This was definitely worth a few thousand FAPs.

What piqued my interest even more were the people carrying these huge glass cases on top of their heads filled with spring rolls. Robert smirked as his eyes followed my eyes following a seller who'd stopped, put her box on the ground, folded a banana leaf into a cone and opened the box. She scooped some sauce which looked like peanut sauce into the cone and then, with a pair of scissors that doubled as tongs, she cut pieces of a spring roll into the sauce.

I asked Robert, "Are those spring rolls still hot?"

"You mean the *lumpia*? No, they're not hot. Do you want some?"

Hmmm, I thought, greasy spring rolls in unidentified sauce. Would the possible upset stomach be worth the food FAPs? I usually would dive into any street (or beach) food offering, but with Adi being busy for the next few days and me being alone during Silent Day and not even knowing where the nearest doctor or hospital was, I could not take stupid risks.

With a heavy sigh I replied, "No, I better not."

Although I stood out like a giraffe among a herd of zebra, I couldn't see beyond a few metres with so many people packed so closely together. It was stifling; the wind couldn't break through the human barrier, and there was no protection from the mid-day sun that beat down on us from above. Robert could see that it was time to take me back to my refuge in Ubud.

The day before Nyepi Day, Robert took me on a tour of East Bali to photograph as many *Ogoh Ogoh* as possible. Ogoh Ogoh are giant paper mâché monsters that the young generation of each Banjar make by hand in their bake Banjar (local community centre). Each village has their own styles and traditions for how they design and construct these freakish Ogoh

Ogoh. On the eve of Nyepi, the young generation hoist their sinister monsters onto their shoulders and parade proudly through the village accompanied by loud gamelan music and fiery torches. The Ogoh Ogoh converge at the main village crossroad to be judged, spun around and around until they crashed into a heap, and finally burnt in a searing bonfire to scare away all the evil spirits on the eve of the Balinese new year.

On Nyepi, or Silent Day, no movement is allowed and everyone stays home. All tourists remain in their hotels, not allowed on the beaches. People pass the day without any work or pleasure – no partying, no sex, no laughing loudly – and without any fire – no light, no cooking, and no working. With the island completely quiet, the Balinese pray that the evil spirits will not find us again for another year.

Adi hugged me tighter as I recounted the awe of being surrounded by his unique Balinese culture. Part of me wished that I hadn't planned a month-long trip to Australia. However, Chinese common sense compelled me to explore any possible romantic options before becoming serious with him. Marty, the friend I was staying with in Melbourne, was a question mark. Marty was also my alibi.

Only Grace knew that I was spending four weeks in Bali prior to my month in Australia; my family assumed that Bali was a short stopover. It was still the era of postcards and landline phones when nobody knew exactly where you were unless you told them.

When planning "my sabbatical from life," visiting Marty had reassured Mom of my safety and sanity. I guessed she had mixed feelings about Marty. He checked many boxes of the perfect son-in-law: Chinese, check. Homeowner, check. Securely employed, check. Called her "Auntie" with proper respect, check. However, the fact that his hometown of Melbourne was on the other side of the world negated all the checks. My mom never had any interest in Australia, and in-laws living "down under" was not an exciting prospect.

I'd met Marty on my month-long trip to Europe in August 1994. He and his brother, Gary, had become my best Aussie mates on the bus of under-thirties. Marty and I were fierce Uno buddies and he'd always lug my heavy suitcase off the bus. Whether we were in Positano or Vienna, I could always depend on his kindness and strong biceps.

In 1996, I'd visited him in Chicago while he was there for work training. Then Marty came for a tour of Canada in 1997. I proudly showed off my hometown of Toronto before we flew to Calgary. From there, we drove out west together, stopping in Banff, Kelowna, Vancouver and finally, Whistler. Without radio reception in the Rocky Mountains, I'd picked up an Alanis Morrisette tape, which probably put Marty off Canadian artists forever – we played that cassette until it broke. At a gas stop off the highway, we froze in front of the newspaper boxes that headlined Princess Di's death.

Now in April 2001, I was heading to Melbourne.

It was 5:30 a.m., and Melbourne's airport was empty except for a small group of Chinese people who seemed to be waving at me. I squinted. Without my driving glasses on, they were an indistinct blur to my sleepy eyes.

"Frances, over here!" shouted a familiar Aussie accent. I could just make out Marty, who had a gorgeous Asian beauty draped around him.

I couldn't believe that Marty had roused his friends out of bed to pick up his Canadian travel buddy at 5:30 a.m. on a Saturday morning. We piled into Marty's Honda CRV and then into a booth at a twenty-four-hour diner for breakfast. Their heavy Aussie accents made it difficult for me to catch the full conversation, but I didn't feel left out. They were so friendly and down-to-earth, no pretension at all.

Marty's girlfriend, Angela, came back with us to his house. Marty had done well for himself; at thirty-one, he owned a lovely two-story home across from a strip of parkland that ran the length of the road. It was the perfect place to settle down and start a family.

When Marty showed me to my room, he whispered, "I'm sorry about Angela. We broke up months ago. She got wind that you were coming to stay and suddenly wanted to get back together two days ago."

I laughed, "She's worried about you and me? Didn't you tell her that you're like my brother?"

"Yeah, sure, I guess," Marty said, shrugging. "I don't mind. Let's see what happens."

"You can let her know that I'm seeing someone in Bali, so she can relax."

Part of me wondered about a future with Marty, but I didn't want to lead him on, so I'd fessed up about Adi in a nonchalant way.

After I'd showered and napped, Marty decided it was time to plan out my time in Australia. He offered the use of his car at my disposal, as long as I could drop him off at work in the mornings.

"Wait, you drive on the other side of the road. And I haven't driven all year in Asia," I said.

"No worries, mate. You'll get the hang of it. There's just this one weird turning lane that I have to show you downtown. Other than that, you'll be fine." Marty grinned.

I appreciated his confidence in me.

Marty continued, "I have so many places to take you. We can start at the Great Ocean Drive."

"Is that like driving from Los Angeles to San Francisco up the California coast? I did that with my mom and brother after my grandmother passed away."

"Well, maybe… Never mind, scratch that. We can drive down to Yarra Valley or Mornington Peninsula for a wine weekend."

Wanting to ward off what could become a romantic getaway, I said, "I think Napa Valley spoiled me for other wine regions, unless of course, you can whisk me back to Beaune and those amazing caves we explored."

"You're a tough person to impress, mate."

"Sorry, don't mean to be difficult. How about the Great Barrier Reef? Do you dive? I've always wanted to learn."

"Yeah! Now we're talking. Somewhere you've never been, doing something new!"

"Okay, let me plan it. I have tons of time while you're at work."

"What else will you do all day?"

"Golf, of course."

The first evening, we met up with another bunch of Marty's friends at a Spanish tapas place tucked in Melbourne's Laneways. It reminded me so much of Europe.

While standing outside saying goodbye to his friends, I exclaimed. "I love Melbourne! The weather is perfect, warm and balmy."

They all started laughing and punched Marty in the ribs. "What lies have you been feeding her?"

"What? Isn't it always like this?" I asked.

"No, it's never like this. In one day, you'll experience four seasons."

That very evening, I woke up shivering in bed. There wasn't any central heating. I pulled on another blanket, but I was still freezing. Taking a shower in the morning was torture. Used to the humidity and warmth of Bali and Hong Kong, my body couldn't do cold weather anymore. None of my clothing was appropriate for Melbourne weather. In the end, I wore a thick fluffy fleece jacket of Marty's every single day and night.

Marty had always told me that Melbourne was "the top of the world," to which I always countered, "No, you're 'down under' and Toronto is 'the top of the world.'"

I finally grasped why he identified with his hometown as much as I related to mine. Unlike many U.S. cities where assimilation and integration were the keys to survival, Melbourne and Toronto were mosaics rather than melting pots. Each had pockets of vibrant ethnic neighbourhoods where traditional cultures flourished. People of all backgrounds flocked there for food as authentic as anything you'd find in Italy or Vietnam.

My days fell into an easy rhythm. After dropping Marty off at work, I'd navigate to the far left lane to make a right turn (like, what?), park somewhere downtown and wander around the Laneways filled with quaint cafés and quirky shops.

One of my favourite haunts was Pelligrini's Espresso Bar, which reminded me both of Rome and Little Italy in Toronto. Marty had taken me there before we caught a musical at the Princess Theatre. The moment I walked into the narrow Italian trattoria where the daily pasta specials were chalked up on a board, I was smitten. The fresh, homemade pasta was sauced lightly with a bit of pasta water, exactly as you'd find if you were sitting in Piazza Navona. The best part was the retro wraparound bar where I'd sit on one of the red vinyl stools and enjoy my gnocchi pomodoro and tiramisu without feeling alone or needing to hide my head in a book. I'd learnt this little trick while I was working in sales at CNET and during my lonely days in Tokyo.

Other days, I'd jump on the highway and head out of the city to play a round of golf.

When I told Marty that I was driving to Portsea Golf Club to play one of Australia's championship courses, he looked a bit skeptical. "That's really far, and I'm not sure the weather will hold out."

"It's okay, if I play there, I'll get so many FAPs!" I said as I pulled away from the curb.

The journey down to Portsea took me past little towns called Mornington and Sorrento where fish and chip places peeked out from in between bakeries selling vanilla slices. I marked them as possible stops for the drive back. The ocean appeared on my right, low grey waves under an even grayer looking sky. *Maybe this isn't the best weather for a day out on the fairways,* I thought, *but I've already driven for two hours so I can't turn back now. Besides, when will I ever have a chance to play Portsea again?*

The empty parking lot should have warned me off, but I continued into the pro shop.

A lanky golfer looked up from the register and stared at me incredulously. He asked, "You want to play in this weather?"

"Yes, please. How much?"

"If you're crazy enough to go out there, you can play for free," he said, shaking his head. "But I'm not responsible for what happens."

"Umm, okay, that's great. Thanks," I said, not paying any attention to his concern.

A free round at Portsea – I just saved seventy-five dollars! I bounced over to the first tee and practiced a few warm-up swings. I tried to tee up for my first shot. The wind was fierce, blowing my ball off the tee repeatedly. Maybe this wasn't such a good idea, but it wasn't raining so I wasn't giving up yet.

I finally got the golf ball to stay teed up. I smiled at my ball and swung. I screamed as my ball flew forwards and then boomeranged back at me because of the force of the wind. If I hadn't ducked, the ball would have hit me in the head with full force. Well, that's just nuts! I stuffed my driver back into my golf bag and ran towards the pro shop just in time; the sky opened up and rain pelted down.

Sheepishly, I said, "You're right, I'll get killed by my own ball if I play today. Just want to say thank you and let you know you don't have to send out a search party. I'm leaving."

"Well, it looks like your ball knocked some sense into you," the man behind the register said, giving me a big grin.

"Yes, and it almost knocked me out completely!" I shook my head and laughed at my foolishness.

The redeeming part of my aborted round of golf was digging into a plate of fresh, piping hot fish and chips while bundled up in Marty's warm fleece as the freezing rain lashed against the windows.

Between days downtown and days on golf courses, I stayed home and cooked, a small way to repay Marty for his generous hospitality. I'd walk to Chadstone Mall to pick up groceries and spend the afternoon making simple meals for two. It was a test drive for me. Living with Marty felt like playing house. This was what married people did. Of course, if I lived here, I'd have a job and eventually kids to take care of.

Marty's girlfriend rarely came over. I felt like I was dating Marty – we went out for dinners, to see shows and even to his parents' place on Sundays. There I saw what life would be like with Marty; his older brothers, their wives, and toddlers running around at the grandparents' with a big lamb roast in the warmth of their kitchen. It was all very tempting.

But neither of us crossed the line. We remained firmly in the friend zone. And my dreams were always of Adi.

Sports-related FAPs alluded me during my whole stay in Australia.

I'd arranged a live-aboard dive trip for Marty and me to explore the Great Barrier Reef. We'd taken the Padi dive course in Cairns, but during the final exam in the deep pool, my left ear started bleeding. The doctor forbade me to dive as I had flights back to Melbourne, onwards to Sydney and then back to Bali in the next week.

Marty was more disappointed than I – he'd lost his diving buddy. I was still eager to live on the boat, despite not being able to dive. I could snorkel. The Australians teased that I'd end up as shark bait. On the boat, Marty's misery increased as he became seasick along with the other divers. Oddly, I didn't get seasick at all.

Floating on my back and looking up at the blue sky, the world seemed endless. How did I find myself in the middle of the Great Barrier Reef, and all by myself?

Marty perked up immensely when a colossal turtle swam close enough to hug. He could not stop talking about the turtle.

After four days on the boat, we longed for hot showers, gourmet food and some pampering. Anticipating our needs, I'd already booked us luxury spa treatments at Daintree Resort, located deep in the rainforest.

Before visiting me in Canada, Marty, a typical Aussie bloke, had never gone to a spa and thought massages and scrubs were only for the ladies. In Banff, I'd convinced him to join me at a mountain spring resort where he'd reveled in the hot mineral pools. Now, Marty eagerly awaited our spa sessions at Daintree and understood why I was dating Adi, a professional massage therapist.

Marty gave me his fleece jacket as my going away gift. I begged him to keep it since I was heading to balmy Sydney and Bali, but he insisted that I take it as reminder of my time at "the top of the world."

Cam said he'd move to Sydney in a second if the opportunity arose. He'd described the city with a dreamy look in his eyes as a cross between San Francisco and Toronto, a cosmopolitan mix of Asian and Western cultures set against dramatic ocean views and iconic surf beaches.

Cam's comparison to our Canadian hometown could be seen everywhere. Familiar street names passed by: Queen Street, King Street, Wellington. The British Commonwealth tied us Canadians and Australians together even though the two countries were geographically worlds apart and both had long ago gained independence from England. Looking around, I noticed even the architecture reminded me of the parliament buildings in downtown Toronto. I ambled down to the waterfront, taking my time to stop and see if I could catch a glimpse of the Opera House between the red brick buildings.

Businesspeople rushed past me, heads bent, entering office buildings with their coffees in one hand and their briefcases in the other. I looked at their grim, unsmiling faces and thought, *I do not want to find myself there again.*

Down at the waterfront, I peeked into the window at Neil Perry's Rockpool in the Rocks restaurant, wondering if I had the gumption to eat there by myself. I wished Adi or even Marty was here. Lunch was more casual than dinner, but it would still be full of suits doing business, not appropriate for solo dining. I walked further along and found myself at a seafood market. It was pristine and clean, a world away from the messy wet markets of Hong Kong. Amazingly, you could pick any seafood you wanted and they would cook it up simply for you. *Ah, this is the perfect solution.* I could sit outside at one of the picnic tables with one of the best views of Sydney harbour.

After lunch, I jumped on a bus headed for Bondi Beach. The bus wound its way through downtown and then through leafy suburbs and seemed to climb forever, up to a very posh area with massive mansions. Strange that a bus route would pass through this type of neighbourhood, I thought. Was I on the wrong bus? Thankfully, once we made it to the other side of the hill, Bondi Beach spread out in front of me. Even on a weekday, the beach was packed with sunbathers and surfers. There was a massive, Olympic-size pool where people were jumping off the very high diving board. It was definitely not my scene.

What was I doing here? I felt utterly alone at that moment. To keep my mind off my loneliness, I decided to shop for a gift for Adi.

I wasn't sure exactly where we were going or if we even had a future together. I hadn't told anyone about him, except for Grace and Marty. And even then, I had kept the details sparse.

Adi was unlike anyone I had grown up with. His world could not be more different than mine. I couldn't imagine how I could stay in Bali, and I couldn't see how he could follow me either, especially since I didn't know where I was going myself. Shaking my head, I simply had to believe that I'd figure this out. *Just go with the flow, Frances. Don't overthink. Don't worry about the future. Enjoy this time with Adi and just see what happens.*

A silver lighter with "Sydney" emblazoned on its side caught my eye. It was subtle and understated, unlike the other cheesy souvenirs. I disagreed with Adi's smoking, but I wasn't in any position to tell him what to do. In the end, I splurged on the lighter and a cool pair of Ray-Bans. At least I'd help protect his eyes. My one other purchase in Australia was a lacy blue lingerie set from David Jones in Melbourne. I wasn't sure if that gift was for Adi or for me.

I took the bus back to the Surry Hills area, where I'd read about an up-

and-coming restaurant called Billy Kwong. The quiet neighbourhood was rougher than I'd expected, but I still went in search of the restaurant. It was a shoebox of a place with tables squeezed together and packed with diners, all laughing and chatting loudly. Without any bar or small tables, I was already intimidated. No matter how yummy the food, I wouldn't feel comfortable in a place like that alone.

I found another Asian bolthole around the corner that looked cheerful and inviting with its front painted in a deep red and a bar looking into the kitchen. A solo stool waited for a solo diner. Looking back now, I wish I had been the girl who could walk into Billy Kwong, with or without a book, and enjoy a meal alone without feeling judged.

The fragrant scent of frangipani wafted from the *canang* offering on Robert's dashboard. Bali assails all your senses when it welcomes you home. My heartbeat quickened as we turned into the driveway of Stardust Cottages Guesthouse.

I elbowed open the heavy antique wooden doors and dropped my black Prada tote on the cool marble floor. Behind the gauze of the mosquito net, Adi snored softly. I tiptoed over and covered his face with butterfly kisses. His eyes fluttered open. I gazed into his dark irises, drawing my hand along his chiseled jaw. He shuddered. My skin tingled as he pulled me down and kissed me deeply and ran his hands through my hair and along my neckline. He flipped me beneath him and let me feel his desire. Without a word, the month away from each other fell away in seconds.

Our legs entwined, I recounted my adventures in Australia while we nibbled on room service from the guesthouse's sister restaurant. Completely satiated, we drifted into our dreams.

Suffering from jet lag, I woke up famished. I flipped on the bedside lamp and gently shook Adi awake.

"Honey, do you think we can get some *padang* food?"

"Um, what time is it?" Adi mumbled back sleepily.

"It's midnight."

Squinting at me, he smiled and laughed, "Of course, darling. Anything for you. I'm hungry too. Padang is good."

I wrapped my arms around Adi's sturdy body as we balanced on his motorbike. He didn't bother with his helmet, which allowed for ease of nibbling his neck as I leaned into his muscular back. It was pitch dark; Adi took it slow around the potholes. Back on the paved main road, Adi sped across town in two minutes. The chill of the wind heightened the warmth of his back pressing into me.

We climbed up the steep stairs to the only lit-up establishment, fondly called "The Padang Place." We didn't know the small eatery's actual name, but anyone in the know would only eat at "The Padang Place," which boasted slightly higher hygiene standards and a quicker turnover than the other places in town. Other padang places piled their spicy dishes in tall pyramids for an undetermined amount of time behind the supposedly impenetrable curtain, while flies took bites of each dish, twenty-four hours day and night.

The server, hailing from Sumatra, pulled back the curtain for us to examine the night's offerings. He piled steaming rice onto banana leaves held in a flat woven plate called *ingka*. He added some boiled cassava leaves on the side of the plate and turned towards me to take my order. I pointed to the chicken rendang; Adi jumped in asking for the chicken leg, not the overly dry breast, in Bahasa Indonesian. I squeezed his hand, in awe that after a month apart, Adi recalled the smallest details, little things others wouldn't notice.

Many other dishes were foreign to me: yellow-coloured blocks of what looked like squished white beans, intestines in rich brown gravies, assorted deep-fried items, including little round patties, some made of corn and others that looked like they had onions and other vegetables in a batter. I recognized slices of fried eggplant smothered in spicy tomato sambal. Adi nodded to the potato *perkedel* – one of his favourites – to be added to my plate, along with generous spoons of green and red chili sambal.

I sat down ready to eat with my spoon and fork, but Adi had disappeared into the back.

"Where did you go?"

"I wash my hands. Do you want to try... eat with your hands?"

"Sure, why not," I said as I got up to wash my hands too.

All Indonesians eat with their right hand only. It's a learned skill, and only for thick-skinned individuals.

"My fingers are burning," I said.

Adi laughed as he swept away several dropped grains of rice from my lap with his left hand.

"What's that?" I asked, pointing my chin to the yellow-coloured block on his plate.

"It's tempe curry."

"What's tempe?"

Adi looked at me with wonder in his eyes, "You never eat tempe? We eat this every day. It's made from soybeans. Like tofu, but tempe is…fermented. I don't really like it cooked this way. It's good deep-fried with Balinese spices."

The next day, Adi worked the later shift, so he didn't have to leave until 11:00 a.m. which allowed us a leisurely morning to nibble at our breakfast and laze around. We worked on Adi's floating skills in the oval-shaped pool adorned with goddesses spouting water over our heads. I plucked frangipani flowers one by one out of the pool, breathed in their amazing scent and assembled them on the stone edge of the pool like wedding decorations.

Adi noticed me holding the flowers to my nose. Later that day, he surprised me with a bottle of my favourite frangipani body lotion. The glass bottle of the pale green lotion was fitted snugly in a handmade batik-designed paper box and tied with a ribbon. The bottle itself was a piece of art, tied with twine under the lip and sealed with gold wax. Adi helped his cousin Suaji make these uniquely packaged spa products, which they sold to hotel spas all over the island. They supplied several of the 5-star resorts, including The Ritz Carlton and Four Seasons, where Suaji was a massage therapist.

The humid, moist weather in Bali suited my skin. I glowed with health. Previously, my skin cracked and even bled in the harsh, dry winters of Toronto, despite the rich moisturizers I lathered all over my body.

In Bali, all the layers fell away – no more business suits, no more thick creams, no more pretense.

I clung to my last few days with Adi.

After Bali, I planned to hang out with Grace in Hong Kong for a few weeks before heading back to San Francisco and Toronto to figure out my next steps. My sabbatical couldn't last forever.

Grace and I shared an unreasonable fear of public toilets, especially ones I'd encountered in China that were simply holes in the ground. We insisted on 5-star toilets if we were outside. My toilet anxiety limited my ability to explore further afield with Adi.

With my time in Bali drawing to a close, Adi insisted on taking me to see the "real Bali" for our last date. He didn't actually say "last date," as neither of us knew what to say. What were we anyways? We'd never discussed any possible future. Adi had learned a saying, "Let's play it by ear..." and figured it described our situation well. These few weeks with Adi, I'd lived moment to moment for once in my life. I didn't have any answers since I couldn't even pose the questions in my own mind.

We drove east towards Candi Dasa in search of a little fish warung that Adi's cousin Suaji had raved about. We inched past *Goa Lawah* (the Bat Cave Temple) so we wouldn't miss the small dirt road heading north.

Our noses followed the scent of coconut smoke and we found a hole-in-the-wall packed with locals. It smelled delicious. There were huge plumes of smoke coming off the satay grills that sat directly on the dirt floor. Young men, teenagers really, fanned the tuna satay, turning them over as they cooked. I stared in awe as the cooks remained perfectly balanced while squatting, skewering more satay and grilling all at once. It was a perfectly choreographed dance of food.

We headed inside, squinting to adjust from the bright sunshine to the dim and dingy warung. Adi pointed to two spots on one of the low wooden slab tables where people sat to eat. Banana leaves of food laid on the same table where they sat cross-legged. Knowing that I couldn't hold that pose, I opted to swing my legs over one side of the low table.

A grouchy-looking girl haphazardly put our food between us. There were two types of tuna satay – *sate tusuk* (pieces of marinated tuna skewered on bamboo) and *sate lilit* (traditional Balinese satay made of pounded spiced meat, in this case, tuna). There was also *pepes ikan* (tuna wrapped and grilled in banana leaves), a fiery hot golden-coloured fish soup, green *Kang Kung* (morning glory) in tomato sambal, and deep-fried peanuts. All of it was served with the killer condiment, *sambal matah*, a Balinese raw spice paste of lemongrass, shallot, chillies, roasted shrimp paste, coconut oil and kaffir lime. When we started eating, we stopped talking. The food was insanely delicious.

From there, we decided to explore a hidden cove called Blue Lagoon. We climbed up a rugged hill shaded by a large tamarind tree. Adi yanked off a tamarind for me to try the tangy, sticky fruit.

I desperately needed to pee, but there weren't any 5-star resorts or even one-star lodgings around. Hidden behind a tree, I ended up peeing on my sandals while Adi laughed his head off.

"Darling, that's why you need to learn how to squat. This is a basic life skill," said Adi as he held me up so I didn't make a total mess of myself.

"Not for me! I'm never coming back here. I'm sticking with 5-star."

"Okay, that's fine, but if you want to see 'real Bali,' you need to squat," Adi said, helping me hobble down to the ocean lagoon to wash off my sandals.

"Why would I need to squat?" I questioned as I walked right into the shallows.

"Balinese homes have squat toilets. Very dirty. Sometimes you can't find a 5-star toilet when you need one." He said, pointing to my wet sandals.

"Ugh, I can't think about this. It's so gross. Let's go back. I need to wash off my feet with soap. And possibly, throw away these flip-flops."

✳

On my last morning, I planned a little trek to collect my last FAPs in Bali. My guidebook revealed a stunning walk that started at Pura Gunung Lebah, a mystical temple deep in the jungle valley, and continued across the Campuhan ridge into the village of Keliki.

After two hours of solid walking, I finally found myself back at the very north end of Ubud, desperate for a washroom. I wasn't ready to try squatting anywhere in the local village, so I ventured down a driveway marked by an impressive stone sign that read "Ulun Ubud Resort," and figured correctly that they'd have decent facilities.

Stepping into the lobby, I circled unique wooden statues of a couple, tall and thin, reaching over 2 metres each.

The front receptionist stepped forward and said, "Those are called *Loro Blonyo* or the 'Inseparable Couple.' They are from Java."

"Wow, everything here is incredible. These tables and sculptures, I haven't seen anything like this in Mas village or elsewhere."

"Our owner has a special collection in the back. Would you like to see more?"

I nodded enthusiastically as she led me across the parking lot, pushed open a pair of wooden doors wide enough for a truck to pass through, and into a lofty warehouse-style building filled with massive dining tables. These were not your everyday Pottery Barn or Ikea tables; they were substantial slabs of solid wood, measuring 4 metres long, 1 metre wide and 10 centimetres thick.

I walked over to one table that was a beautiful patina of coffee colours, with uneven cuts and unusual solid legs at each end. I rubbed my hand across the wood, feeling the smooth finish. Another table with a matching bench called out to me too. The designs were utterly unique, one-of-a-kind pieces. I was in love.

An eccentric elderly man with white streaks in his black hair, which was tied in a low ponytail, came in from behind me and introduced himself as Gusti, the owner. "These are very unique tables that I collect and finish here in my workshop. I'm very selective. The wood talks to me." Gusti patted one of his tables fondly.

I was thinking, this is a whacked wood guy, probably the best person to get a wood table or anything wood from. "I see. So how much would one of these tables cost?" I asked.

"Well, I usually don't sell to the public. I sell to hotels like Begawan Giri.

Last week, one of their guests – a fashion designer, Donna or Karen, or something like that – bought some tables.

I coughed, "You mean, Donna Karan? She bought tables from you?"

"Yes, yes, that's her. You know her?" he asked me back so innocently, as if every tourist knew each other.

"Well, I know of her. She's kind of famous. Do you mean I can't buy one of your tables?"

"Are you looking for a table?"

"Well, not really, as I don't have a home yet. But I agree with you, each table is unique. I may never find another one like this." I bent down to touch the first table that I liked and muttered more to myself than to Gusti, "You're right; I don't even know why I'm asking. I don't even have anywhere to put it."

"I can see you love that one. If you want to buy it, you can leave it here until you get a home. Then, we can ship it to anywhere in the world."

"That's very kind of you, but I don't know where I'll end up or even if this long table will fit." My heart ached a bit, not wanting to admit that I had no real future with Adi. That I was untethered, homeless.

"That's okay. These tables are rare and valuable. If you buy them now, I'll store them here. If you can't find a big home next time, I'll return your money."

"Really? You'd repurchase the table from me?" my eyebrows raised, wondering if this was a scam.

"Yes, I can easily resell the table."

"Wow. I absolutely love this table and even that one there with the matching bench." My outlook changed to optimism, thinking about how these tables could anchor me. In my mind's eye, I could see my future dining room in my dream home – a warehouse loft, somewhere in the SOMA district of San Francisco or near St. Lawrence Market in downtown Toronto.

"If you take both tables and the bench, I give you a good deal," Gusti said smiling, looking confident that he'd landed the sale.

I rarely went shopping; I preferred to collect unique items as they appeared. Often, serendipity interceded and treasures would appear in the most unlikely of places. This was how my massive dining tables sat in his warehouse until I found my forever home.

*G*race gushed over my new persona. "Look at you, rockin' a sarong! Only you can get away with wearing that sexy lace top and walk around Hong Kong like you're on a beach. You look like a Balinese goddess!"

"And you're glowing like Aphrodite," I responded.

"Ugh, no, I feel like a beached whale," Grace said as she rubbed her pregnant belly. "You're slim and tanned. I've never seen you look better."

Ah, what best friends are for? To lift you up when you're feeling despondent. Thank goodness I was staying with her, Jonathan and Ashlyn to keep my mind off Adi. I felt like a fish out of water now that I was back in Hong Kong. I missed everything about Bali. The blue skies, the clean air, the smiling faces, everything. What I missed most was waking up beside Adi and knowing that day would bring another adventure.

"Are you sure you're up for Shenzhen tomorrow?" I asked Grace.

"The thought of shopping and feasting with you and Rachel is what's keeping me going," Grace answered.

I shook my head in disbelief as I lugged ten massive shopping bags behind two waddling ladies. Grace and Rachel had the same due date, August 16th. How were they not exhausted?

The two of them had cleared out entire shelves of knock-off designer purses in the wholesale shops of Luohu Commercial City. They convinced me not to miss out on deals of a lifetime; I succumbed under the power of the super shoppers and reluctantly bought three decadent confections posing as purses. In a moment of clarity, I picked up two simple, black, pocket-sized shoulder bags: one a fake Prada and the other knockoff DKNY.

I carried their parcels while begging them to sit down for some dim sum, but they were relentless in their pursuit.

The following evening, Grace and Jonathan had to attend a black-tie fundraising event.

I wandered along Wellington Street aimlessly, feeling nostalgic. I wavered in front of a Thai restaurant that I'd tried once with our HungryForWords team, back when we were a small, tight group that ate every meal together.

I didn't want to go in alone, but I was starving. I stood a bit taller, pulled open the door and made my way up the stairs to a buzzing restaurant filled with boisterous groups around big round tables. I hesitated. *Stop being ridiculous*, I told myself, *just find a quiet table in the back.*

As I navigated around the tables, I heard someone shouting my name. I turned and saw Cam, Audrey and Jake sitting at a table tucked into a side nook. I was mortified. Of all the millions of people in Hong Kong and the thousands of places I could have chosen to eat, how did I find myself at the one place where three of the only people I know in Hong Kong were dining at that exact moment? I breathed in and walked over to their table.

"Frances, you're back!" Audrey got up and hugged me.

"Wow, you look gorgeous...looks like Bali suits you," Jake said. His appreciative eyes travelled down my lacy top and over the mint green silk sarong wrapped tightly around my hips.

"Ah, thanks," I said, leaning closer to Audrey.

"Are you alone?" asked Cam innocently, not meaning to drive the lonely stake into my chest.

"Ah, yes, I'm grabbing a bite before meeting Grace later," I lied out of embarrassment.

"Don't just stand there, sit down and join us," he said as he pulled back a chair.

"No, no, it's okay. I don't want to disturb you guys," I said, looking around for a table to escape to.

"Are you kidding? Just sit down already," Audrey said and pulled me down in the chair beside her.

I'd never felt so uncomfortable in my life. The conversation kept stalling. Nobody could or would say what we were all honestly thinking. Things had been so different just sixteen months earlier when the four of us were the best of friends, thinking that HungyForWords was going to conquer the world. And that even if it didn't, we would have so much fun trying. I quietly sighed in relief when the bill came.

As we were parting ways, Jake said, "Frances, let me treat you to afternoon tea at the Shangri-La. I know how much you love The Library there. Or let's do a spin class together."

I wrinkled my forehead with confusion. He'd betrayed me, bad mouthing me while I was in Tokyo and tainting my friendship with Cam. I thought, *What an asshole, as if I'd ever trust you again.*

With a bright smile, I blew him air kisses, squeezed his arm and said, "I'd love that. Let's get together soon."

In the taxi on my way back to Grace's place, I pressed speed dial to my trustworthy travel agent, Raj. "Please book me a flight to Bali, departing two days from now."

There wasn't a reasonable explanation for Dad, Mom, or my godmother as to why I was rushing back to Bali. I'd just returned from a two-month sojourn. They expected me to get back on track and figure out my next steps.

I fabricated that I longed to golf in Kunming, China, and had to do it before moving back to the States or Canada.

They all asked the same question: "You're going to Kunming? By yourself?"

I lied, "It's an organized golf tour, I won't be alone. I'll stay in a luxury 5 star resort. Don't worry, I'll be fine."

*L*imited by my dwindling savings for this unplanned trip back to Bali, I'd booked us into Sayan Terrace. The small boutique property of seven stand-alone cottages offered the same views as Four Seasons Sayan, but at a fraction of the price. No matter how hard I tried, it was impossible to capture the breathtaking view on my camera. I was literally a tiny spec in the grandness of it all.

Adi and I basked in the oval infinity pool, perched high above the rainforest jungle and rushing Ayung River. Around this communal pool, we met an assortment of characters right out of a timeless travelogue: two eloquent Asian hoteliers, an eccentric English lady living out her retirement in paradise, a couple of Dutch honeymooners constantly canoodling as if they'd just rolled out of bed.

My relationship with Adi shifted when I bought that ticket back to Bali. My actions spoke volumes. Adi knew that he was no longer a casual holiday fling. We acted and felt like a couple.

When we walked into a café, Adi exuded a quiet confidence, tossing out silly remarks that made all the waitresses laugh.

His eyes peered at me from beneath his long lashes. "You know, if you could speak Balinese, you'd think I was really funny."

Squeezing his bulging bicep and pecking him on the cheek, I said, "Honey, you're hilarious even in English. And all those girls giggling and batting their eyes at you are proof enough."

English was Adi's fifth language, so words danced from his lips. His favourite pastime was messing with me.

"Now let me practice my Bahasa Indonesian," I said, motioning a waitress over. "*Saya mau satu kelapa muda.*"

"No, honey. It's *kepala muda*," Adi corrected me kindly.

I shook my head in frustration, and repeated, "*Saya mau satu kepala muda.*"

The waitress bent over laughing as Adi slapped his leg and howled.

I swung around and punched Adi in the arm, "You tricked me again. I just ordered 'young head' instead of 'young coconut,' didn't I? You're the worst teacher ever. I'm never going to learn."

"No, this way you'll remember two words, not just one," he said as he tapped his young head with his fingers.

"Okay, okay. I now know two words. Progress. Let's eat and get back to the hotel. It's too hot to be out and about."

Adi was a kind, considerate and polite human being, treating every single person we met with respect. Whenever I was excited about something, which was often, I was always super enthusiastic, bordering on manic. He showed me a quiet confidence that perhaps spoke even louder than someone who was always talking (namely, me).

For a Balinese man to be with a foreigner seriously was almost unheard of at that time. We drew stares everywhere we went. It could be that my giggle, which sounded like a goat bleating, attracted the attention, but Adi assured me that it was us, not me.

Even lying together in the privacy of our suite, we could almost feel the curious eyes of the staff watching us, wondering what we were doing together.

I lay my head against his chest as Adi tried explaining the complexities of me being with him, but I didn't fully grasp the implications at the time. He told me that for native Balinese, every single person in your village knew everything about you, and each Balinese person was intimately tied to their community within the Banjar structure. Once a woman married into a community, she took on responsibility for intensive Banjar obligations to help at every ceremony, whether in happiness (a birth or wedding) or sadness (a funeral).

No foreign woman in her right mind would sign up for a lifetime of this. I assumed that growing up in a Chinese household with a practicing Buddhist mother and having to perform duties whether you wanted to or not had prepared me well for Bali. I'd later learn why my professors at business school preached, "Never assume anything. Never."

I brushed off Adi's concerns as I looked into his kind eyes. "Honey, I can learn fast. And I love the Balinese culture; everything here is so beautiful and romantic. And I have you, the most patient teacher, right?"

Springing out of bed, I carefully balanced a plate of fruit on my head that teetered dangerously as I attempted to glide across the room.

Adi laughed, "Darling, a plate of fruit salad is not the same as a tower of fruit offerings."

"Watch me! I've never been scared of anything," I challenged.

"Okay, okay, let's take it slowly, okay?"

I reached over and kissed him, feeding him a morsel of fruit from the plate.

We decided to take one of the hotel owners, William, up on his offer to stay for free at his family's hotel in Jimbaran. This way, I could splurge on my last three nights at Waka Gangga, the sister hotel to the Waka Di Ume where Adi and I had first kissed.

After we turned off the main road in Jimbaran, we found ourselves bumping along a rugged path strewn with white rocks and gravel through an arid area without any trees.

Convinced that we'd lost our way, Adi kept asking, "Are you sure we're in the right place?"

"These are the directions that William gave me," I said as I held on to the enormous flapping paper map. It was not easy navigating on the back of a motorbike.

As we rounded a particularly tight corner past a couple of cows who looked as thirsty as we felt, a low, flat building appeared with an understated sign: "Jimbaran Hills." I carefully got off the bike, still with my legs spread out as if I'd gotten off a horse. My butt was so sore after the hour and a half of bouncing on the back of the motorbike. I was even more grateful for Adi at that moment, thinking of how he made that ride every day to Tanah Lot, worked nine hours, and then drove another hour and a half back to Ubud to be with me. Thankfully, Adi only had one more day of work before taking four days off for his first vacation ever.

Adi pulled my heavy bag off his bike and escorted me through the small, dark lobby. It was particularly dim coming in from the blinding sunlight and white stone road we'd travelled. At check-in, the receptionist expected me, informing me that all my meals could be taken in the hotel restaurant since it was far from any cafés. I raised my eyebrows as Adi was heading back to work and I'd be alone there.

"Darling, you can have *lunner* here, and I'll be back late tonight."

I laughed when the receptionist looked bewildered, "Honey, *lunner* isn't a real word. I just made it up as we always have our main meal between lunch and dinner, so I called it *lunner*. It's a meal that I only have with you," I said as I hugged Adi tightly.

"Oh, okay. The pool looks good. Relax and see you tonight."

I imagined that a highway motel room would look something like what I found when the receptionist opened the door to my room. While relatively clean, it looked like nobody had stayed there for years. The furniture was plain and non-descript. If real tourists ever stayed here and thought this was Bali, it would be a real shame. I really couldn't complain since I was staying for free, but we'd leave tomorrow.

I picked up the phone and called Waka Gangga to let them know Adi and I would be checking in a day earlier than expected.

e were back in the land of lush green rice fields as far as the eye could see. Instead of turning left towards Tanah Lot, Adi took us right and further west into Tabanan Regency. There were no longer any signs of tourism. We zoomed past local children who turned to wave and smile at us as we passed. Older women, shirtless and braless with towels wrapped like turbans on their heads, bathed unabashed in the little streams that ran alongside the narrow road. Instead of hiding themselves, they showed us toothless grins. I felt totally at home.

The road wound down towards the sea. Holding on to Adi, I peeked over his shoulder to see the glittering black sand behind five or six little thatched, cone-shaped cottages. It was a dramatic view from our high vantage point. Adi took us along the paved driveway to the entrance of the hotel.

"Welcome to Waka Gangga, Miss Frances." The smiling bellboy took my duffle bag off Adi's motorbike. "Your driver can park over there."

"He's not my driver. He's my boyfriend who's also staying here," I corrected him with a glare.

Casting his eyes downwards, the bellboy apologized, "I'm sorry for my mistake. We don't have many locals stay with us."

I shouldn't have shown my anger. This remote part of Bali was a world away from tourist hubs like Ubud or Kuta. In Bali, local guys didn't seriously date foreign women. There were beach playthings, aptly named

"Kuta cowboys," who attracted lustful cougars, but rarely did you find a Balinese man courting a *tamu*.

Tamu translated politely to guest. In fact, I only knew of one tamu who had married a local, namely Brenda, the Australian who'd married Gede and ran Stardust Cottages. Adi later explained that the official translation of foreigner was *bule*. Tamu was polite terminology used by the hospitality industry and had become the standard way Balinese addressed foreigners.

Time stood still for us at Waka Gangga. We sheltered from the scorching sun in our cone-shaped cottage. We languished in a massive terrazzo bathtub, seduced by each other and our surroundings. I felt like a butterfly breaking free from a cocoon of my own making.

"Breathe" by Faith Hill played softly as I watched Adi sleep, following the rise and fall of his muscular chest. Not wanting to wake him but not being able to resist touching him, I gently caressed his face, meticulously etching every feature into my memory.

Eyes still closed, he reached for my fingers, kissed the tips and murmured, "*Titiang tresna tekan adi.*"

"Honey, what does that mean?"

Adi opened his eyes and smiled, "I love you."

"I love you too." Curiosity overtook me in this most romantic of moments. "Why did you say 'Adi' if you love me?"

Adi laughed, understanding my confusion, "'Adi' refers to you, a girl, meaning 'I love you, girl.' When you say I love you to me, you say, '*Titiang tresna tekan bli.*' 'Bli' means brother."

"*Titiang tresna tekan bli, Adi,*" I replied.

My heart hammered as Adi pulled my face towards him and smothered me with his kiss.

At sunset, we sat in the shade of palm trees while I pestered Adi with questions about his childhood. Although we'd grown up worlds apart and in different economic circumstances, we'd both worked continuously from a young age. Adi raised pigs starting at ten and made thousands of *sate* in the early mornings before dawn to put himself through high school. My first job at thirteen had been at Baskin Robbins where my arms ached from lugging heavy tubs of ice cream and scooping cones at warp speed when movie goers spilled out of the theatre next door every two hours like clockwork.

As we watched a pack of local boys kick a ball across the black sand beach, Adi suddenly blurted out, "I want a whole soccer team of babies with you."

"What?" I laughed nervously, "But...we're just getting to know each other better."

Adi reached over to brush a few strands of my hair away and looked me straight in the eyes. He said calmly, "I know enough. I want to marry you."

"You're not serious..." I sputtered.

"How do you feel?" Adi asked as he peered into my face.

I couldn't hide anymore. He knew. I wanted nothing more than to spend the rest of my days learning more about this person whom I felt I already knew.

I'd finally found my 4Cs, but it was up to me if I had the most important C - courage.

On our last night before I was to fly back to the States and Canada, we decided to have a proper date. We dressed up for the first time and headed to KuDeTa, a brand-new beachfront restaurant in the up-and-coming area of Seminyak. The restaurant had a club-like vibe, which I didn't expect. The glamourous waitress, decked out in a tight black skirt and low-cut blouse uncommon for Balinese women, directed us to a table on the deck where the sky lit up for a spectacular sunset of tangerines, violets and cotton candy pinks. Both of us were quiet, lost in our own thoughts. The heaviness of my leaving the next day with no set plans to come back weighed on us both. I can't even remember the food we ate, even though this was the fanciest place that I'd been in Bali.

After dinner, we met Adi's cousin Suaji at a bar in Legian. It was my first time meeting any of Adi's friends or family. Suaji, a spa therapist at Four Seasons Jimbaran was confident and spoke English well. I could see why Adi was close to him. We quickly moved on to Double Six, the most famous disco in Bali at that time. It was already midnight, several hours past my regular bedtime, and definitely not my scene. I didn't want to look rude to

Suaji, but I could not help yawning. Adi looked at me, took my hand in his and led me out of the disco while Suaji trailed behind us.

I'll never forget that last night; it was pitch black with no street lamps in the remote villages that we zoomed past. There wasn't another soul around. The roar of Adi's motorbike pierced the silence. Suddenly, the road broke into a clearing of rice fields and thousands of stars twinkled above us. Adi slowed down and I gasped, wrapping my arms around him even tighter; I never wanted to let go. He stopped the motorbike and turned off the engine, then pulled me off and held me close. Our heartbeats fell into the same rhythm.

The sounds of night were completely foreign to my ears – field frogs croaking, crickets chirping, fruit bats clicking – but in Adi's arms, I was home. We looked up at the magical sky, and I like to think that we were both wishing for the same thing.

2 3

Surrounded by bits and pieces of my past life in San Francisco, I picked through what to keep, what to sell, and what to donate. My furniture and the remnants of my former life as a media sales executive littered the floor of my friend Maggu's exquisite dining room. Taking inventory of my possessions was a sobering exercise that showed me how much I'd wasted on clothes, handbags and shoes that had never suited me. I wanted to be rid of my business suits, but instead I zipped them into garment bags to be stored in one of Maggu's guest rooms until I decided my next step.

Regardless of where I would end up, I planned to live lighter. I was splitting my summer between San Francisco and Toronto, hoping I'd figure out what to do with my life. I wanted to hop on a plane back to Bali, but then I'd have to tell the world about Adi.

Ironically, the first three items sold were the brand-new fake Chanel, Prada and Dior bags that I'd bought in Shenzhen against my better judgement. I kept two small black nylon bags, the size of wallets, that could be slung over my shoulder (hopefully for when I could be back on Adi's motorbike). I coveted a different life now – one without a need for fancy clutches or beaded finery.

I'd had enough for the day and got up off the floor to go see what Maggu was cooking up. She was my ski buddy and disco partner from business school who'd conquered first London (Sky TV), then Whistler (full-time skier, part-time shopgirl) and now Silicon Valley (ground floor of Amazon and now Google). Having ridden above the Dotcom bust, she'd plunked down newly minted cash for a gorgeous Victorian near Haight and Ashbury. Luckily for me, she was busy spearheading Google Commerce and let me run my own shop (a Craigslist garage sale) out of her unfurnished dining room.

Leaning against the white Formica island, I watched Maggu prepare the beautiful Californian greens for our dinner. My tongue was tied. I was dying to divulge my secret romance, but I didn't know how to frame the situation in a palatable way. "I've fallen in love with a Balinese guy and I've decided to move to Bali" sounded insane even to me.

I ventured with another approach, "Hey, Maggu. Have you thought about your life goals?"

"Hmmm, of course, I want a healthy relationship. It doesn't have to be marriage, but I'd love to have a strong partner who can handle my success."

"Would you be okay if you didn't make that much money, just as long as you were in a happy relationship?" I asked, hoping she'd agree.

"No, no. I've always stuck to my goals; make my first million before I'm thirty…"

"Wow, I never even thought about that." My eyes widened as I realized how different my values were. "I mean, I want to be healthy, have balance in my life and eventually raise a family, but a set amount of wealth has never entered my mind."

"Well, you need to set your goals to achieve them instead of aimlessly working with no end in sight. It's about focus."

"I'm already thirty-one, so I've missed the million-dollar mark," I said, hiding my doubts behind a nervous giggle.

Lying on the pull-out sofa that night, I stared up at the elaborate corniche detailing on Maggu's elegant living room ceiling. Would I be okay to be poor? I'd always worked hard, even taking on three jobs one summer to finance my house at university. I doubted that one could earn any significant money in a developing country like Indonesia. Should I be setting financial goals too? Make a couple million before retiring to Bali? Adi could wait for me, right?

My other side argued back. What are you talking about? That is so NOT you. You're the carefree wanderer, remember? FAPs! Life is about collecting FAPs, not dollars. Adi is like winning the FAP lottery. You can figure it out as you've always done. Just go with your heart.

I tossed and turned all night, waking up just as tired as I was the night before. I sighed and reminded myself I needn't ponder life goals or lay out a five-year plan right now. Decisions of what to keep and what to sell were more pressing.

I opened the door of Maggu's front door and found Stephanie. A very pregnant Stephanie.

"Oh! I had no idea. Like, what?" I asked, my eyes wide with shock.

Stephanie, a mutual friend of Maggu and mine, leaned in and hugged me. "This is why we decided to meet here first before heading out to the restaurant," she said.

"So is the baby Jim's?" I blurted out. Jim was "The One" that Stephanie had been dating very seriously when I'd left for Hong Kong.

"No, the baby is not Jim's. It's a long story. Jim and I broke up shortly after you moved to Hong Kong. I was crushed and desperately needed to get away. So I took off for Argentina. I hooked up with a guy for one night, and here you have it," said Stephanie, tapping her tummy with affection.

"Noooooo…." I was shaking my head in disbelief.

"I'd gone off the pill after the breakup, and I just wasn't being smart. Anyways, I decided to keep the baby. I've told the father, but I don't expect him to be involved at all since I only met him that one night. The good news is that Jim and I are back together. He's willing to help me raise this baby as his," she said, rubbing her belly protectively.

"Wow! I'm so, so happy for you, Stephanie! I know it's not what you expected, but this is so beautiful, and you're glowing! Now, let's go feed the two of you!" I said and pulled her off the couch to head out to the restaurant together with Maggu.

That night, as I stared at the ceiling again, I wondered at how happy endings can happen when you least expect them.

I finally hinted to Maggu that I'd met a guy in Bali named Adi. I was still hesitant to give details, but I did confess that Adi was ten years younger. I wanted to gage Maggu's reaction to the big age difference. When she didn't flinch or even bat an eyelash, I poured out my fears of possibly leaving corporate life, not knowing what other options existed in Bali. Knowing her views about wealth accumulation, I didn't divulge that Adi was a spa therapist. While I thought I'd hit the jackpot, I knew others wouldn't agree that a lifetime of warm massages made up for the lack of cold hard cash.

"I'm going to be poor but happy, right?" I asked, looking to my wise friend for her approval.

Maggu took everything in stride; one of her best friends gets pregnant from a one-nighter, and the other says she's going to Bali with no plans in sight. Her response was pragmatic as ever: "You'll be fine. You've always figured things out. And this one is worth figuring out, right?"

The next day, my cousin Darren and his girlfriend Miche zoomed up in their BMW to park behind Maggu's gleaming Mercedes convertible.

They'd lived in Hong Kong when I was there, but we rarely saw each other because we were all working the crazy Dotcom nightmare. When the market went bust, they'd retreated to San Francisco, where they had both lived before moving to Hong Kong. Darren and Miche came over to help buy some of my stuff. I'd been over to their brand-new loft the day before, which was still sparsely furnished. Their loft was my dream home. I'd always wanted to live in a loft. So much so that Dad had renovated the third floor of his last home in Toronto to be that loft. My brother Ken and his wife Patricia had lived there for a couple of years, but I never did.

Miche chose the massive stand-up easel that my dad had given me when he'd moved to Hong Kong. My heart smiled, knowing that it would stay in our family.

What I really needed to sell was my Audi. Crazy that despite the total bust of the Dotcom market, everyone was still driving around in super expensive cars. I had no idea if there would be any buyers in this market but looking at the impressive line-up of luxury vehicles parked outside, I figured anything was possible.

Crystal, another best friend from business school came by for afternoon tea. I observed how she glowed with health, pregnant with her first baby, as she got out of her cranberry red Saab.

I pushed down the uncomfortable question – *Is everyone having babies but me?* – as I hugged Crystal gently so as not to squish her precious tummy.

I'd gift-wrapped one of my childhood keepsakes for Crystal as I would not be there for her baby shower. She pulled the fragile, porcelain, castle-like contraption out of the tissue.

"This is exquisite!" Crystal said as she turned it around in her hands.

"I know, right? It's such an unusual music box. Grace's mom gave it to me for my tenth Christmas," I said as my eyes lingered on my old treasure.

Crystal turned the brass key and the delicate figurines twirled round and round as a lullaby tinkled out from the vintage music box. "You cannot part with this, Fran. It's too sentimental. You need to keep it for your future children."

"No, I want you to enjoy this with your baby. It's too fragile for me to be carting it around the world when I don't even know where I'll land. And who knows if I'll ever have children? I'm not going to hold on to a pipe dream."

Crystal carefully asked, "Have you met anyone else, Fran?"

I hesitated and then said, "Actually, I met a guy in Bali."

"Bali?" Crystal sat up a little and patiently waited for me to continue.

"Yes, his name is Adi and I've spent about five weeks in total getting to know him. He's the kindest and funniest person I've ever met. Even though, we haven't known each other long, part of me feels like I've known him all my life. I just don't know how to move the relationship forward. So far, I've only told you, Grace and Crystal about him. Nobody else knows," I said, wringing my hands in my lap.

"Oh, Fran. Just see what happens with Adi. It's been so long since Vern."

I winced, annoyed that his name still had the power to hurt. Crystal had been one of the Fab Four to hold me up when I fell apart that Christmas. She, Grace, Keitha and Elaine had done everything console me. Little did any of us know that it would take seven years and a Balinese man named Adi to finally heal my heart.

24

After San Francisco, I crawled back to Toronto.

This was the first time I was going to live in Toronto in over three years. Instead of returning as a hero, having lived in her dream city of San Francisco and then conquered the Internet world in Hong Kong and Tokyo, I felt like a Pekinese dog returning with her tail between her legs.

Mom's condo didn't feel as welcoming or cozy as it had the Christmas before when I'd finally decided to leave HungryForWords. I felt walled in. Unable to move without being questioned.

Mom was being as sensitive as she could be, but there was this unasked question hanging over us all the time: "What are you doing with your life?"

To survive, I spent as much time out of her condo as possible.

Upon Grace's brilliant suggestion, I signed up for a sculpture class at an art school downtown. Maybe now was the time to go for my other dream of being a sculptor in Venice in the winter months. I'd been there for Carnivale 1994 after skiing in the Dolomites. This had been one of my ultimate FAP-collecting adventures. After the fantastic week swooshing down the Italian Alps in Cortina, I meandered around a melancholy Venice – one so much more romantic in the winter when the little laneways were virtually empty of tourists and the mist would rise off the canals, lending it an otherworldly atmosphere.

Since that trip in 1994, I had marked Venice as a possible place to live and work as a sculptor. Imagine all the FAPs – walking into a café, downing espressos in one shot, imitating that nonchalant Italian flair at the counter and flouncing my hair as I stepped out for another day from my artist loft where I'd spent the morning with my hands buried in clay. A move to Venice might be more palatable for my family who respected art and culture. Maybe by throwing myself into another passion, I could forget about Adi.

My human form sculpture class turned out even better than expected despite the male model being a middle-aged man with bulges where I would have preferred a six-pack. But because of this, I let my mind wander back to the most perfect torso that I'd been intimately wrapped around for the past few months. I could conjure Adi's exact body in my mind, and my hands seemed to move of their own accord, moulding the clay torso with confidence. I manifested Adi in my mind and brought him closer to me in my art.

Another bonus of the sculpture class was its location on Queen Street West, known to Torontonians as "Queen West." During lunch breaks, I'd indulge in the myriad of ethnic cuisines that lined the street. I could sit down at a sushi bar for a delectable selection of sashimi or grab one of the best burgers in town. To work off my caloric meals, I'd wander along the street full of quirky shops selling one-off items and peep into shady bars, remembering times when Grace had dragged me into a place called Bovine Sex Club well past midnight.

Walking down Queen Street transported me instantly back to those days right out of university in 1992 when I was still dating Vern and had all my closest biz school friends living in Toronto. We'd extended our university days by holding tightly to each other. We lived within a one-kilometer radius of each other and often congregated at one apartment building where Grace, Nate and Ian lived in three of the total six units there. Many a night you could find a handful of us catching an up-and-coming band at The Masonic Temple or drinking "tea" in some greasy place in Chinatown.

Then, one by one, we scattered around the globe. First Grace to Hong Kong, then Nate to Singapore, Elaine to London, Ian and Crystal to Harvard and then San Francisco, Keitha to Saskatoon, Cam to China, and me to San Francisco and then to Hong Kong. Elaine was the last of our gang to leave Toronto for a backpacking trip across India and China with her future husband. Despite the distance, we'd diligently kept our friendships alive in the early years, before the weddings and the babies.

Spending this summer meeting up with happily settled friends in San Francisco and Toronto, I found that a chasm had emerged. Back in business school, I'd always been called "weird" or "too artsy" while everyone else chased the money jobs like consulting or investment banking. Even back then, at twenty-one, I'd craved a balanced life. Now, a decade later at thirty-one, I'd experienced a wider scope of life experiences than many of my friends.

Was it just that we were in different life stages? My female friends jabbered on about mommy groups and the best neighbourhoods to upgrade to, while my male buddies discussed potential investment possibilities or how many crates of Opus One they were hoarding. I'd tune out, daydreaming about life somewhere other than here. Did I embody fundamentally different values?

At one dinner, a trophy wife started mocking me when I mentioned that I had taken the bus to the party.

She said, "Oh my God! Frances takes public transportation now."

My eyes narrowed. I'd worked hard to buy my cars, including the Audi that I'd paid for in cash at the age of twenty-six and that had sat unused in my brother's garage for almost two years. This heavily jeweled woman had quit her waitressing job the second she moved in with her plastic surgeon husband-to-be. Her entire life was funded by him.

Who should be mocking whom? But I kept my lips pursed in disgust, figuring that any cutting remark would fly over this airhead. Wasted words are best left unsaid.

How had the social structure of my wealthier friends in Toronto devolved into this? The obsession to register children before they were born at the most elite private schools, the need to spend thousands on real name-brand bags and shoes, and the sad emptiness that flickered from their eyes when they thought no one was looking.

Spending time with my more down-to-earth and creative friends from *The Toronto Star* was akin to being back with a family you'd chosen. We shared a lot of laughter thinking back on the old times. Nothing significant had changed in the past five years at the newspaper, which had plodded along like always while I'd lived at the threshold of the Internet boom as it shot forward at lightning speed. The Internet was in a difficult position since the market crashed, but entrepreneurs and techies were resilient and already moving on to the next big thing.

I craved the balanced, contented life that these newspaper friends lived, but I aspired for more – more adventure, more creativity, more culture, more discovery, more inspiration, more travel, more FAPs... Bali certainly ticked off all the boxes, but it was also on the other side of my world, not just physically, but in every other way too.

25

I pitied my mother. In the Chinese community, the expectations were high. Although she didn't say it out loud, I knew Mom hoped that I could have the happily ever after that she had been denied.

Every auntie and uncle, related to us or not, doted on me. My mom and dad were respected (read: feared) Chinese parents. A step out of line meant that we went to the kitchen drawer and chose a weapon of choice. We'd hand over the utensil and Dad would smack us hard on our open palms. I always went for the floppy plastic spatulas and wondered why my brother always selected an unyielding wooden spoon.

Dad's hits were not always contained to those moments in the kitchen. He suffered from severe manic depression and often lost control, but his target had always been Mom. When I was sixteen, Dad broke my younger brother's arm when Ken had raised it to defend me. I'd called the police immediately, and the aftermath of that incident finally freed us from his violence. Mom had been desperate to hold her family together, but when Dad struck her children, she divorced him. It was at this time that Mom revealed that she'd hidden her first marriage from us because Dad had forbidden her to let anyone in Toronto know she'd been previously married. In one moment, we lost our dad but gained our older half-brother, Andrew.

Despite our well-known family problems, a few of these aunties still pegged me as good daughter-in-law material: seemingly obedient, wide hips fit for childbearing and the ability to cook. When I graduated from business school, I became the prized pig. I avoided all dim sum lunches for fear of being married off to the first available good Chinese boy.

"Why aren't you eating the *si ziu ngau ho*? It's your favourite," Mom asked, offering me the plate of pepper and black bean beef rice noodles.

"Well, I like *wat daan haa jan caau ho* more."

"But you don't like eggs!" Mom said, exasperated that I wanted another noodle dish, especially one that featured slimy scrambled eggs and prawns.

She shook her head and said, "You've changed. You were never like this. What's happened to you?"

"What? It's a noodle dish, Mom. What's the big deal?"

"That's not what I'm talking about. You…you wander around all summer. Not trying to get a job. What are you doing?"

Change for me had been gradual, but Mom saw me maybe once a year now so maybe my transformation was more pronounced, leaping up like spikes on a line graph for her each time we met up. I could see how maybe it seemed like I'd gone through some weird Bali portal. Coming back to Toronto (a.k.a., the real world) revealed what I already knew – I didn't belong there anymore.

"I want you to be happy and safe. Did you burn out? What's wrong?" Mom asked, peering at me with worry etched on her face.

"Nothing, Mom. I just need some time to figure things out. Let me eat some more of those noodles. You're right. I did love them before." I bent over my bowl and shoveled the rice noodles into my mouth so she'd stop interrogating me.

My sculpture of Adi took its permanent form by the end of the summer. And out of the clay, the next steps of my life emerged. I realized that Adi had taken a permanent place in my heart. I couldn't pretend otherwise.

When I lugged the massively heavy torso of a naked man into her condo, my mom gave it a once over and said, "Where are you going to keep that?"

"Here?"

"No, no. I can't display that," Mom muttered, shaking her head.

"You don't have to display it. I'll store in the guest room closet in a box," I mumbled as my forehead broke out in sweat.

I gazed at my project of love. If Mom reacted like this to an inanimate sculpture (albeit a nude body), I cringed thinking what she'd do if she knew the real man existed.

I'd furtively bought a phone card so that I could call Adi without it showing up on Mom's phone bill. Adi had one of the only cellphones in his village at that time, but he kept it in his locker when he worked. He'd proudly told me that he was the first person in his entire village to buy one, saying that the phone number alone cost a million rupiah, almost his entire month's salary in 1998. It was harder than expected to stay in touch with him. With the thirteen-hour time difference and his long work hours, I'd resorted to calling his hotel's main number only to get the spa receptionist. She was the same polite woman whom I'd terrorized on my second day in Bali.

Adi and I could only get snatches of conversation in the whole summer, but this time, I was telling him something I needed to hear myself, "Darling, I'm coming back to Bali. Wait for me."

I finally admitted to Mom that my time in Toronto would end soon. I explained that I'd be going back to Bali in September. I planned to figure out how to work there. I'd pointed out that Four Seasons, Canada's premier hotel brand, had two resorts there. I could work in their marketing and sales department. Honestly, I had no idea how I would just break my way into tourism hospitality, but I figured how hard could it be?

I'd always been described as the salesperson who could sell ice cubes to Inuit. Selling some of the most beautiful resorts in Bali should be a walk in the park (or golf course). Four Seasons was a Canadian company. I was Canadian. Their head office in Toronto would be overjoyed to have a Canadian over in Bali. Fingers crossed.

"Bali? That's so far away! Hong Kong was bad enough, but at least I knew you were with Kai Ma, your dad and Grace. You don't even know anyone in Bali."

"Well, that's not true. Remember Robert, the driver? He's my friend. And there are lots of expats. Don't worry, Mom. I make friends easily. And Bali is only a four-and-a-half-hour flight from Hong Kong."

Mom knew that it was useless trying to change my mind. The "changed" Frances was no longer obedient. She seemed to do whatever she wanted. She no longer needed her family's approval and had long ago stopped needing them for any financial support.

In the end, we flew down to San Francisco together. Mom had decided at the spur of the moment to bring her favourite aunt, Great-Aunt May, on an epic journey along the Silk Road. Great-Aunt May, whom I'd lived with briefly at her orchid-filled home up in the foggy hills of Mount Davidson, San Francisco, was the perfect travel companion for Mom.

Travel was and always would be Mom's number one reason for being, even more than her kids. She was a trailblazing traveller and completely outside of the social norms of her conservative Chinese community. I'd hazard a guess that by age sixty, she'd travelled to as many countries as the number of years she'd lived.

The irony was not lost on me. Could Mom not see how I was actually following her adventurous footsteps?

I still had to sell my car and donate a few leftover items to be entirely unburdened by my old life.

Selling the car was easier than expected. Despite residing in San Francisco for close to three years, my Audi was in pristine condition.

Have you ever seen how San Franciscans street park? It's horrifying to watch. They swerve into a parking space 10 to 15 centimetres shorter than their car. The driver bangs his way forward and back until the car is fully squeezed into the spot. All over San Francisco, you'll see the most luxurious sportscars with deep scratches and bent fenders. My Audi had avoided this fate, protected as it had been since it moved from Toronto, first in my apartment's well-kept parking garage and in CNET's management team lot, and later in my younger brother Ken's garage, shielded from other cars and the weather.

Another benefit of selling my car was finding my tiny automatic camera in the trunk as I showed it to the eventual buyer. My compact black Olympus camera had hidden in the shadows since June. The film inside held the photos from my last Bali trip with Adi! Using my found treasure, I took one last photo of my Audi in Ken's driveway as a keepsake.

My precious Audi was going to help fund my future adventures with Adi.

The next day, Kevin, one of Ken's best friends who'd become my golf buddy during my time living in San Francisco, picked me up in his hunter green Saab. We headed out for a farewell round at the Presidio, one of the best public courses in the U.S., with some holes having uninterrupted views of the Golden Gate Bridge.

"So what will you actually be up to in Bali, Fran?" Kevin drawled, having picked up the typical Californian accent since moving down from Toronto. "I've known you for a long time, and you're never one without a plan."

"Well, I'm hoping to land a cushy sales job at Four Seasons, of course."

"Have you applied yet?

"I figure that I'll have a better chance applying in person."

"So you're just going to Bali without anything set up? Come on, there's something else going on here."

I blushed, and Kevin pointed at my face. "Ah, there's something that you're not telling me. Your whole family is so confused. And worried too."

"Okay, okay. I met this Balinese guy. His name is Adi. He's seriously the nicest person I've met in like, forever. I know it's a bit crazy, but I have to figure out what I'm going to do."

"Oh wow! You're upgrading from an Audi to an Adi," he said, nudging me jokingly.

His words were a revelation to me. That was the first time that someone had given me a refreshingly different perspective of the changes that I'd undertaken. When I'd announced my extended sabbatical back to Bali, most of my friends had averted their eyes. Some questioned why I'd toss out things that represented stability and security. One girlfriend even begged me to keep all my Armani suits as a "back-up." They all meant well, coming from their own place of comfort; they thought if they wrapped me up in the same armour, I'd be protected too. But I didn't want to be safe. I wanted to be free.

Kevin was right. Adi was an upgrade, not a downgrade of my life. I was chasing something that truly mattered to me.

The sound would not stop. What was that ringing in my dream? I finally realized that I wasn't dreaming. I sat up in the bed, at first confused about where I was, and then reached over to grab the phone, glancing at the digital alarm clock next to it – 6:33 a.m. Who the hell is calling so early?

"World fall down, world fall down!"

"Auntie May, what's wrong? Are you okay?"

"World fall down, world fall down!" My Great-Aunt May was hysterical.

"Wait, I'll get Mom. I don't understand."

"Turn on the TV!!" she screamed.

"Okay, okay, just wait a minute while I find the channel changer."

When the TV flickered on, I didn't understand what I was looking at. It looked like a scene out of a "Die Hard" movie. A plane was crashing into a building… I suddenly realized, "Wait, that's the World Trade Centre. Is this for real?"

Mom came out of the bathroom in her curlers and rumpled nightgown, rubbing her sleepy eyes, and asked who was calling.

"Mom, Mom. Look." I could hardly get the words out as I pointed to the TV.

My mom slowly sat down beside me with a look of horror matching my own. We could not believe what we were seeing. Vast plumes of smoke and fire engulfing the top floors of both towers of the World Trade Centre.

"Get dressed. We have to be with Ken and Patricia," Mom ordered.

We were staying at a hotel down in Fisherman's Wharf. I was leaving that very day for Bali via Hong Kong. Mom and Great-Aunt May had flights to Beijing that day too. We'd planned to go to the airport together around 10:00 a.m. for my 1:00 p.m. flight, with theirs scheduled to take off an hour later.

We checked out of the hotel as quickly as we could and jumped into a taxi to Ken's place.

Relief washed over Mom's face when Ken opened the door. "Thank God, you're home."

Ken, a stockbroker, was always in the office before 6:00 a.m. San Francisco time to be there for when the markets opened in New York at 9:00 a.m. He said that shortly after 6:15 a.m., everyone in his office building, the Transcontinental, the tallest landmark in San Francisco, was ordered to evacuate and go home immediately. The authorities said they were worried about more attacks. Sadly, they were not wrong.

My sister-in-law, Patricia, eight-months pregnant, was huddled under a blanket with her eyes wide in terror as more and more unbelievable images flashed across the TV. I sat down gingerly beside her and grabbed her hand, tears rolling down my face. My older half-brother, Andrew, was already slouched in the armchair.

All flights were suspended. The news told everyone to stay home. Do not go to the airport. Do not use your phones as they needed the lines clear so people looking for their loved ones could get through. I desperately wanted to call Marnie and Bertram, who both worked on Wall Street, but families were the priority, not biz school buddies.

We must have sat there frozen on that couch for hours as news about the two other planes came through.

The CEO of Cantor Fitzgerald flashed onto the screen. There was anguish and pain in his voice as he whispered that he'd been late to the office after dropping his child off on his first day of kindergarten. He broke down completely, blubbering incoherently that his brother was up there. All his employees were up there. He wailed that he should be the one there, not them. His company took up floors 101 to 105, exactly where the first plane exploded into the North Tower.

There were now images of people leaping off the rooves of the burning buildings. I couldn't watch any longer.

"I'm going out for a drive. I'll be back soon."

I jumped into Ken's car and swerved onto Geary Blvd, a street usually packed full of traffic and public buses. It was completely empty. Not one car or pedestrian. I drove thirty blocks without seeing a soul. I turned right into Presidio Park, mine the only vehicle in the parking lot.

Leaning forward on the steering wheel, I took big gulps of air to calm myself down. I got out slowly and walked into the deserted park. If it wasn't for the reason why the park was completely empty, I would have loved it. Without traffic noise or anyone about, you could hear all the birds singing in the trees, the wind rustling through the early autumn leaves and see the Golden Gate Bridge, gleaming and proud, another icon of America – another possible target.

My fists tight with rage, I looked up at the astonishingly clear blue sky and wondered out loud, "How can you let this happen?" I wanted to scream at God.

My heart hurt, a physical pain deep in my body, thinking about all those children who had gone to school for the first time that morning and one of their parents not coming home that night. How would they ever feel safe again? Would they ever want to go back to school, ever? I thought about how, in one horrific moment, thousands of lives were destroyed. I knew deep in my heart that life would never be able to go back to a time of innocence. People would now live with a deep fear.

I sat down on a park bench, under the shade of a huge tree, and bent my forehead on top of my hands, clasped in prayer. I prayed for all those souls who'd left us too early. I prayed for the pain that their families and friends would have to endure. I prayed for myself and the growing uncertainty of my going to Bali. I prayed for the world to heal.

I looked up as a couple stopped walking nearby; they smiled a sad greeting and asked if I was okay. I smiled back and answered, "Thank you, it's just all a bit overwhelming. I couldn't watch TV anymore."

"Yes, that's how we felt. We needed to come outside and get away from it."

"It's weird how peaceful it is here? Isn't it?"

"Yes, it's a bit eerie. Not one car on the roads."

"I better head back before my family panics."

"Take care."

"You too."

A few days passed in a numb fog before we could go to the airport to check what we could do about our flights.

Mom was still determined to travel the Silk Road with Great-Aunt May. Somehow, their journey had become more precarious than mine because the Silk Road route crossed close to Afghanistan – now known in every household as the country that harboured the evil terrorists. Meanwhile, Bali was the same safe and peaceful oasis as before. Any misgivings about my travels were unsaid on Mom's part. She longed to escape from the world situation as much as I did.

Life is meant to be lived. It could be extinguished so quickly and violently for so many. Knowing that made me feel a greater urgency to live for now. Nobody could fathom what the future held.

When I took my ticket out, I noticed that my flight had been scheduled for 1:00 a.m. on 9/11/2001, not 1:00 p.m. as I'd thought.

I'd actually missed my flight before the 9/11 attacks had even transpired.

As a business traveller who flew on planes the way others rode buses to get to work, realizing my mistake was surreal. I'd somehow misread my departure to be 1:00 p.m. American Airlines didn't use the twenty-four-hour clock at that time. They used 1:00 a.m. and 1:00 p.m. I'd never been so thankful for making a mistake.

If I had been on a plane on that date, albeit flying above Hawaii at the moment the first plane hit, my mom would have had a heart attack. For Mom, Ken, Andrew and me to be in San Francisco all together, when we were usually in different countries, had been a godsend.

The airport was in complete mayhem. The harassed-looking airline counter staff only glanced at my ticket, saw it was dated 9/11/2001 and shoved a new ticket across the counter. I checked my flights carefully this time. I had a one-night stopover in Hong Kong before continuing to Bali the next morning. My return flight back to Toronto was set for December 19th. I'd have a total of three months in Bali.

27

BALI, SEPTEMBER 2001

Walking through Bali's airport was surreal. I was one of only a handful of tourists. It really hit me how this one event on the other side of the world had tilted everything out of balance. Everyone shared the collective pain, no matter how far they were from New York. It wasn't enough that thousands in the U.S. were killed on 9/11, the terrorists' attack reverberated from that centre and affected even more innocent lives around the globe.

Robert was his same cheerful self as he lugged my heavy suitcases into the back of his van. I jumped in the front seat beside him as usual. A now familiar canang greeted me on the dashboard; a few colourful petals fluttered away as we took off. "I'm glad you came back,

Frances. I'm very sorry about what happened in your country."

"Thanks, Robert. I've been very sad too, but the attack was in the States. I'm from Canada. We're different countries."

"Still, they're your neighbours. So their pain is your pain too, right?"

"Yeah, you're right; their pain is our pain."

"We say here in Bali that we are here for you, in happiness and in sadness. That's why we help each other. For ceremony. A baby born or someone dead, doesn't matter. We help."

"That's so beautiful, Robert. Yes, planes were forced to land in Canada because the States closed all their airports. Many people in my country took strangers into their homes and took care of them."

I looked out the window as we passed Kuta Beach, the sun still high in the sky, making the blue water shimmer. Everything seemed so peaceful; beach sellers laughed with each other underneath the coconut trees while the odd surfer floated on the horizon. I'm not sure that these innocent people understood the ramifications of 9/11 yet, how the ripples would be felt even in this seemingly untouchable paradise. How tourism would likely grind to a halt as people became afraid of travelling on planes that could now be used as weapons.

Adi had already checked into our room, Room #6 at Stardust Cottages. He was napping peacefully when I pushed open the carved wooden doors. Adi woke with a start and hopped out of bed to help me with my luggage. He was constantly amazed by how much stuff I brought with me.

As he reached out to hug me, I held up my hand, "Don't touch me. I'm disgusting after the flight. Let me jump into the shower first."

"I don't care," said Adi as he pulled me in for tight hug and a wet, slobbering kiss. "We can shower together."

The pain of the world had sat heavily on my heart since I woke up to my Great-Aunt May screaming, "World fall down." When Adi pulled me into his arms, I felt a soothing balm envelope my body and soul. My pent-up tension dissolved as tears streamed down my eyes.

"Why are you crying?" Adi asked as he brushed the hair away from my face.

"I don't know. I feel guilty for being able to escape to Bali. So many are suffering. Don't get me wrong, I don't want to be anywhere else but here with you. But am I just running away from real life?"

"This is your real life. You decided to come back before 9/11 happen. You aren't running away. You run to me."

His eyes spoke with such sincerity; this gentle person stayed calm and introspective through the worst of times. Adi didn't say much but when he did, he spoke words that I could hang on to. Words of wisdom. I've always had a fiery nature; I would blurt out exactly how I felt without a thought. I redefined the saying "You wear your heart on your sleeve." My face was a massive highway billboard lit up with emotion, a book splayed open for all to read. My open honesty was my biggest strength and weakness. Adi was my opposite, and his words healed like a calming balm.

"Okay, enough of my moping. Let's get into that shower."

We spent the rest of the evening reuniting after months of being apart. I was amazed at how we immediately fell so comfortably back in place.

When we were together, it was as if time were suspended. As if I'd known Adi in another lifetime. That our souls had moved through eternity, meeting each other time and time again. This time, it just so happened he was a Balinese man in love with a Chinese Canadian woman.

Stardust Cottages was pretty much empty. Adi said that when 9/11 happened, people rebooked their flights, checked out and went home to the safety of their families. Future bookings had been cancelled as people decided against travelling.

I got a call one morning on my cellphone, which surprised me as my phone rarely rang in Bali. It was Yosh. He and Marie planned to wed at The Ritz Carlton in October; however, their friends and family in the States were scared to come to Bali. He needed some local reassurances that Bali was safe.

"What do you mean? Of course, it's safe. You've been here. I don't understand."

"Frances, Indonesia is the biggest Muslim country in the world."

"Yeah, so? Bali is Hindu. We're on an island."

"Well, the media is freaking everyone out, and there's been major backlash and racism towards Muslim people in the States."

"What? That's crazy!"

"I'm actually surprised that your family allowed you to move to Bali at a time like this."

"Yosh, how do you and Marie feel? Isn't that what's most important? If I went along with everyone else's fears, I would go crazy and never be able to live."

"Well, we really want to go ahead with the wedding as we had planned. And I don't want to move the wedding to the States. Bali is really special to us."

"Of course, it's where you asked Marie to marry you in March. I think you guys need to go with your gut."

"Thanks, Frances. Talking to you reaffirms what we thought all along. We're getting married in Bali, even if it's just the two of us, and you and Robert the driver are the only ones who show up."

Yosh's call was disconcerting, even for a super optimist like me. After talking to Yosh, doubts crept in and woke me up to the new reality of post-9/11. I couldn't ignore the fact that getting a job in Bali was previously going to be tough, and now it would probably be impossible. Even if there were jobs, how could I fabricate a hospitality career out of thin air? I only spoke a few words of Indonesian like *sate* (satay) and *selamat pagi* (good morning) – words seldom needed in business to negotiate hotel deals with hard-nosed travel agents.

Despite this, I pushed on. The following day, I confidently bounced into the lobby of Four Seasons Sayan with my resume in hand. My shoulders fell upon discovering that their Sales and Marketing department was centralized down at their Jimbaran headquarters, ninety minutes south of Ubud, and that they were not hiring.

I walked away from the lobby and reassured myself. Relax, I don't have to work yet. I've budgeted ten dollars a day for food and thirty dollars a day for the guesthouse. This stay in Bali is about Adi and me – time to devote to our budding relationship and see where it goes. For once in your life, just enjoy yourself. It's only for three months. Not forever.

2 8

After a torturous summer away, all I wanted was to spend carefree days and romantic nights with Adi. But Bali ceremonies had something else in store. Ten days of island-wide ceremonies were coming up, from the opening celebration of Galungan to the closing day of Kuningan. Galungan was the most important ceremony in the Balinese Pawukon calendar, when the ancestral spirits returned to earth to celebrate good triumphing over evil.

Adi had to help his parents prepare for the ceremonies on his days off. I had no idea what the ceremonies entailed, but I did know that the only reason I was in Bali was to be with Adi. I was desperate to make some concrete decisions in the next twelve weeks before going home for Christmas. Now two weeks were wiped out before I even got started.

Although I was seething inside, I couldn't show my real feelings to Adi. It was too early in our relationship.

I wanted to scream, "I flew across the world a week after 9/11...to be with YOU! I'm going against every belief that I grew up with and disappointing every other person in my life by not climbing the corporate ladder as expected. I have no fixed address!" But I didn't say that, for fear that Adi might jump on his scooter, never to return. Instead, I clamped my mouth shut.

Determined to exude a graceful and calm persona, I wrapped a delicate silk sarong around my waist and strolled down narrow laneways that I'd never explored when preoccupied with Adi. I happened upon a man and his young son decorating a bamboo pole tucked away on a street called Jalan Kajeng.

"Wow! What are you making?" I asked, admiring the craftsmanship of their work.

The father smiled proudly, "It's called a *penjor*. It's a special offering. Every family makes this together for Galungan."

Seeing my interest, he invited me to help them attach round cylinders made of pale yellow leaves to the bamboo, which was wrapped with shiny yellow fabric.

I thanked him but shook my head and said, "No, go ahead. I'll just watch."

Watching the little boy learn his culture in this intimate setting, my heart felt heavy. Despite us being in the nascent stage of our relationship, I wished that I'd been included in Adi's ceremony preparations, instead of being pitied by some strangers.

I spent a couple of days by the pool, trying to read but failing, constantly rereading or skipping words while impatiently waiting for the ten-day Galungan ceremony to end. Without Adi's presence, my thoughts swirled between fuming about his absence and romanticizing him in my head. I tossed my book aside and made a conscious decision to stop wallowing and wasting my idyllic time in Bali. Who knew if I'd be back? Tourism in Bali had evaporated overnight so my chance to get a job was definitely zero now. The way things were with Adi, it seemed like I wasn't an important part of his life. I'd better just get on with it and enjoy all the island offered before going back to reality.

During my wanderings around town, I'd happened upon a book titled *The Tropical Spa* which described a magical spa called "The Source" at Begawan Giri Estate. For decades, the British owners sat on the mystical piece of land in the village of Begawan Giri, translated as Wise Man's Mountain, before they carved out one of the most unique resorts in the world, featured in many architectural and design coffee table books.

I longed to experience the property but couldn't afford its thousand dollars a night price tag. No harm in asking, I figured. When I called, the front office suggested a lower-priced option to me, a private yoga class and picnic lunch at The Source, their spa, where I could experience three rockpools fed from sacred mountain springs. I'd been granted a way to experience Begawan Giri for a song.

One of the estate's butlers carried a wicker picnic basket as he led me down to The Source open-air Balinese spa pavilions scattered amongst the ferns and foliage above the roaring Ayung River. My neck stretched left and right as my eyes tried to memorize every detail. We ducked under a crumbling stone gate and the butler advised that I watch my footing as we proceeded down the uneven stone steps to the riverside rockpools.

We arrived at a rockpool flanked by a wooden deck with six cushioned sunbeds. The butler unfurled a large white towel on one and pulled up a small square table. I sat down in this jungle paradise, not even caring that my mouth hung open. I clasped my hands in delight as he unpacked my lunch. Out came little baskets woven from banana leaves. One held a leafy green salad, another contained skewers of tropical fruit, a third revealed a smoked salmon roll and finally, a delectable brownie in the last square – a feast for a jungle fairy. Looking at this lovely meal before me, I couldn't help but wish I were enjoying it with Adi.

Halfway through my ten days of torture, a gregarious American couple showed up at the pool. The second they started talking, I knew we'd become friends.

Nicole and Clint were on their honeymoon, having just gotten married in their hometown of Santa Cruz. They were blown away that I'd previously stayed in Santa Cruz and had even dined at their favourite place on the seaside. They recounted how their wedding was almost called off because of 9/11 and then how everyone had freaked out when they said they were going ahead with their honeymoon in Bali.

We bonded over our daring. That we were the ones willing to get on a plane and fly halfway around the world to the country with "the biggest Muslim population in the world" while everyone else cowered in front of their televisions, fixated on the bombs being dropped on Afghanistan.

Clint and Nicole, being new friends, were totally outside of my usual social circle. For the first time, I could freely dissect and analyze my relationship with Adi with someone outside of my own head. I disclosed my unasked questions aloud to Clint and Nicole – how I wasn't sure that I could live in Bali long-term, how I hadn't met any of his friends or family yet, and how I felt completely excluded during this Galungan ceremony. Their reassurances eased my concerns and helped still my spinning mind.

I patted myself on the back for maintaining my patience and grace; I'd been able to talk to others about how I felt about Adi without being too emotional. But I broke down the second Adi came back to Ubud.

We had our first fight.

Through tears, I told him how lonely I'd been for the past ten days. I spat out that a stranger on the street pitied me and invited me to work on their penjor. I gulped back my pride, put my head down and whispered that I felt abandoned by him. Adi took me in his arms and kept apologizing. He understood how it might look to me since I didn't know anything about Balinese ceremony. He tried explaining that being the only son and the only child in his tiny family, he and his mom and dad had to do the work of many people.

I said, "I am a person, right? I could have helped."

Adi looked at me, "Are you sure? You're ready to meet my parents?"

To be honest, I wasn't ready to take that step yet, but I was ready to take our relationship to another level.

This was when Adi and I became a public couple. Previously, Adi and I existed in our own bubble, me afraid to show Adi to my world and him afraid to show me to his. We still weren't ready to cross those lines, but Clint and Nicole helped us recognize what we were because we were reflected in them – a couple in love. Also, there wasn't any history between us. They weren't my friends, and they weren't Adi's friends. They were "our" friends.

With Clint and Nicole in tow, we explored Bali through new eyes. We discovered La Lucciola, an iconic beachfront restaurant accessed thought the parking lot of Petitenget Temple and therefore, only frequented by those in the know. We celebrated Nicole's birthday (October 5th) and mine (October 10th), sitting on mats in an expansive garden of a new Indian restaurant up in the artist colony of Penestanan. Close to the end of their three-week honeymoon, Clint and Nicole were wholeheartedly rooting for Adi and me.

Nicole whispered in my ear as we leaned back into our cushions, looking up at the bright stars peeping through the coconut trees, "You guys totally belong together."

I nodded in agreement, thinking, *Yeah, I just have to figure out how to make that happen.*

"Frances… Frances, are you up?"

"Wait, I'm coming," I answered. I pulled my silk robe around me and opened the creaky wooden doors. Adi had departed before sunrise to make his 7:00 a.m. shift at the resort.

"What's up, Clint?" I asked, squinting into the morning sunlight.

"I told Brenda about you, and she wants to talk to you."

"Brenda? You mean the owner? I've never met her."

Clint was practically leaping out of his skin in his excitement. "Just listen! Last night, Nicole and I were coming in around 10:00, and we saw a guy standing on that bench peering into your room. I said, 'Hey, get down from there,' and he scurried away. So this morning, as we were checking out, Brenda happened to come by. I explained that I was a bit concerned that her staff were peeping into Frances's room. She said, 'Who's Frances?' So I told her all about how you're this total marketing whiz who's practically living here. It's kinda weird that she doesn't know who you are when I think about it. I mean many of the other guests here know who are because you're like the welcome wagon at the pool."

"What? A guy was peering into our room?" I was a few steps behind Clint, still trying to recall what Adi and I might have been up to around 10:00 p.m.

"I know, I think it's a serious security issue, but Brenda said not to worry, that the Balinese are like little kids, just curious."

"Well, okay. I guess." I pulled my robe around me a little tighter.

"Never mind about that. Listen. I told Brenda that maybe she might need someone like you. She has this guesthouse, two restaurants, a gift shop, a bakery, and six kids. I really don't know how she does it. So she said she'd come talk to you."

"Wow! Thanks, Clint, for doing that. I don't know if anything will come of it, but I really appreciate your support. I'm going to miss you guys so much!"

"Yeah, I can't believe that Nicole and I have to go home today. It's going to be so depressing. You'll have to keep in touch and let us know how things work out. Give Adi a big hug from us, okay?"

I closed the doors and sat down, thinking about how Clint had described me to Brenda. That was incredibly kind for him to say all those things. I'd only known him for three weeks, and here he was selling me to the owner. I didn't expect that she'd actually come to talk to me. This was my third stay here, and she didn't even know I existed. Maybe that's why she needed someone like me. She must be overwhelmed if she wasn't aware of guests who stayed in her ten-room guesthouse that wrapped around her own home. Six kids alone could make you go in circles, never mind the empire that she was running. *Anyways, don't get your hopes up,* I warned myself.

Later that morning, Brenda appeared on my terrace and introduced herself. She was a petite, regal-looking woman wearing a crisp fuchsia cotton blouse and a flattering A-line skirt with her blond hair twisted up neatly in a tight bun.

Brenda spoke with a soft but distinctive Australian drawl, reminding me of Marty. "Clint told me all about you. And that you might be able to help me out at Pala."

"Pala?"

"Yes, that's my restaurant up the hill. I need help with marketing and improving the service there. Would you be interested in that?"

"Sure, that sounds amazing."

"I can't pay you, but I can offer you free room and board for each day that you help out."

I felt like I'd won the lottery. While I wasn't gaining any income, my expenses would be cut significantly.

Trying to keep my cool, I answered calmly, "Yes, that'll be fine. I'd love to help out. When should I start?"

"Can you come with me now to Pala?"

"Um, okay."

Pala was a five-minute drive from the Stardust Cottages. I envied Brenda having her businesses so close to her home. For me, proximity to work equalled life balance.

I'd never had a long commute to work. I'd always lived within a thirty-minute drive or, in the case of Hong Kong, a few minutes' walk to the office. The air travel that I'd endured between Hong Kong and Tokyo was made better by my sushi takeout boxes and the peacefulness of having no Internet access.

I'd never had a typical 9-to-5 desk job where I'd quickly wither away. Being in sales and then an entrepreneur meant I was always running from one place to another, or travelling from one city to another, meeting new people all the time. I thrived on diversity.

Walking into Pala transported you into a land of fairy tales. The restaurant resembled a majestic Italian villa crossed with a Balinese palace. Pale pink and white stone walls housed ornately carved statues in cave-like holes. Towering Corinthian columns soared from the marble floor up to the ceiling, which was covered in woven bamboo. And the view. The view was out of a movie. You faced an uninterrupted view of a valley ridge with ancient coconut trees reaching towards the skies above from each of the two terraces.

Brenda walked over to the bar and ordered a cappuccino. She then turned around to see if I wanted one too. I shook my head as I marveled at the restaurant's architecture. Brenda sat down at one of the heavy square wooden tables and invited me to sit to her right. I had no idea how indicative this position would become. Brenda was frank; she confessed that Pala had been a challenge for her, as her husband Gede had built it during her sixth pregnancy. I nodded along. Her priorities were for me to train the staff, particularly the wait staff, to provide better service. She discussed cross-promoting Pala using her other businesses, but she didn't have the time to implement her multitude of ideas.

For the first time in a long time, I felt inspired to work again, especially in areas that I was passionate about – food and service!

Back at *The Toronto Star*, I'd dabbled in food-related marketing. Whenever I sat across the desk of a media planner, I often asked for a piece of paper to quickly sketch an idea for an upcoming campaign. I was supposed to sell advertising space, not ideas. I'd expended insurmountable amounts of energy to force through innovation at the 100-year-old dinosaur of a newspaper. Even when I'd already sold an idea to key clients like IBM and Bell Canada, I'd have an even harder sell to convince *The Star* to produce it. *The Star* may be Canada's largest newspaper, but things operated in such a reactive way. Corporate was known for saying no. Some of my closest clients at Ogilvy and Mather and BBDO thought I belonged in the creative department, not sales. The most senior VP at Leo Burnett once said, "If you want something new done at *The Star*, ask Frances. She'll break down walls for you."

My final year at *The Star* had been the most invigorating, when I'd made record numbers in ad revenue, created unique ad products and turned client entertainment into a collection of FAPs. But it hadn't been enough. I became bored and longed to explore the new media forefront of San Francisco. Yet instead of finding innovation at CNET, I discovered that a greed mentality had already set into Silicon Valley and the Bay area. Before Cam arrived in San Francisco in 1999, I was contemplating a move to Seattle and Portland, where it seemed all the creatives and hippies had relocated. Instead, Asia found me.

Sitting across from Brenda, looking at an epic view, I smiled knowing that I'd reached another new frontier.

$\mathcal{Y}$osh and Marie's wedding was fast approaching. They'd asked if I could arrange a lunch in Ubud and a tour for about thirty guests. I was back in my element.

I begged Adi to accompany me to Begawan Giri. Their signature restaurant, Kudus, would be the perfect place for Yosh and Marie's lunch event. Kudus was located inside an antique wood *joglo* (a carved Indonesian teak building), dismantled from one of the royal palaces in Java. The owners of Begawan Giri had shipped all the pieces across Java, over the ocean, and to Bali. Situated high above the Sayan River, artisans had rebuilt the joglo, piece by piece, carving upon carving, in the tropical jungle where one could dine as kings and queens had in bygone eras.

Adi hesitated before grudgingly agreeing. He said that the hotel wouldn't take me seriously if I showed up on the back of his motorbike. I'd hoped that I'd left that superficiality behind. I wasn't going to let other people's small mindedness prevent Adi from seeing Begawan Giri for himself. Thankfully as we pulled up to the lobby, the resort staff were accommodating, kindly pointing us to the parking lot without assuming he was my driver.

The resort was just as magical as the first time I'd visited. We followed the reception staff through the modern white archway – a clever window to the expansive gardens and the grove of soaring coconut trees. I carefully watched my step on the smooth white stone pathway which turned slippery in the current rainy season. A chef in whites introduced himself as Chef

David. We met with him and his team to discuss the event's details, but to our dismay, Kudus couldn't accommodate thirty guests, so we had to settle for the resort's sister restaurant, Glow. Glow's layout wrapped around in an L-shape with small square tables each set for two to four people, so it wasn't ideal, but it would have to do as we were a week away from the lunch.

After the menu for Yosh and Marie's event was decided, the front office staff asked if we'd like a tour of the residences. I was beside myself with excitement. Customarily, only staying guests could enter the suites. We had the extraordinary privilege of being able to tour every single residence as occupancy was near zero from the ongoing fall-out of 9/11.

Most other resorts in the world were usually one massive building block of rooms. Begawan Giri was a collection of five exquisite residences, each designed around a singular theme. There was *Bayugita* (Windsong), *Tejasuara* (Sound of Fire), *Tirta Ening* (Clear Water), *Wanakasa* (Forest in the Mist), and lastly *Uma Bona* (House of the Earth Son), a two-bedroom royal palace. Each residence comprised of five suites, ranging from an entry-level deluxe suite up to a lavish master suite.

When I stepped into the Master Suite of Tirta Ening and turned my head to the right, my heart leapt. I blinked my eyes in disbelief as I took in a massive rock pool and waterfall (yes, an actual waterfall!) in the suite's outdoor bathroom. I pulled Adi in and pointed as my mouth gaped open.

I jumped up and down in glee, the total opposite of professional and collected. "This is it! This is where I want to get married!"

Adi's eyes opened wide in absolute astonishment, but he calmly replied, "Ah, okay, let's talk about this later, darling."

He gently tugged me out of this bathroom, which was beautiful beyond words. The front office staff giggled as I turned and stretched my neck to get one last glimpse of my wedding dream.

The funniest part of our tour was when Adi walked into Uma Bona and stopped in his tracks still with his eyes practically popping out of his head. Unlike me, being the wise man that he was, he showed no other signs of excitement. Uma Bona was an opulent villa of dark mahogany wood carvings and gilded brass fixtures. It was reminiscent of a luxury yacht with low divans covered in cream linen and an eternity pool accessed either from polished wood steps leading from the main living room or the peekaboo window from the massive marble master bath.

Adi turned to me, "Okay, this is it. I agree."

When we got to the parking lot out of eyesight and earshot of the staff, I resumed jumping up and down excitedly. "Really? Can we get married here? Are you serious?"

"Yes, darling."

"How? How are we going to do this? It's insanely expensive here."

"Why, we can do it right here," Adi answered as he grinned widely and spread his arms out, "Here in the parking lot."

"Very funny, honey." I pouted as I pulled on my blue motorbike helmet.

Adi had already stated his intention of marrying me. I'd gone along with him even though I had no idea how we were actually going to make it happen since none of my family knew of his existence yet. Nevertheless, I was a die-hard dreamer. I truly believed that if you thought it, somehow, the thing you imagined would magically manifest.

As if in a dress rehearsal for our own wedding, I dreamed up the perfect Ubud guide for Yosh and Marie's wedding guests. I quickly sketched a hand-drawn map on Ubud, pinpointing all my favourite shops and cafés. I'd start the tour at Saraswati Temple with a quick explanation of Balinese culture, and from there people could fan out to explore on their own using my map. After a morning walking around Ubud, Robert and his family of drivers would bring all of us to Begawan Giri for lunch and an optional spa session afterwards.

I insisted on using handmade paper. Adi thought my project was a bit too ambitious and asked if it wouldn't be better to hand draw just one map and make thirty copies.

"Nah, that's sooooo boring. I don't want plain old paper. I want this to be totally unique, handwritten with my hand-drawn map on handmade paper," I replied with my face set in a stubborn frown.

Seeing that he couldn't dissuade me, he confessed that he remembered seeing a shop on the south end of Ubud selling cards and paper. Bingo. I had my handmade paper. As I embarked on a project Adi perceived as a bit too ambitious, I finally realized by map five that there was no way that I'd get the maps done in time. Adi shook his head quietly and sat down every night after a long day of work to help me hand draw all the Ubud tour maps. I knew then, as I do now, that he would always be the wisdom and the rock holding me down when my head flew in the clouds with my whimsical, impossible ideas.

31

*A*di and I sheltered under one of the only trees at Jimbaran Beach. The sun was scorching hot, so nobody else was on the beach. The ocean sparkled blue, but the reflection on the water was almost blinding to look at. We were at the middle part of the beach, where the local fish warung was located. We were splurging on this seafood feast because I wouldn't see Adi for the next five days. I was going to Yosh and Marie's wedding as a "single."

When I told Adi that last time, Robert had taken Mom and me to a proper café near the fish market, Adi shook his head. "That's where all the expensive places are for tourists. This is where locals eat."

Through the smoky haze of the open fire barbecue, the waiter appeared, looking like a gangster with a long ponytail and tattoos up his muscular arms, on which he balanced a massive tray of seafood that he placed carefully onto the wooden table before us. My mouth watered as my eyes took in the charred whole fish and butterflied prawns. Alongside them sat grilled clams and tiny skewers of squid satay covered in tomato sambal.

The waiter asked if we wanted rice or potatoes, and we both answered, "Rice, please," at the same time, smiling at each other.

He returned with a woven basket of rice and *kangkung* (morning glory) mixed with tomato sambal as well as four little dishes of sauces.

To my surprise, this tough looking waiter proudly announced, "I make this sambal myself. This is *sambal matah*, this is *sambal tomat*, this is *kecap manis*, and that is garlic butter."

Not wanting to disrespect the gangster, I commented politely, "Wow, that looks amazing! Thanks. What's your name?"

"My name is Made," he said, pronouncing it *Maah-day*.

"That's Adi's name too! So you're second-born," I said and then realized that I might be bringing up past pain.

"You know Bali names. Good…good," he said as he gave me the thumbs up.

Seeing Adi's furrowed brow, I reached over to him thinking that I'd just reminded him of Wayan, his older brother. Adi rarely talked about his family. All I knew was that his brother had been killed in a car accident when he was four years old. Actually, Adi wasn't thinking about Wayan, he was worried about how I'd get to The Ritz Carlton as he had to rush back to Kerobokan for a ceremony.

"Don't worry, I'll ask Made to find me a taxi."

Overhearing our conversation, Made offered, "You need taxi? I take you. Ritz Carlton is close to here. Just up the hill."

Adi shook his head slightly at me, looking extremely skeptical.

"Do you have a car?" I asked, ignoring Adi's overprotectiveness.

"No, I take you on my bike. You come on his bike, yah?" Made asked with a nod of his head toward Adi, who now glared at Made.

What could I say? Made placed my black Prada duffle bag in front of him and off I went on the back of his motorbike. When we turned onto a deserted dusty road without any houses or even any other traffic, I started to panic.

"Are you sure this is the way to The Ritz Carlton?" I asked, recalling a curvy but well-paved road we travelled the last time I stayed at The Ritz in May.

"Yah, yah. This is a shortcut."

Hope it's not a shortcut of my life, I thought. I prayed Adi's skepticism about this gangster-waiter person was unfounded. We were the only motorbike going up and up; the road was a deep valley with towering white rock cliffs on either side of us – a perfect place to ditch a body. The landscape was dry and rugged, unlike the lush green jungle of Ubud. We wound around a curvy road and found a big Ritz Carlton Bali sign carved out of the same white stone that we'd just driven past. I breathed an inaudible sigh of relief.

Made swerved into the lobby and slammed on the brakes. Three staff gaped at the sight of me as I hopped off the motorbike, took off the helmet and shook out my ponytail. Made handed me my duffle and zoomed off.

I turned around, and one of the staff asked, with more than a hint of arrogance, "May I help you?"

"I'm checking in."

The other two staff jumped into action when I said this – one rushed to hit the massive brass welcome gong and the other placed a flower lei of bright orange marigolds around my neck.

"This way, ma'am," said the first staffer as she took my bag and led me through the lobby to the reception desk. As I gave my name, she stood there holding my duffle bag, looking me up and down, assessing my light blue cotton camisole and capris, which showed off my deep tan.

To her total astonishment, the front office receptionist said, "Welcome back to The Ritz Carlton, Ms. Tse. We've upgraded you to a Club Room."

A Club Room had the same layout as the entry-level Resort Room that I'd shared last time with Yoko. My barter deal with Brenda cut down my daily expenses but staying at The Ritz Carlton for one night typically equated to one month of Adi's salary. The three nights for the wedding events would already have been an extreme indulgence even when I'd been earning a significant salary in Hong Kong. I was able to afford The Ritz because of the fallout from 9/11. Without any tourists, I paid less than a hundred dollars a night.

Despite the room deal of the century, 5-star resorts still charged exorbitant food prices. A bottle of water cost the same as a meal elsewhere. The Ritz's *nasi goreng* (Indonesian fried rice), deliciously reimagined with steak-sized beef satays and served in a massive wok, sold for twenty-four dollars at a time when nasi goreng on the street sold for a dollar. To save money, I figured that I'd stuff myself at the included buffet breakfast, skip lunch and ration my welcome fruit bowl over two nights for dinner since one dinner would be the wedding reception.

When the bellboy finished showing me the features of the oversized room (my dad's three-bedroom apartment in Hong Kong was the same square footage), he directed me to the Club Lounge. I followed him into the elevator – a novelty in Bali, as there are only four floors maximum to each building. We went two levels down and he opened the double doors into the luxuriously carpeted Club Lounge.

Out of the stifling October humidity of south Bali and into a calm oasis of comfort, I felt like I'd come home. In the blink of an eye, I was sucked right back into the luxurious trappings of my old life. Everything here was familiar; the fluffy scones dotted with raisins, the silver dish of whipped cream in a bowl of ice, the smoked salmon finger sandwiches, and even the tiny *lumpia* (spring rolls).

The Club Lounge butler explained that as a Club Room guest, I could take all my meals in the comfort of the lounge.

Not trusting my ears and thinking there must be some kind of language error, I questioned, "Do you mean that the food here is free?"

"Yes, Miss Tse, you can enjoy breakfast, lunch, afternoon tea and dinner as well as unlimited drinks here. If you prefer a buffet breakfast, you can go to Padi restaurant," he answered.

I nearly kissed him! The Club Lounge became my refuge for the next four days.

Not to waste a second of my new-found haven, I immediately sat down in a traditional English armchair with an exceptional view of the Indian Ocean and ordered Earl Grey tea with cold milk on the side.

Most places in Bali – in fact, in the world – failed at making tea properly, usually giving you a cup of tepid water with a tea bag on the side of the saucer. I watched the butler put down a white porcelain teapot filled with steeping tea, a tea strainer, a silver jug of cold milk and a wedge of freshly sliced lemon. I shook my head, smiling. The Ritz actually serves loose leaf tea! Loose-leaf Earl Grey in a tea pot! I was home.

My next thought was, Adi should be here. What was wrong with me? Yosh already knew about Adi, kindly inviting him to both the wedding and the Ubud tour and lunch at Begawan Giri. I'd lied to Yosh and said that he couldn't come because of ceremonies. I hadn't told Adi that he'd been invited either.

As I sat there sipping a drink that I hadn't known that I'd missed, my insides chilled despite the piping hot tea. I'd judged Adi when nobody else had.

When I was with Adi, all I saw was his very essence – the kind, gentle, wise soul that I'd fallen in love with. But I feared that everyone else saw him as unsuitable. For starters, I was a head taller than him; I was unusually tall for a Chinese girl, and he was unusually short for a Balinese man.

The most taboo part of our relationship was that Adi was ten years younger than me. We looked the same age, as strangers often mistook me for ten years younger than I actually was, but that didn't matter. My family and friends knew that I was an over-the-hill, unmarried thirty-one-year-old.

In terms of occupation, Adi being a spa therapist was completely outside of the realm of my friends: bankers, consultants, marketers and entrepreneurs. I feared their judgement of Adi and of me for choosing him. Part of me wanted to protect Adi from them, but a bigger part wanted to protect myself from being judged.

Going to a formal event like Yosh and Marie's wedding meant that appearances mattered. Our clothing mattered. Everything mattered. But I'd forgotten what mattered most: Adi.

I have stunning photos of the wedding day, of me looking like a Balinese girl in my mom's Spanish vintage crocheted top and my favourite soft green and cream silk sarong. I envied Marie who exuded confidence and knowing in the bridal preparation villa when the photography team was there to document every second of her journey from bride to wife.

Marie glided gracefully down the flower path of frangipani towards Yosh, who waited under a Balinese pavilion at the ocean's cliff edge. Perfectly matched in height and age, they epitomized a model Japanese couple.

I'd been to so many weddings; this was my tenth in the past five years. All the brides had been close friends and had chosen grooms who, at least outwardly, matched them in every way.

When I was a teenager, Mom laughed at me as every time we dined at exceptional venues: Tavern on the Green in Central Park, The Red Room at the Hong Kong Club, the sculpture gallery at AGO. I'd excitedly remark, "This is where my dinner reception will be!"

Mom would roll her eyes and ask, "How many times are you getting married?"

None, actually – that was the problem.

My wedding dream never featured the actual wedding ceremony. My focus had always been the dinner reception.

I hated white even if bridal magazines dressed it up as champagne, cream, eggshell or pearl – it was still white. I'd die before donning a fairy tale gown. Another image that I couldn't envisage was walking down a church aisle supported by my dad, a man who rarely supported me in real life. I'd hoped that by seeing alternatives to churches as I had at Crystal's garden wedding in Carmel and this ocean-cliff ceremony, I'd somehow envision a way and a place where my wedding could come true.

Instead of tasting sweet inspiration, I swallowed the bile of shame.

I sat beside Robert, who'd come for the wedding and dinner reception. His presence cut through my pretense; Adi should have been the one smiling back at me. Robert had been brave enough to come to this event where he was the only Balinese represented.

Why hadn't I seized this opportunity for Adi to show up with me? I knew why.

Despite being half a world away from my mom, I still feared that she wouldn't approve of Adi. No matter how far I'd come, my instincts were to please my family and reassure my friends that, yes, I was the same as them.

32

Witnessing Yosh and Marie's wedding made me re-examine what I was doing in Bali. Did I really want to marry Adi? Did I even understand what that entailed?

Adi alluded to the vast responsibilities that a Balinese wife took on. As he was the only son in his family compound, many duties rested on his shoulders alone. As his wife, I too would help at the numerous ceremonies for his neighbours, around sixty-five other families. In any given month, this could take up to a week of one's time. Balinese did not have time off, let alone vacations. Any days off work were taken up with ceremonial duties.

I'd have to learn to speak Bahasa Indonesia, and even better if I could speak low Balinese. I was horrible at languages – growing up only speaking Cantonese until I went to kindergarten, I even butchered well-known English sayings.

These unknown, unwanted duties that came with becoming Adi's future wife made my head spin.

Not wanting to divulge my fears to Adi, I kept quiet and looked for activities to occupy my mind and push out any unsettling thoughts.

Becoming a sculptor in Venice still sat in the back of my mind so I opted to learn one of Indonesia's most revered crafts, batik painting. I jumped on my rental bike and whizzed across the main road, down Jalan Hanoman and back up the hill at Monkey Forest Road to the place I'd seen a sign: "Make your own batik."

My eyes adjusted to the dimness of the musty-smelling batik

studio/shop where handprinted indigo cotton sarongs hung from the low ceilings. I brushed them aside to find the batik artist in the back pulling wet fabric out of big buckets of indigo-hued water the same colour as his hands. Seeing me, he wiped his hands on his worn sarong and explained that the course was one-on-one; I could come as many times as I needed until I finished my batik.

My work at Pala accounted for only two or three days a week. Considering I had hours and hours to kill on the other days while Adi worked, I handed over my deposit right away. With such flexibility in the course, I could still monopolize Adi's precious days off.

The artist, Bapak Nyoman, led me over to an open cement floor and sat down cross-legged, motioning for me to do the same.

"Sit on the floor?" I asked, already worried that he'd say yes.

"Yes, please sit here and watch."

This was already more challenging than I expected. Most Westerners like me did not sit on the floor to create art for hours. We sat upright in a chair or stood in front of an easel or large table, depending on the artwork involved.

"Okay," I said as I lowered my sturdy body onto the floor and crossed my legs.

"This is hot wax...be careful," Pak Nyoman warned as he dipped his metal tool into the wax and drew a pattern onto the square of cloth that he held in his other hand.

I shrunk back. Hot wax? What had I gotten myself into?

Pak Nyoman explained that artists created batik by painting patterns on the cloth with hot wax. Once the wax dried, the cloth would be dyed and the wax peeled away, leaving the painted pattern, like relief printing. This was a lot more complicated than I had expected, but I was curious to learn.

He looked at my wide eyes and smiled, "Don't worry, you go slow. I teach you."

And he did teach me, as promised. A few weeks later, I'd show my finished batik, the size of a napkin square, to Adi. As an added bonus, I'd gained the ability to sit on a hard floor for thirty-minute intervals before having to get up and shake off the pins and needles – a skill that would serve me well in the coming years.

❋

As the weeks wore on, I became more and more distant from Adi. Usually a non-stop chatterbox, I talked less and less. Sometimes I wouldn't even hear Adi talking to me.

Worry creasing his brows, Adi asked me, "Are you okay?"

I didn't want to hurt our relationship by saying that I was scared, so I'd pasted on a smile and said, "I'm missing home."

This could not have been further from the truth; I dreaded having to leave Bali. Even though I had this little stint with Brenda, it wasn't a paying job nor even real. There was no way my mom would accept me just being in Bali. I could hear her worry in my mind: *How are you going to live there? Why do you want to live there? You don't even have a job!* So many questions that I didn't have any answers to. I couldn't reveal to Adi that I didn't have a plan. The only thing I knew for sure is that I'd only completed one small corner of my batik. I was hoping by the time it was finished, I would have also created a way to stay in Bali.

One day on the way to my batik class, I noticed a small jewelry shop. Usually, I wasn't interested in jewelry, so it was a bit odd that I pulled my bike over to check it out.

As the glass door closed with a bang, the salesperson looked up and smiled at me. He was exceptionally tall for a Balinese man and dressed formally in a white button-up and pressed black pants – also unusual. Catching myself staring, I peered into the glass display near the window, feigning interest in some earrings and a necklace.

"Would you like to try them on?"

I said, "Sure."

He responded with, "Do you mind?" as he leaned in to brush my hair back meaning to help me put the necklace on.

I ducked away from his hand. Nonplussed, he casually passed the unclasped chain to me. As I secured the clasp on my own, he watched me in the reflection of the mirror.

"Hmmm, I'll think about it."

"Are you staying here for long?"

"Sort of," I said, not wanting to sound too friendly.

"What's your name?"

This was always the first or second question that all the super friendly Balinese people would ask a tourist, so I did not find it pushy or prying.

"My name is Frances," I said, pronouncing it slowly, knowing the "Fr" sound was difficult for Balinese to grasp.

"Nice to meet you. I'm Ketut," he said and reached out to shake my hand.

I was a little taken aback by the gesture, as most Balinese did not shake hands. They might nod and smile, or if you're close friends and a guy, slap you on your back and grunt. But shaking hands – that didn't happen.

He grinned and said, "Maybe you can come to visit again. It's really boring here, there aren't many tourists now."

"Okay, see you later," I said as I walked out with no intention to return.

On my way to my batik class the next day, Ketut was sitting on the shop's step.

As I passed, he shouted out, "Hi Frances!"

I waved back and continued zooming down the hill, past the Monkey Forest to gain enough momentum to make it back up the other side. Every day after that, if I was going to my batik class, I would see him sitting there on the step or cleaning the glass storefront. He didn't do anything obvious, but it seemed like he was always waiting for me. Ketut always smiled and waved as I flew by. Deep in my heart, I knew that I shouldn't smile back, but I did.

33

Taking my half-brother Andrew's advice to get to a little-known country before the backpackers and tourists, I was heading to Laos via Thailand for nine days.

During my final summer days in Toronto, I'd known that I wanted to travel to Laos during my Bali sabbatical. I didn't know when I'd be back in Southeast Asia with this much free time. I'd flipped through the travel brochures at the Gap Adventures office and booked an eco (as in, economical) trip to northern Thailand where I could add an option to explore Laos. This itinerary was the only one that included Laos, my ultimate destination.

Adi, rightly so, worried about my ambitious trip to trek among the Thai hill tribes above Chiang Mai, followed by a two-day boat trip down the Mekong River to Luang Prabang, Laos. While I thought this was a fast-track to more FAPs, Adi reminded me that my definition of adventure meant trying new canapés at the The Ritz Club Lounge, not sleeping in mountain shacks made of bamboo.

He looked at my beaded sandals, my crisp cotton camisole and my black Prada bag, shook his head and said, "I'm taking you shopping."

This was my first time to Denpasar, Bali's biggest city, which in any other part of the world might be considered a large country town. We drove through a leafy neighbourhood called Renon where massive mansions lined the road. We zipped past some government buildings, none taller than the coconut trees, and stopped at a busy crossroad where a two-story department store called Matahari helmed one corner.

I leaned into Adi and shouted into his helmet, "Is that where we're going?"

He shook his head and called back, "No, that place is expensive."

Adi took me around the corner and parked in front of Ramanaya Department Store – I looked up at the white concrete three-story building. My shopping in Bali so far consisted of quaint little shops and the local market in Ubud. Department stores in Bali were uncommon and even more uncommon was the escalator in the open-air lobby. We broke into a sweat the moment we entered the stiflingly store where rows and rows of clothing were packed together without any air conditioning for relief. This was not the gleaming department shops of the west where designers held separate areas.

As I passed the racks, I couldn't recognize any of the brands – Adi pointed out his favourite brand, "Watch Out." I admired his taste in the stylish and funky brand. The rest of the store felt like we'd gone back to the '70s with brands like "Leah" denim; its Americana emblem disguising its Indonesian origins.

The backpacks were hidden at the back. Most came in bright pinks or purples with big flowers or cartoon characters until we dug out a plain black and grey school pack.

My hiking shoes were stranded in Ken's closest (I'd only used them twice in the whole year that I'd lived in San Francisco). Adi brought me a long-sleeved button-up shirt of his dad's and hoped that my running shoes would suffice.

Arriving in Bangkok after more than a month in Bali was jarring. Serene scenes of farmers quietly toiling away in rice fields were replaced by insane motorbikes, cars, buses and *tuk-tuks* jostling for position on the roads, sidewalks, anywhere there was an empty inch. The constant din of noise assaulted my ears. The smog of the city infiltrated my pores. The poverty of so many tore at my heart. I wanted to jump back on the plane to Bali.

On my first night, I met my assigned roommate Pavla, a tall, chestnut-haired Czechoslovakian woman about my age. She clung to me like a life board, glad to find someone who knew how to navigate an Asian metropolis.

Her first request was to visit the Royal Palace. Although I preferred to seek out Thai street food, I was compelled to protect Pavla from the crooks (i.e., the tuk-tuk drivers). Keen to flaunt my street smarts, I was still no match for the hard-wired tuk-tuk drivers. One particularly unscrupulous driver veered in front of a gem store and announced this was a necessary stop on the way to the palace. I nudged Pavla, and we jumped out.

I sneered back at the driver, "This was a necessary stop for us," as we stalked off without paying.

Another lied straight to our faces, saying the palace was closed but he could take us to (you guessed it) the gem shops! In the end, we took the least expensive way and walked.

Pavla and I became fast friends as we bargained our way through Chatuchak Weekend Market and dug into greasy pad thai while sitting on plastic stools on the sidewalk in Khao San Road, the infamous backpackers' district.

Together, we boarded the overnight train from Bangkok to Chiangmai. When we met the tour guide at our hotel in Chiangmai, he was shocked that I didn't have a Laos visa yet. For having a super organized, A-type personality, I'd somehow lost all basic travel skills – I'd missed my flight on 9/11, and now, I'd failed to get a travel visa. Thankfully, for a small fee of twenty dollars, he could arrange my Laos visa by the time we got back from the hill tribes.

Chiang Mai was a refreshing change. We walked through the quiet streets to a lively night market for dinner.

I'd signed up for an extra option – one of the best decisions of the whole trip – a day learning Thai specialties at the Chiang Mai Cookery School. Every aspect of this experience woke muscle memory as we sliced and pounded away with our individual mortars and pestles to make a spicy feast of five dishes: pork noodle salad, green curry chicken, massaman pork curry, stir-fried vegetables and, for dessert, mango sticky rice. Each of us made enough to feed four people; how I wished that Adi was with me.

Ten of us piled into an uncomfortable open-air *bemo* for the hour-long drive to the beginning of our hill tribe trek. The rickety transportation was an ominous sign for me, and it took every bit of conviction and FAP-bargaining with myself to stay on the bemo instead of returning to the relative comfort of our two-star hotel. Pushing down my growing fear, I followed Pavla and the group into the jungle. We climbed all day to the hill tribe village. When we arrived at the bamboo shacks, I thought, *That wasn't bad at all. I can do this!*

After hours of uphill climbing without anything but water, we were ravenous. We devoured platefuls of the simple, flavourful, nourishing vegetable curry and rice. Our local Thai guide was from these mountains and shared generations-old folk tales as we ate.

With a serious face, he leaned into the bonfire and said that he had to give us some information about the next day's trek, "Do you know what to do if you see a snake?"

All of us city dwellers on the edge of our seats solemnly shook our heads. With the flames illuminating his face, he shouted, "RUN!!!" We fell off the logs laughing.

This was rustic redefined. This was not the shabby chic of Pottery Barn. There were no mattresses, no showers, and no toilets. We slept on bamboo slats raised above the ground, splashed our faces from one bucket of icy water and shared a communal outhouse. Pavla was grateful for the warmth of my blanket (thanks to Adi's foresight) and the warmth of my body as we cuddled each other to survive the night.

My trip literally went downhill from there. Without proper trekking shoes and wearing worn-out running shoes, I slid the entire way down the muddy mountain. Why did I pay for this? They should be paying me!

I was saved by the shower – the most beautiful thing I'd ever seen – a long bamboo pipe that gushed crystal clear mountain spring water. I washed off the outer layer of mud. For the most part, it was a futile effort.

The next challenge was to ride an elephant bareback. I can't believe that I'd thought this would be cool. It was disgusting. Flies flew all over the elephant and, therefore, all over me. When our small herd started stomping through the jungle, the elephant in front of mine decided that the whole path was his outhouse. I was so relieved to finally slide off the elephant at the end of our trek. If my butt wasn't sore enough from sliding down the mountain, it was likely bruised black and blue from this bouncing ride.

Could it possibly get worse? Of course it could. We clambered onto rickety bamboo rafts to travel downriver, passing one village after another. Clinging to our rafts, we listened to our guide tell us that the villagers did everything in the river: their bathing, their laundry, everything. Their outhouse sat at the bottom end of the river, which doubled as the top end of the next village. We were knee-deep in that river, our raft bobbing in and out of the murky water... Eeeeewwwww!

When I got back to our hotel room, I stripped down at the entrance and dumped all my clothes, including my useless shoes, into the trash. I dropped the blanket on top of the pile. After that trek, the two-star hotel room felt like coming home to The Ritz.

Only six of us, including Pavla, remained from the hill tribes tour. The Laos portion was an extra add-on tour. For me, it'd been the other way around. Laos was the main reason I'd booked the Gap Adventure tour; I was determined to get there before the rest of the world crowded in. My half-brother, Andrew, had spent six months travelling through India and Southeast Asia. Of the ten countries he'd travelled, he'd urged me to get to Laos, a country still unexplored.

Laos had recently opened back up to the world after decades of war and genocide. In the Vietnam War, the Americans dropped millions of explosives over Laos which continued to kill innocent farmers and villagers as undetonated bombs exploded in rice fields or somewhere in the jungle when someone made the wrong step.

We clambered onboard the rickety old longboat, ducking our heads to avoid hitting the low ceiling. This longboat would serve as our home for the next two days as we meandered down the Mekong, stopping for one night in Pak Beng village. Not the most comfortable mode of transport, but the view from the river was priceless. My already battered and bruised butt became numb from sitting on the hardwood slat seats, but I hardly noticed. I was mesmerized with life along the lush jungle edging the riverbank.

From time to time, we'd pass a single bamboo structure raised high above the ground or a small village of ten to twenty homes clustered together. Laughing children splashed in the muddy water while little ones clung to their mother's sarongs as the women scrubbed laundry in the river.

The overnight stop was reminiscent of our bamboo shack on the Thai mountain, but thankfully it was dry and warm.

We travelled onwards early the following day, stopping at the weaving village of Pak Ou, where I started what would become a mad obsession with handwoven Laos silk. Weaving silk was a traditional skill passed from mother to daughter, something a busy mother could do for an hour while waiting for rice to steam or after coming back from a day in the rice fields, the sound of the loom clicking late into the evening. A 3-meter by 50-centimetre silk weaving might take six to eight months to weave in between the chores of daily life. The silk itself is often spun by hand and dyed with flowers, nuts and seeds. These exceptional weavings were prepared for the most important Laos ceremonies, such as weddings, when the groom would move into the bride's home – the opposite of Bali's social structure.

Rounding the river, Luang Prabang came into view. This town, the second largest in Laos, sat high above the river. We climbed up the stairs carved into the riverbank for our first glimpse of quaint little streets lined with French colonial shophouses. There weren't any cars or motorbikes; instead, graceful Laotian women clad in silk sarongs, a basket on one arm and an umbrella in the other, glided past on old-fashioned metal bicycles. I held my breath, watching this sublime moment of artistry go by.

Luang Prabang felt like a mystical dream, one that had always been on the periphery of my consciousness. It now manifested into reality as I wandered into one weaving shop after another where women sat with their fingers flying over looms making a rhythmic clickity-clack as they wove luxurious lengths of silk. Indigo blue, soft rose, and rich coffee hues. Mythical nagas (dragons) crossed with diamonds in intricate patterns. I imagined that Luang Prabang was the Ubud of twenty years earlier. A time before tourists, before 5-star resorts, before direct flights.

The architecture of the town whispered of the rich history lived in these buildings. Many of the colonial shophouses were in a decrepit state with a few renovated ones dotting the street, a backpacker café selling baguette sandwiches or crêpes – a reminder of the town's French past – or an Internet café selling a minute for a dollar, just enough time to send a quick email home.

A little bell rung as I stepped into the Internet café. I reluctantly coughed up five dollars for five minutes to quickly check for urgent emails.

Surprisingly, I found an email from Will, an ex-client from *The Toronto Star*, and nearly fell over when I clicked, open.

"Frances, I know this is coming out of the blue. I want to know that I've fallen for you, babe..."

What? I reread the email.

I never stepped out of line, even when I'd been insanely drawn to Will years before.

Back when we worked together five years earlier, Will had described how his buddy had set up his girlfriend in a luxury condominium in Vancouver, and he'd hinted that he could do the same for me. Heartbroken over Vern, I'd daydreamed about being this well-kept woman pampered by Will. I'm not going to lie. Living on the West Coast of Canada, away from the eyes of my family, golfing and skiing at Will's expense, was tempting. But when I imagined his young daughters and his wife, I knew that I would never have an affair with a married man.

I replied asking if he was still married. And left it at that.

Walking down at the riverfront, the sunset was as dazzling as the view from the water. Shimmering across the river, mesmerizing shades of cotton candy pink and blood orange lit up the opposite side of terraced greenery. It looked like a sweets shop on display.

In one of the silk shops, I donned a deep indigo silk sarong which had been sewn onto my body in mere minutes. I didn't have the grace and finesse of the Laotian goddesses, but the young Aussie blokes from our tour were visibly astonished by my transformation from mud-covered, inept hill tribe trekker to a feminine Chinese girl. One immediately asked where he could buy a similar skirt for his girlfriend back home.

The Laotian cuisine was just as delicious as its sunsets.

I tried fiery hot *larp*, grilled fish minced with fresh herbs such as coriander, dill and green onion and mixed with pounded rice powder, Thai chillies and a generous squeeze of lime. *Luang prabang* salad became another favourite. I usually avoided salads of any type, especially in Asia where hygiene and water were highly questionable. Our trustworthy local guide, Phayvanh, insisted that I try it and my resolve broke. The watercress looked just picked, dressed in a light and creamy dressing, topped with ripe tomato slices. I'd only eaten cooked watercress in my mom's pork broths and had no idea that watercress could be eaten raw. I polished off the whole plate as the others remained skeptical of the salad. To this day, it was the best salad I'd ever eaten. Thankfully, my stomach was strong enough to handle it too.

It was surreal to walk the entire length of the main street and see only the five other people from my tour group. There were no other backpackers, usually the first to explore uncharted territory, let alone tourists.

The light here reminded me of Bali – whether it was sunrise or sunset.

One of my lasting impressions of Luang Prabang was "giving alms" to the Buddhist monks at sunrise. Phayvanh suggested that we buy snacks, such as cookies and chips, that the monks rarely receive. Phayvanh woke us before dawn and led us in the dark towards the main crossroad where only an occasional bicycle passed. A silent cluster of monks drifted towards us and fell into line, their saffron robes flapping gently as they held their woven baskets.

We held back as local villagers put bits of cooked rice and vegetables into the baskets of each monk. My forehead wrinkled as I worried about the mish mash of different food that the monks had to endure each day. Once the locals left, we stood motionless, not sure what to do.

Phayvanh smiled at me and motioned me forward. As I approached the first monk, he opened the lid of his basket and I dropped a packet of biscuits into it. I did this for about six monks before my goodies ran out. Pavla stepped past me to the seventh monk and started giving too.

Watching from a distance, I was in awe of the monks' devotion. And I understood that I was the one who'd received the real gift from these young monks as the sun rose behind them.

35

*B*ack in Bali, my old habits came roaring back.

I threw myself into work at Pala, coming up with one creative idea after another. I enjoyed working with Brenda and admired her endless energy. We shared a passion for food and creativity. I saw how a natural-born entrepreneur operates and flourishes.

At the crack of dawn, Brenda, still in her nightgown, could be found in the sewing room choosing vibrant fabrics for cushion covers to sell in her homewares shop. Afterwards at Pala, we'd meet over breakfast and talk about the latest idea or concoct a new recipe in the kitchen. Whenever Adi worked a late shift, I'd join Brenda for dinner at her first restaurant, Clove Café. Her husband, Bapak Gede, sat with his friends at a nearby table. I thought it odd that we didn't sit together and mentioned this to Brenda.

She laughed it off and said, "Boys will be boys."

If I wasn't here, who would she eat with?

Brenda quickly became my Bali mentor — a Westerner who'd fallen in love with a Balinese man and chose to live in Bali.

She described Bali of the '80s when she'd started dating Gede. In the early days, they rented a café on Monkey Forest Road. When that lease ended, Gede built Clove Café and then Pala while Brenda was busy having six children. Gede added a few rooms around their house for friends; this morphed into the Stardust Cottages over fifteen years. Her colourful stories fascinated and reassured me that dreams do come true. I could follow my heart, figure out how to be with Adi and still be financially successful.

Some days, I remained at Pala when Brenda rushed home to change for a ceremony or help at her Banjar. I didn't fully understand the implications of this; instead, I was mesmerized by her transformation from an Australian mum to a Balinese Ibu when she reappeared in a lacy kebaya and batik sarong. Seeing this, the warning signs that had been lurking in the back of my mind started to flicker; Adi often told me how so and so was getting married or his parents were helping at a cremation for the next three days in his village. I started to wonder what life as a Balinese wife really entailed.

Brenda wanted service improved at Pala, so I'd role-play with the waitresses during the afternoon lull. First, I'd ask Yuni, Ayu and Kadek, three of the more senior waitresses, to pretend they were the guests and I was the waitress. I showed them, step-by-step, what 5-star service looked like. It was hilarious when they couldn't decide what to order, having never been put in this situation before. They would giggle and scan the menus (that they knew by heart), looking scared to order too much. I had to remind them that they weren't paying for the imaginary meal.

When we switched roles, another waitress, the regal looking Jero, joined me as a guest. I became a most demanding guest, asking for extra this and complaining about that. The waitresses had a hard time dealing with these challenges; they'd freeze in fear when someone got angry. The Balinese were raised to hide their anger, especially in the hospitality industry where the customer was the king.

Each waitress exuded her own unique charm in the orange sarongs and feather-weight white blouses that accentuated their hourglass figures. How could guests get angry at any of them?

Then again, just a year before, a "stressed out" Frances had stormed up to a timid spa receptionist to complain. My unwavering standards had led me to Adi. If I hadn't complained about Puji, I might never have met my love.

Inexplicably, I'd been given the task to instill the same level of excellence that I myself demanded. I believed that anyone could be taught new skills. That it all came down to one's attitude and character. I continued to work at lightning speed, having not yet adjusted to the slow pace of island life. Being Chinese, certain character traits such as diligence and reliability were not only expected but had been hammered into me from an early age.

For Balinese, it seemed that ceremonies and staying dry took priority.

Wine distributors or cutlery suppliers (the salespeople!) simply wouldn't show up if threatening clouds appeared on the horizon.

When I called their office, they said, "It's raining."

I'd answer back, "Yes, I know it's raining, but you were supposed to be here an hour ago."

"No miss, I don't come when raining."

Pala had sixty staff for a hundred-seat restaurant where we served forty customers during the busiest time. This was mystifying because in Canada or the States, a handful of waitresses handled a hundred diners at a time.

One rainy morning, the head chef came up to me and said that three of our cooks couldn't work that day. My floor supervisor piped up and said that two of the waitresses and one of the bartenders needed the day off too.

Baffled and wary of the weather, I asked, "Why are they just telling us now? Shouldn't they request a day off in advance?"

"Ibu Frances, someone died in their village last night," Yuni, another waitress, explained.

"I don't understand. Doesn't it take time to plan for the cremation?" I asked, "Why is everyone going there now?"

"When someone dies, we must go to their home right away," said Suryani, my right-hand assistant who was going over a new menu with me. "The village helps prepare for the ceremony and stays with the family," Suryani explained.

"All of them?" I asked. I couldn't see how a whole village could crowd into the home of the deceased.

"Yes, this is what we do in Bali. There's a lot for you to learn here," said Suryani.

A lightbulb finally turned on. I now understood why we had to double up on staff. We could never predict when half of them might not show up on any given day.

Suryani was the friendly receptionist who'd shown me around Stardust Cottages when I'd first stayed there back in March. She was the only one out of 200 staff of the two restaurants and guesthouse who knew how to use a computer. If I wanted anything printed, I'd find her in the main house, just outside Brenda and Gede's bedroom.

Recounting my days to Adi, he'd chuckle with amusement and shake his head.

"What? Why are you laughing at me?" I asked crossing my arms over my chest.

"Darling, you're working with Balinese. Our culture is more important than work," Adi said in his cautious way, looking up at the ceiling to carefully form his words.

"So that's why we have so many staff?" I asked, "So people can attend ceremonies?"

"Yes, darling, that's right. Ceremonies. We're tied to our Banjar and our temple," said Adi patiently.

"Wow. This is so different from what I'm used to where work always comes first. Suryani is right. I have a lot to learn. I'm so used to dealing with what's urgent that maybe I've missed out on what's important."

36

I'd fallen into a nice rhythm: working three or four days a week, batik classes on one or two days, and the highlight of my week was spending two full days with Adi.

I relished every moment with him, but as we got emotionally closer, I got more scared. Adi talked more and more about what life might be like when we married. An only child and Balinese, Adi was responsible for his parents and ancestral family compound. When we married, we would have to live with his parents in their family compound in Kerobokan. This was the way things were always done in Bali, it wasn't an option to choose otherwise. I couldn't even pronounce the name of his village properly; Brenda had corrected me when I asked if she knew this village. To her and Adi both, I didn't know how to voice my fears, so I stayed quiet.

We entered the rainy season in November. When Adi worked the late shift, he braved the two-hour journey from Tanah Lot to Ubud, departing at 10:00 p.m. from Le Meridien through torrential rain in pitch black darkness along slippery, unlit roads. It took all his concentration to avoid deep potholes as well as territorial stray dogs on the road. I'd sit up on edge until he arrived safely.

Adi often got in past midnight, trailing rain as he dragged himself in, looking like a drowned puppy. He wore many layers, including the orange fleece (his favourite colour) that I'd bought him from Old Navy in San Francisco. Even that and my bright yellow CNET windbreaker couldn't keep him warm.

Despite jumping into a prepared hot bath, his face remained a bluish colour with dark puffy bags beneath his gentle eyes. I'd often have a spicy nasi goreng from Pala to warm him up, but Adi still shivered with cold, teeth clattering when he climbed under the thin sheets and wrapped his arms around my warm body.

We decided for his safety and health and my sanity that he'd only come when he worked mornings or on his days off.

When I look back, this was how a gap opened for another to fill. I'm ashamed to even write about Ketut from the jewelry shop and how I allowed him to enter my life.

Ketut was a patient pursuer. And he knew how to draw me in. He stopped waiting on the step. He no longer showed me any interest.

My first and only love, Vern, had been interested in me for over two years at university before anything happened between us. It was only when he stopped holding out for me that I finally noticed him. Somehow, I fell right back into the same pattern.

Vern first noticed how cute I was on the bus on the way to an event at Storybrook Gardens during frosh week, the first week of university. He and I were sitting on a log with our mutual friend, Ally. He turned to me and introduced himself as Dave's roommate. Dave had been my high school prom date. He and Vern had been roommates for years at UCC, a prestigious boarding school in Toronto. Seconds after we were introduced, Ally pulled me up and dragged me into the river to compete in one of the frosh week competitions. Vern looked on as we ran screaming with laughter in the water.

After that, I paid him little attention. Sometimes, I'd look up in the canteen and find him staring at me, but I'd quickly look away. I often skipped my Calculus and Algebra classes, as they were complete repeats from my advanced-level high school courses. I'd later ask Vern if I could copy his notes. I could always find him bent over his books at the library, and he always agreed. I'd score one hundred percent with my student number stacked above Vern's, a close second.

Vern would shake his head and say, "How do you do that? You don't even go to class. It's so unfair."

At the end of our first year at university, he came to my dorm room and sat on the floor to say goodbye before we all left for summer break. I was in so much shock that there was a guy in my room, I could hardly respond to him.

In my second year, Vern came to my birthday party with a box of chocolates, hoping to finally ask me out. His face fell when he saw me laughing with another guy on the couch and left abruptly. Vern avoided me for the entire second year until the very end, when we bumped into each other on campus. He shyly asked me to an Asian dance that weekend. I thought, *Why not?* That ignited a small flame.

We started writing to each other that summer, when he was in Montreal and I was in Toronto. In these letters, Vern let his guard down, and I felt free to write how I felt without the intensity of his eyes burning on my skin. On a whim, I convinced a girlfriend to accompany me to Montreal to visit Vern. I wanted to see the person behind the letters.

When we got to Montreal, my friend suddenly had to rush back to Toronto.

This is how Vern and I found ourselves having dinner alone at the most romantic French restaurant. We closed the place down, laughing and drinking each other in. I wondered, *How had I not noticed how devastatingly handsome he was?*

It was stiflingly hot, too humid to sleep in the bedrooms, so Vern and I slept in the living room, on sofas across from each other. Hot and bothered all night, I decided that I wanted to be with Vern. Every cell in my body ached to walk across that room and lay on top of him. But girls like me didn't do things like that. I had to wait for him to make the first move.

Unfortunately, the next morning, a rather plain Chinese girl showed up and greeted Vern with a kiss on the mouth. I was in total shock. Vern looked at me sheepishly and introduced me to his "friend," at the same time asking if she and her brother could grab a ride in my car back to Toronto. His "friend" had suddenly decided to tag along and stay at Vern's for a few days. I was livid.

Vern had the courtesy to sit beside me as I drove. I fumed for the entire five hours drive back to Toronto. He'd totally led me on – in our letters, agreeing for me to stay with him in Montreal, and definitely during our dinner the night before. My car sympathized with me and become equally overheated, forcing Vern to get out every few kilometres to cool the engine down with water. I snapped and hissed, becoming increasingly grouchy as we got closer to Vern's family home. Unable to hide my rage, my face was still set in a scowl when I met Vern's parents for the first time.

The next day, Vern picked me up in his red sports car with his "friend" ensconced in the passenger seat beside him. Squashed between Dennis, Vern's best friend from boarding school, and the brother of the "friend," I stewed in the middle back seat. We tumbled out at Queen's Quay Terminal, my favourite glass arcade at the waterfront where Dennis and the brother tried to entertain me while Vern, hand in hand with his "friend," trailed behind us.

Simmering with jealousy, I marched over to Vern and announced, "I'm not feeling well. Please take me home."

"Now? We just got here." Vern asked, looking totally confused.

Knowing how Vern really felt about me, Dennis saved the day by agreeing that I didn't look well. He insisted that Vern take me home while he took care of the "friend" and her brother. Vern had finally gotten my attention.

This same inattention, this time from Ketut, drew me right back into his shop.

A little bell chimed merrily as I walked into the small shop. Ketut came out from the back, buttoning up his shirt. He smiled widely when he saw me standing there.

"Hi, Frances. I'm happy you come back."

Ignoring his implication that I had come back, I looked around for an excuse to be there. "Ummm, I'd like to see the necklace again. Do you still have it?"

I didn't really have a plan. As if pulled in by an invisible magnet, I just needed to see if Ketut was still here. Now I was considering buying a necklace? My bloody curiosity was expensive.

"Let me see." He took three long strides and suddenly he was right in front of me. He brushed my arm lightly as he reached into the glass display case. "This one?" he asked, holding up a delicate, filigree silver necklace.

I leaned in a little to take a closer look, "Yes, that's it."

"Do you want me help you put on?" he asked, his eyebrows raised.

I knew that I should say no, but I nodded, as if under a spell. Ketut lifted my hair as he secured the clasp, his warm breath whispering against the back of my neck. He emitted a strong cologne that was a bit off-putting but not enough for me to step away.

Looking over my shoulder into the mirror, he asked, "Do you like it?"

"I'm still not sure," I replied, trying not to stare at the image of us standing like a couple.

He cocked his head, reflected in the mirror, "You can stay here. Until you decide, that is."

I looked up at him and shivered slightly, my skin tingling. *What was I doing? I needed to leave. Like ten minutes ago.*

"You know, nevermind. I don't have any cash on me right now. I don't know what I was thinking."

"That's okay; maybe I bring the necklace to your hotel. You can pay me later."

"Um…" Wrinkling my forehead, I thought hard.

I didn't really want him to know where I was staying. At the same time, I wanted to somehow keep talking to him. What if he bumped into Adi? No, no, I can tell him to come when I know Adi is working. Why am I trying to hide this from Adi?

"Excuse me?" Ketut peered into my eyes questioningly. "Do you need more time? Why don't you sit down?" He pointed towards a stool.

"Sure, sure. Umm." It was as if I'd become mute. I couldn't even string a coherent sentence together.

"I saw you go by. Many times. Where do you go?"

"Oh, I was going to my batik class," I said, finding my voice again.

"You make batik?"

"Well, you could call it trying to make batik," I said, giggling as I always did when nervous or unsure. It was something I was hardly conscious of doing but drew many stares. People even turned their heads to see the source of the strange sound emanating from me.

"You have a funny laugh."

"You think?"

Now it was Ketut who laughed, "Yes, it's…how do you say? Unique."

"I've had this laugh all my life. I think it's because I couldn't speak English when I first went to school, so I laughed instead. Maybe to fill the silence."

Not missing a beat, Ketut pushed forward. "Where are you from?"

"I'm from Canada."

"I think you are from Singapore or Japan."

"Yes, I get that a lot here. People are surprised when I say that I'm from Canada."

"Doesn't everyone speak English in Canada?"

"My parents are from China. I was born in Canada, but my parents only spoke Chinese at home. I only started learning English when I went to school."

"I understand."

"How is your English so good?" I asked, trying to turn the conversation away from me.

"Not so good. I talk to tourists like you."

"Yes, that's the best way to learn. I need to learn more Bahasa Indonesia too."

"I teach you, and you teach me English. How about that?"

"Umm." I stalled while thinking to myself, *Now's the time you say that your boyfriend, Adi, can teach you Bahasa Indonesia. Come on, there's no need to spend another second here. What are you doing?* Instead, I heard myself saying, "Sure, why not?"

Ketut smiled as he held up the necklace, "How about this? I can bring it to you. Where are you staying?"

Before I could stop myself, I blurted out, "Stardust Cottages."

"I know that place. On Jalan Bisma. I work near there before."

Instantly curious, I asked, "Really? Where?"

"At the photocopy shop."

"There's a photocopying place? I never noticed it."

"I know the guesthouse where you stay. What room?"

"When you come, I'll meet you at the front reception," I countered, finally getting some of my senses back as I got up and headed towards the door. "Come at four tomorrow afternoon, okay?"

"Okay, see you tomorrow, Frances." Ketut smiled as he held the door open for me to pass.

Sitting on the floor of the batik shop, I went over every word that we'd exchanged as I dipped the metal tool into the hot oil and drew carefully on my square of cotton. What was I thinking? Now he knew where I was staying. This was a bad idea, but I didn't seem to be able to help myself.

I wished I could talk to Grace about this. She was four years older and had left dozens of broken hearts in her path. As a teenager, I'd idolized

Grace, who'd shared every detail of her romantic and sexual forays during our weekly sleepovers. When I'd been crazed with devastation over Vern, Grace had been my most ardent ally, sympathizing with my heartbreak when others had lost patience. She was an expert in the area of men where I had little experience.

I wasn't married to Adi, but I knew his intentions. I loved Adi and wanted to marry him, but I didn't see how it could work. Being the only child in his house, Adi explained that if I married him, he didn't have the option of moving away, not somewhere else in Bali and definitely not to Canada. He was worried that I wouldn't be comfortable living in his family compound or able to take on the immense responsibilities of being his wife. In Bali, I'd only stayed in quaint little guesthouses or 5-star resorts.

When I was with Adi, I didn't see how I could ever be without him. I felt completely safe and cared for in his presence. His every move was considerate and kind. And he was the funniest person I knew.

Often, when I looked deep into his eyes, I felt like I'd known him for many lifetimes. Adi felt the same way, that somehow we'd always known each other. Balinese Hinduism and Buddhism both subscribed to the idea of reincarnation. I'd read in my trusty guidebook about a Balinese king marrying a Chinese princess in the fourteenth century.

I'd pointed it out to Adi and said, "I think this was us in our previous life."

"I think you're right. In every life, we will always find each other," he said, reaching over and pulling me into him.

But when I was alone and thought about the reality of the situation – could I really live in a Balinese family compound with Adi's parents, whom I hadn't yet met? Did I want to? Could they accept a foreigner in their home? Adi said that there were no other foreigners married to Balinese in his village. Our relationship was already the talk of his hotel. His friends at the spa couldn't believe that Adi drove two hours most days to see me. Most Balinese didn't travel further than ten minutes away from their home.

My thoughts and actions defied logic. Why was I even remotely interested in Ketut? He was a random Balinese guy whom I'd spoken to for a total of fifteen minutes in our two interactions. I knew nothing about him.

I studied every aspect of my relationships, albeit I'd only had Vern and

Adi to speak of. But there had been other opportunities such as Will and Marty, which were both significantly more substantial and appealing than a random, unknown Balinese man like Ketut. I usually tread very carefully when it came to matters of the heart. Yet, I'd willingly walked into a lion's den and practically offered myself up as a meal by inviting Ketut over. *What have I done?*

*a*di left at sunrise for his morning shift. I averted my eyes when he kissed me goodbye, already feeling guilty for my unspoken thoughts.

The devil on my shoulder pulled me back: *Guilty? For what? For wanting more friends in Bali? For simply buying a necklace that supports the struggling economy?*

The angel on my other shoulder countered: *Really? Then, why did you change three times just to go to Pala? Perhaps, you're anticipating the "date" you've set to receive that necklace from Ketut at 4:00 p.m.?*

Work was less than productive as I daydreamed, perched on the bright purple cushions, staring mindlessly at the spectacular views of the valley. My breakfast was eaten by flies. Every minute felt like an hour. Antsy, I kept checking on the staff, wandering down to the kitchen where the cooks sat on the floor and peeled mountains of garlic and tiny Asian shallots.

Not needed there, I checked on my waitresses who were gathered around the heavy marble table behind the bar. Every morning at 10:00 a.m., their able hands created Balinese offerings; some for the Gods, others to be hung as decorations from the ceilings or to adorn the edges of the oxidized copper flower vases.

Each waitress had a different job in the offering assembly line. One ripped the young, pale-yellow coconut leaves away from the central spine. The most experienced and bravest waitress held up the floppy coconut leaf and sliced it quickly in the air to shape the leaf and make cuts or holes for a specific offering. The others took one of these cut pieces, folded along the cut lines and skewered the ends together with a thin bamboo stick called *semat* to form a small square frame. Someone else skewered three same-sized pieces into a flat square. A final assembler attached one of these flat squares to a frame to create a container called a *ceper*. I finally learned that the square saucer-like container that I saw everywhere was called a ceper.

The ceper (the square container) held a *porosan* (a dry offering of betel leaf), a *duras* (a woven ribbon of young coconut leaf) a variety of colourful flower petals, and finely sliced pandan leaves to make a *canang*. A canang was the most common offering in Bali. It took hours of woman power to make them every day.

Each day, millions of canang were offered all over the island. Once offered and left for a few minutes or hours, the offerings were taken down from the shrine, tossed to the ground, swept up and discarded. It went against Western logic – all that work for seconds of devotion.

When I got back to Stardust Cottages, I couldn't decide whether to wait in the reception area or wait in my room. Would I look like I'd been waiting for him if I waited at the reception? Was it too personal if the staff brought him to my room? I finally settled on the terrace in front of my room. Here, I could look busy reading my book and relaxed when Ketut arrived.

Devil: *Yes, perfect. Look nonchalant. Be hard to get.*

Angel: *Excuse me, but why are you even thinking about this in such detail? Hard to get? You're already taken. He can't get anything. Does the name Adi mean anything to you? Hello? Hello?!?!*

"Hello, Frances." I woke from my reverie to see Ketut rounding the corner, waving in greeting.

"Um, hi. Oh great, you're here."

"Yes, you asked me to come at 4:00 p.m."

"That's right. Thanks so much for going to all this trouble to bring the necklace."

"It's no trouble. It's my pleasure," replied Ketut smoothly.

Angel: *Are you really buying into this? He's a playboy. Run!*

At this point, the devil in my mind took a swipe at the angel and knocked her out cold.

I didn't take heed of Angel's warning as I fixated on Ketut's dimple that deepened as he smiled. Just like Vern's.

"Do you want to try it on again?"

"What? Ah, no, no, that's fine. Let me just get the money."

Ketut sat on the daybed, looking around curiously, "So, how long have you been staying here? It must be expensive."

"Actually, it's not bad. I'm kinda working for the owner, Ibu Brenda. I stay and eat for free. That's why I can buy this necklace," I said as I handed him the cash.

"You work here?"

"No, not here. I'm helping at Pala."

"Pala, the restaurant?"

"Yes, the one up the hill."

"Yes, I know it. So you live here?"

"Sort of. I'm trying to figure out how to stay here."

"Really?"

Say it, say that you want to stay here because of your boyfriend, Adi.

"Ah yes, I love Bali." *You mean you love Adi!* coughed the Angel who'd just regained consciousness. "Well, thank you for bringing the necklace," I said as I tilted my head to the reception area.

Ketut got the message and got up and said, "You're welcome. Whenever you want to practice Bahasa, you know where to find me."

"Yes, I know where to find you," I said, averting my eyes for the second time that day.

My face showed everything I thought, and I didn't want Adi or Ketut to know what I was thinking.

Equally terrified and thrilled, I went from buying a necklace to speeding past rice fields on the back of Ketut's menacing black motorbike. I cannot explain how this happened. Nothing made sense. I didn't tell anyone I was leaving. Somehow, Ketut had convinced me to go with him on his motorbike.

We drove south for over an hour. I wasn't familiar with any of my surroundings and yet, I didn't feel scared. Ketut said we were in Denpasar as he led me through a warren of laneways and into a room.

Glancing around his friend's dingy room, Ketut patted a disgusting mattress with repulsive stains on it. Something in me refused to sit down.

Ketut stood up, wrapped his arms around me and kissed me. I drew away reflexively. *Yuck, that was gross, like kissing a wet fish with slimy, salty lips.* I trembled – not with desire but fright – and whispered that I wanted to go home.

Ketut countered that he wanted to marry me. My eyes few open in confusion.

Being the fourth child, Ketut said that he could live anywhere, in Bali or in Canada. He offered to take me to his village to meet his mother so I would understand that he was serious. For now, he agreed to take me back to Ubud.

Back on his bike, my thoughts spun.

He was closer to me in age. He was tall, dark and handsome (Kai Ma had warned me about this lethal combination, but I pushed her voice out of my head). His outward demeanor could be respected by my social circle back home. Why was I listing his qualities like I was checking off specs for a laptop? What was wrong with me?

How had I gone from seven long years of nothing to three willing suitors?

Famine or feast. Drought or flood. Why couldn't I find balance? I was teetering, my footing unsteady. A fall was inevitable because I couldn't seem to right myself.

38

$\mathcal{I}$ woke up more confused than ever. Why was I compelled to see Ketut? I needed to talk to Grace but calling her was not an option with long-distance rates at a dollar a minute. I'd touched on my conundrum in a quick email to her, but Grace rarely checked her email; if she wasn't nursing her newborn, Raine, she was too busy chasing after Ashlyn.

Out of desperation, I confided in Brenda. I figured she was married to a Balinese man, she'd met Adi, and I could depend on her experience in Bali. Brenda was supportive, smiling knowingly as I discussed my dilemma of choosing between Adi and Ketut. She didn't offer an opinion, but thankfully, she revealed my secrets privately to her husband and to Suryani.

That afternoon, I went up to the office to get something printed.

Suryani pounced on me immediately. "Frances, I hear you break up with Adi because of other guy."

"What?! No, no, actually, I don't know what I'm doing," I said, looking around for an escape, my heart clamouring with fear. *Oh my God, everything travels at a snail's pace here but news travels at lighting speed!*

"Adi is a really good man. I mean it. Not so many like him here."

"Yes, yes, Adi is perfect. It's not him, it's me. I'm the problem." Tilting my head down in shame.

"What's your problem?" Suryani did not back down. She looked at me fiercely, daring for me to challenge her.

"Well, I don't really know for sure, but I think I want to be with this guy, Ketut," I said, wavering as even to my ears, it sounded off.

"Ah Ketut, yeah. Brenda told me about that. He's no good. Did he touch you?"

"No, no, it's nothing like that," I said as I shrank back.

"You don't understand. I think Ketut do Black Magic to you," Suryani replied, clicking her tongue and shaking her head in frustration.

"Black Magic? What's that?" I asked, my head starting to pound.

"It's hard to explain. Never mind about that. The big problem is he already married."

Shaking my head in confusion, I said, "What are you talking about? Ketut isn't married. I don't understand. You're just saying that so I'll stay with Adi."

"I know this Ketut. Before, he work down the street. He even show me a photo of his baby."

My voice shook, "His baby? Where's his baby?"

"Maybe he hide his wife and baby in the village."

"That doesn't make any sense. Ketut wants to bring me to meet his mother in Singaraja in a few days."

"What? No, no, you can't go there. You don't know anything about this guy, Frances. I must tell Adi. This is not safe."

Overhearing Suryani's panic, Brenda's husband, Bapak Gede, came out of the master bedroom. He rarely said anything to me, just nodded whenever I walked by.

Shockingly, he looked me in the eye and warned, "Frances, be careful. You're new to Bali."

"Um, okay, Bapak Gede. I'll be careful. Don't worry, it's not like that," I said, cringing, appalled that I must look like a loose woman, running around meeting Balinese guys everywhere.

"Okay, don't do something you'll regret later," cautioned Bapak Gede as he went downstairs.

Sweat poured from my forehead, not only from the humidity but from the heat emanating off Suryani as she punched the keys on her computer. "If you don't believe me, ask the staff at the photocopy shop. Maybe you look for the photo with his wife on the wall there."

"No, I believe you, Suryani. I'm sorry. This is just shocking because Ketut never told me any of this. He even said that he wanted to marry me… not that I'm thinking about that. I mean, I'm just trying to figure things out," I rambled in complete confusion.

"Going to Singaraja is not option. Understand? It's not safe. You're acting crazy." Suryani grabbed my hand. "Please talk to Adi."

I couldn't put it off any longer. I had to tell Adi about Ketut. Although nothing physical had happened except for that horrible kiss, this was still betrayal.

Adi arrived before dinner in the orange fleece that he now wore every day. He had a bag of mangosteens for me. My heart broke looking at his innocence.

My tears trailed down my face as I told him that I couldn't be with him anymore.

Adi's eyes widened in disbelief, "Is this because of that guy? I saw you with him last night."

"What? What are you talking about? When did you see me?" I quivered, fearing the worst.

"I saw you and that guy. I thought you saw me too," Adi said angrily as he tossed the mangosteens onto the desk.

"When?" My voice croaked.

"Last night. You…with your knapsack, the one I helped you buy. On the back of his motorbike." Adi choked out the words, hurt visible in his eyes. "You were laughing, and you hugged him. Then, you looked at me and walked away."

"What? I didn't see you. What are you talking about?"

"How did you not see me? You looked straight at me." Adi's face was pierced with pain. "I just left. I couldn't believe it."

"I'm so confused. I swear I didn't see you. It was dark…I didn't have my glasses on. I would never do that to hurt you." I cringed at the thought of Adi seeing me hug another guy.

"I came from work, but you weren't here. You never said you were going out. I waited in the room…for a long time," Adi said as he sat down on the edge of the bed.

"Oh my God, I don't know what I was thinking. I just went along…I'm not even sure how that happened."

"I waited a long time. One of the room boys told me that a guy picked you up. I had no idea what was going on. I was so confused. I didn't know what to think."

"Oh my God, Adi." I dropped my head in my hands in shame, "I'm sorry, Adi. I have no excuse for my behaviour. Really, I understand if you never want to see me again." Tears rolled down my face. How had I not seen what I was doing to Adi?

"I thought you wanted to be with me. And then...you're suddenly with this other guy. Were you looking for someone else?"

"No, it wasn't like that. I don't know. Nothing happened between us. I swear. He kissed me once, and it was gross."

"Then, why do you want to break up with me?" asked Adi, who looked even smaller than usual.

"I can't string you along. It's not right when I'm so confused," I muttered under my breath, closing my eyes and rubbing my temples with my fingers.

"Did I do something wrong? I don't understand."

I looked back up at Adi as tears leaked from my eyes, I whispered, "You didn't do anything wrong. I can't see how we can be together...long term."

"So you're just going to run off with another guy?"

Hesitating for a minute, I grasped at a reason and blurted out, "Ketut said he wants to marry me."

"I want to marry you!" Adi shouted, throwing his hands up in frustration.

"I know, but your situation is so complicated. I can't decide now that I'll live at your house forever. I've never even been there."

"That's it? You want to see my house? Let's go. Let's go right now," Adi said, his dark irises challenging me.

"No, that's not what I mean. You told me about all these responsibilities. That we must live with your parents and attend all these ceremonies. How will I work there? There are no jobs, people are getting laid off because of 9/11."

"I can take care of you. Maybe not to the level you are used to. But I make more money compared to other Balinese. And you can work in Seminyak when things get better..." Adi's voice trailed off as he stared at the ground.

"I know. It's not about the money...or not all of it. How can I decide now that I can live at your house forever? I'm used to living and working wherever I want. Even more than normal people. Freedom is really important to me."

"So this Ketut guy can give you that?"

"I think so...that's what he said. Ketut doesn't have the same responsibilities because he's one of four children. He said that we can live anywhere. I'm going to Singaraja to meet his mother."

"What?? You can't go to Singaraja. Do you even know where that is? Or even what village he lives in? This is crazy." Adi looked completely baffled.

I reached out to Adi and said, "I'm so sorry. I don't want to hurt you."

Adi flinched and shook my hand off. "I'm not hurt. You'll get hurt. Okay, you don't have to be with me anymore, but you're not going to Singaraja. That's not safe."

"It's okay. Suryani says she knows Ketut."

"What did she say?"

"The same thing you're saying. Even worse, Suryani says that Ketut's already married."

"Why aren't you listening to Suryani? She wouldn't lie to you."

"Well, maybe she's mistaken."

"You just said that she knows this Ketut guy."

"Well, not really well. I guess."

"Why would you risk going four hours north to some village where we can never find you again?"

"I don't feel that way. Ketut won't hurt me."

Adi breathed in, unconsciously clenching his fists while he paced back and forth. I watched him, knowing nothing he said would change my mind.

That night, Adi climbed into bed beside me and leaned in to kiss me. I turned away in shame, "Adi, I can't do this with you anymore."

He looked at me with so much hurt in his eyes and turned over to sleep.

The next morning, I found him curled up, sleeping on the floor at the end of the bed, fully clothed and wrapped in the orange fleece. My heart broke again. What was I doing? I must be crazy. I was destroying my relationship with Adi for a total unknown. This was beyond reckless. But I couldn't stop; Ketut had somehow bound me to him.

I shook Adi gently awake. He looked dazed, confused for a minute as to why he was on the floor. The realization of my insanity crossed his face as he rubbed the sleep from his eyes. I cringed as he cracked his neck one way and then the other to rid the kinks.

Adi asked in a resigned voice, "When are you going to Singaraja?"

"On Saturday," I replied.

"How about this? I'll go with you too. I won't stand in your way if you really want to be with this guy. But I have a responsibility to make sure you're safe."

"You don't have any responsibility to me. I can't hurt you like that."

Gritting his teeth, he said, "I'm going to protect you whether you like it or not."

Unbeknownst to me, Adi questioned Suryani further about Ketut. Suryani really believed that Ketut was using Black Magic to control me. Magic, both white and black, are deep spiritual beliefs in the Balinese culture. Those who want to control or hurt others use Black Magic as a weapon. They might obtain the Black Magic from a powerful master in the manner of a curse or possibly an object. The Balinese rarely talk about this openly as it is taboo and shrouded in darkness.

Suryani was adamant that Adi do something.

I hadn't seen Ketut since we'd made plans to go to Singaraja. I was to meet him down the street from Stardust Cottages, at the photocopying shop where he used to work. Adi was determined to keep me safe even if that meant him driving to Singaraja with me.

Adi showed up at dawn on the Saturday I was to go and tried to reason with me. "Look, I talked to Suryani. She thinks that you're being controlled by Black Magic."

"Can you tell me what that means? I don't know how I can be controlled by Black Magic."

"We don't talk about Black Magic openly... Honestly, I don't really believe it exists, but most Balinese do," Adi said carefully as he looked up to the ceiling, searching for words.

"I still don't understand," I said, my forehead wrinkled in confusion.

"When Ketut touched you, he might have put a spell on you," Adi said hesitantly.

I choked out a laugh, "That's crazy. I've never heard of anything like that."

"This is hard to explain to you, but it's possible that Ketut is controlling your mind. Did he touch you the first time when you met?"

"Well, maybe. I was trying on a necklace, so he might've touched me. I just don't see how that means anything," I said, but I recalled how he'd swept my hair aside and tried to put the necklace on me before I ducked away.

"Don't you think it's a little weird that you suddenly want to marry a guy that you hardly know?"

I shook my head, "I don't know…my head hurts from thinking about all this. Look, I'll figure it out when I meet him, okay?"

Adi wanted to come with me, but I needed to talk to Ketut alone. I reassured Adi that if I didn't come back within thirty minutes, he could come get me.

Ketut stood up and gestured for me to sit down at the small table under a big tree.

My voice wobbled despite trying to remain calm, "I need to ask you some questions before I can go with you to Singaraja."

"Sure, is something wrong?" asked Ketut as he reached for my trembling hand.

Staring into his eyes, I blurted out, "Are you married?"

"Married? What are you talking about?"

"So you're not married? If I went into there now and asked the staff, what would they say?" pointing my chin towards the photocopying shop.

"Who told you this?"

"It doesn't matter. I need you to tell me the truth." I spat out the words in rage as I could clearly see that he was hedging now. It's like I suddenly woke up from a nightmare dressed up as a dream.

"Tell me who told you this," said Ketut through gritted teeth.

"No, you need to tell me the truth! Are you still married? Do you have a baby?" I was now shrieking.

Ketut glanced around nervously, "Calm down. Let's just go to Singaraja. You meet my mother. You see everything."

I started laughing hysterically. "Everyone warned me that you'll do anything to get me to Singaraja. There's no way in hell that I'll ever go with you anywhere again. You're a liar!" I stood up, backing away.

"That's enough. You must believe me. I don't know who told you this," said Ketut as he grabbed my hand in desperation.

"You haven't denied anything. I still don't know if you're married or not. This is insane. What am I doing here?"

I yanked my hand out of Ketut's grasp and ran back to Stardust Cottages, holding in angry tears. I was a fool.

Adi sat at the front reception talking softly with Suryani. I hesitated. My head bowed in total remorse, I inched closer to where they sat.

Suryani mumbled something about having to get back to the office and scooted away.

Wiping away my tears through hiccups, I stammered, "I'm an idiot. I can't believe I did this to you, to us. I'm sorry."

"I'm relieved that you're safe," replied Adi in a flat voice.

I didn't know what to do next. I didn't deserve Adi's kindness or forgiveness. I didn't even really understand why I had done what I had done. How could I explain it to Adi? There were really no excuses. I'd mistreated him badly. I'd thrown away his love.

Adi led me back to my room and sat down on the daybed outside, not wanting to go in.

"But…you still wanted to go to Singaraja," Adi said, shaking his head, looking dejected.

"I know it's completely crazy. I don't understand myself. This is not who I am." I said, my voice fading into a whisper. I slumped down beside him feeling dazed and bewildered.

"I don't know who you are. Maybe it was Black Magic like Suryani said. Maybe you don't love me enough. I don't know, " Adi said, running his hand through his hair.

I turned and looked into his eyes, seeing my vulnerability reflected in his. And in those eyes, I also saw unwavering love. A love I couldn't lose.

"No, no. I love you so much, Adi. I was out of my mind." I grabbed his hand and pulled him to me, "Please, please…just stay."

39

The next few days were torture. I had only a week left in Bali before going back to Toronto. I'd torn apart my relationship with Adi. My work at Pala had only been a temporary gig.

Ketut tried one last time to see me. He'd come to Pala to give me my backpack which I'd left on the table when I ran off. I refused to talk to him and asked one of the waitresses to retrieve the bag. When he looked up from the parking lot, I turned and walked away. His spell was finally broken.

Despite my actions, Adi diligently drove up to Ubud every day or night to see me. He said that we'd put Ketut behind us. That it was likely Black Magic, as per Suryani's expert judgment. Not an inherent flaw in my character. I was not convinced of my own innocence, nor of Adi's total forgiveness. While Adi said that he was coming to see me every day because I was leaving soon, part of me thought he came every day to make sure I didn't wander off again. I didn't blame him. I didn't trust myself either.

I badgered Adi with questions about Black Magic, but he'd shake his head and warned, "The less you know, the safer you are."

"What does that even mean? If Suryani is so sure that I was a victim of Black Magic, why won't you tell me more?" I pressed on, "Then I can protect myself."

"You trust me, right?" Adi asked.

"Yes, of course. More than anyone."

"I'm protecting you...by not saying more. Just believe me," Adi said simply and firmly.

If the first few notes of Sade's "Smooth Operator" came on, I would stop my Discman, take out the CD and replace it with Shania Twain's "Still the One." I decided to give Adi my Discman and CDs. It wasn't a way to absolve my guilt. Or was it?

When Adi wasn't in the room, I would pace back and forth, frustrated that I still didn't have a way to live in Bali permanently. A way to move our relationship forward.

Adi ate with me more often at Pala or at Clove Café. Brenda and Bapak Gede seemed genuinely pleased that I'd untangled myself from the love triangle I'd created. If Bapak Gede was at Clove Café, he asked Adi to sit with the boys, leaving Brenda and me to eat together at another table.

The good thing that came out of this separation was that Brenda and I became closer and closer. I had confided in her about my boy problems, which made us friends. I wasn't just a temporary person helping her out at the restaurant. Brenda asked about my future plans. I told her that I wanted to stay in Bali, but I'd need a real job, not just room and board. That just wouldn't cut it, especially for my parents, who already thought I'd lost my marbles.

Brenda gave me a glimmer of hope when she responded, "I've loved having you here at Pala. Your energy has really brought up the staff. I can't promise you anything, but I'll see what I can do about a more permanent position for you."

Walking back to Jasmine that night, I complained to Adi, "Why can't we sit together at dinner? We could easily get a bigger table."

"That's not the way here in Bali. Men hang out with the men. Women sit with women."

"I'm not okay with that. I don't think Ibu Brenda likes it either."

"What's wrong? You can see where we are. We're not away gambling...or have another girl on the back of our motorbike."

"Not funny. I'm sorry, okay? Isn't it behind us?"

"Yah, yah. As long as you're *behind* me on a motorbike."

Ignoring his slight (and the "yah, yah," which translated to "whatever, I don't really agree with you") I continued, "What I mean is that I want to have dinner with you and the others. Why do we have to sit at separate tables?"

"It's the way it is here. You cannot change our culture in one day."

"I'm not saying that. I just want to know if that's what my life would be here. If I marry you, is this how it is? That you'd always be off with the guys."

Adi turned to look at me, finally realizing my fear. Then he said reassuringly, "Darling, I will not leave you alone. There are times when I'll have do things with only the men, but I promise that I'll try to make you comfortable. In new situations."

I looked into his gorgeous dark brown eyes, which always seemed to twinkle at me. Brushing the tips of my fingers along his soft long eyelashes, I reached over and kissed him, "I love you so much, Adi."

"Hey, not here! Everyone can see us," Adi said as he glanced around shyly.

"So what? I want everyone to know that I'm yours. Now and forever," I answered, chasing him up the hill and laughing as he pretended to run away.

40

Arriving in Hong Kong felt foreign to me. I wasn't used to all the city people anymore, rushing around to pass me wearing sombre suits or dressed to the nines in designer clothes. I looked like them, wearing my black yoga plane outfit, Prada tote, and practical black sneakers, but I didn't belong. My outer appearance no longer matched my true inner being.

When the elevator door opened at Airport Express at Central, Audrey squealed, "Frances! Oh my God, you're here."

"Oh my God, you're pregnant!" I stepped back, in total shock from randomly running into Audrey. A very pregnant Audrey.

Audrey got off and we sat down on a bench as I tried not to stare at her huge stomach.

"Wow! I thought you couldn't get pregnant."

"Yeah, that's what the doctors told me, but I guess they were wrong," she said, pointing to her tummy.

"I'm so happy for you! I know you've always wanted to have children. How are you feeling?"

"We were in total shock at first and…Cam had a hard time wrapping his head around this," Audrey said with a sigh as she patted her stomach.

"Yeah, I can't imagine how stressful it must have been when you first found out," I said, reaching over to hold Audrey's hand.

"It's okay now. It's sunk in that this is really happening," she said wrapping her arm protectively around her stomach. "With my mom and my church friends, I have a lot of support. The baby is due in February."

"That's around Cam's birthday!"

"I know, right? Maybe it's fate?" Audrey laughed. "Enough about me, tell me all about your 'Kuta Cowboy.'"

My face blanched. I stuttered, "No, who told you that?"

"Yosh gave us an update that you're dating some hot Bali beach boy."

"Ugh, I could kill him!" I said, shaking my head, "Adi is not a beach boy, and he's definitely not a 'Kuta Cowboy.' He won't even swim in the ocean."

"So tell me about this Adi. None of us know what's really going on with you," said Audrey, her eyebrows raised in anticipation.

"I'm not sure either, but I think he might be 'The One.' I'm scared to admit it, even to myself. It's a really long story and my family doesn't even know he exists," I said, clasping my hands together.

Audrey squeezed my hand, smiling and said, "Wow really? Finally. I'm so happy for you. Your parents must suspect that something is up. Why else would you spend most of this year in Bali?"

"We'll see what happens. I'll need to get a real job which is hard to find in Bali."

"You'll figure it out. You believe in fairy tales just as much as I do. I know it'll work out somehow," said Audrey, "I better go, I'm meeting some friends for tea."

I stood and helped her up. "You look gorgeous as ever."

"Don't lie to me, Frances. I know I look like hell. But that's really nice of you to say."

"I love you, Audrey. Take good care, okay? I'm going back to Toronto in a few days. And then, hopefully, back to Bali soon…"

On the bus to Grace's place, I couldn't believe that I'd literally bumped into Audrey's bump. I knew a total of ten people in all of Hong Kong, a city with a population of over six million. What were the odds of me bumping into one the second I arrived at the airport?

Grace held a gorgeous babe in one arm while propping the door open with the other.

"Look at her! She's another mini-Grace!"

"Yes, meet Raine. Your second goddaughter."

Now two and a half, Ashlyn redefined the meaning of "terrible twos" as the nanny chased her around the apartment. I loved being back with Grace. She doled out the best advice, especially around matters of the heart.

When I told her about Will's proclamation of love and the Ketut saga, she looked at me with what I might call pride. "Wow! You really stepped it up. I mean, nothing for seven years after Vern, then you go on a tear."

"It's not something to be admired. I hurt Adi so badly."

"You didn't even do anything. You had one, as you said, *disgusting* kiss. Get over it. I've done way worse."

"I'm not you, Grace. You know me. Maybe I'm super old fashioned. For me to even think about another guy already seems like a betrayal."

"Vern was insanely possessive of you. He really did a number on you. He made you think that if you even looked at a guy, you were cheating. He couldn't even look at an Alfa Romeo without cursing and wanting to beat it up, even though you made out with that Italian guy in Rome three years *before* you dated Vern! That's just crazy!"

"Okay, yeah, maybe you're right. But I never cheated on Vern. I told Adi that I wanted to marry another guy!"

"Look, I can see how much you love Adi. I think that the fact your love got tested and you came back even stronger means you'll go the distance."

"Well, I have no idea how I'm going to make it work. How will I tell my mom? She's going to freak out."

"Maybe yes, maybe no. Give your mom some credit. I mean, she went to Canada all by herself in her twenties with your dad following her. All in the name of love. So she might understand how you feel."

"Well, the other thing that might be even more of a no-go is that I don't even have a job. Brenda said that she was going to talk to her husband, but she didn't confirm anything by the time I had to leave."

"Don't worry, you always make it happen somehow. I believe in true love."

"You're such a hopeless romantic, Grace. And that's why I love you. Thank you, for always giving me hope."

41

This time, back in Toronto, I wasn't going to miss Christmas by oversleeping for three days.

Walking back into *The Star* felt like coming home. How I missed the camaraderie of my fantastic team. I couldn't wait to see all my old buddies, especially my old boss and mentor, Drew.

As the elevator door opened on the third floor, I remembered just in time not to get off. The advertising sales department had moved up to the fourth floor – which I thought was ominous since the number three in Chinese sounded like *growth*, while four sounded like *death*. Not the best floor to relocate your revenue-generating ad team. I shrugged; my former colleagues couldn't care less about ancient Asian superstitions.

I walked into the management offices, which were now separated even more from the sales floor. I didn't know any of the secretaries who sat in cubicles outside the director's offices, but I smiled at each one as I looked for Drew's new office. Jen, Drew's assistant, waved me over when she saw me. I'd never met her in person, but she'd put me through to Drew a hundred times since I'd left *The Star*. Only a 100-year-old newspaper would still employ assistants to screen calls.

I peeked into Drew's office. His back was towards me, and I could see him typing with his two index fingers.

"Ah, some things never change," I teased.

"Frances!" He turned around at the sound of my voice and immediately got up to give me a big bear hug. "You look great. So tanned and healthy compared to us pathetic pale faces."

"Thanks, Drew, you look okay for a pale face." I giggled as I looked up into his baby blue eyes. I'd forgotten how tall he was after being in the land of tiny Balinese people.

Backing away, I noticed his lush plant by the floor-to-ceiling window, "Talking about healthy, your plant looks great. How did you bring it back from the dead?"

Sheepishly Drew confessed, "Actually, that's your plant. I took it when you left."

I doubled over in laughter. "Ha! So you finally admit that my talking to the plant made a difference! Not to mention all the laughter that it shared in my office with my team. My happy plant." I fingered the leaves and counted eight sprouting from each stem, visible proof that it was indeed my "happy plant."

"Yes, we've all wilted a bit since you left. Would there be any chance of you coming back?"

"I would in a second, but I've met a guy."

"Whoa, Frances has met a guy?" Drew said, eyes widening with curiosity.

"Well, it's complicated. He lives in Bali."

"Bali? Ah, the mystery is unfolding. So what does this…this guy, do?"

"His name is Adi, and he's a spa therapist."

Without hesitation, Drew blurted out, "That's the guy you're going to marry."

"What? How can you say that? You don't know anything about him."

"He's a spa therapist. Is there anything else I need to know?"

I can't remember where we ate or what was said in the next few hours. All I held on to was that one of my closest friends and mentor knew in a flash that Adi was the one I'd marry. Drew might have said it in jest. I don't know. But I took his prediction at face value.

I'd been through the challenges of trying to call Adi from Toronto the previous summer. Before leaving Bali this time, I'd set up a Hotmail account for Adi and shown him how to use email at an Internet café, but I had no idea if he'd remember. I didn't have high hopes; Adi had never used a computer in his life. Bali was lightyears behind San Francisco when it came to technology.

When I found an email from Adi one morning, I was elated. He'd gone to the only Internet place in his village on his day off and figured out how to email me. I was so impressed with his determination. The few sentences he typed probably took him an hour, so I appreciated every precious word. Even in email, he made me laugh. He'd decided that he'd teach me an Indonesian word a day while I was home in Toronto. After that, I couldn't wait to wake up each morning to see if Adi had sent me a new word. But the most exciting email arrived shortly before Christmas.

Dear Frances,

When you left, I felt like I'd lost my best friend.

I talked to Gede, and we'd like you to be the manager of Pala and for you to help me out with other things as well.

We can't afford what you'd get back at home, but we can give you full room and board, including two rooms, giving you an extra one where your family and friends can stay when they visit, as well as ten million rupiah per month.

Of course, if you'd rather rent another place, within reason, we can arrange this instead of the two rooms.

Please let us know as soon as possible.

Warm regards,

Brenda

I was shaking when I read the email. I had to read it a few times to make sure I wasn't dreaming. This was it. My ticket back to Bali – back to Adi.

4 2

$\mathcal{E}$ven with a job in hand, my mouth still couldn't form the words, "Mom, I met this guy…"

Instead, I used her own words as the starting point for the ultimate "sell" of my life.

Contrary to what most Asian mothers advocated, since I was a young child, Mom had proclaimed loudly that health and happiness were the most important things in life. I babbled on and on about how healthy and happy I was, for the first time in years! Mom studied my radiant face closely and shrugged, unable to argue back.

I strategically displayed laminated photos of my time in Bali all over the condo – strewn on the coffee table, peppered here and there in the kitchen, scattered on her desk. Like a shopper stuck in the maze of Ikea, no matter where Mom looked, she encountered images of my dream: kebaya clad women balancing fruit towers on their heads, scenic landscape shots of terraced rice fields and a glowing Frances surrounded by smiling waitresses at Pala. Absent were the handful of photos of Adi and me.

Adi was cautious when I told him that I had a solid offer from Ibu Brenda. "Darling, I want you to come back to Bali. But it must be for yourself. Not just for me."

"But you're the main reason why I want to live in Bali."

"Yes, I understand. But this is a big decision. Vacationing in Bali for a few months is different than moving here."

"Are you scared now? You don't want me to come back?" My heart tightened as I spat out the words accusingly.

"I'm not scared. I want you to come back. But this is a big sacrifice for you," Adi said, exceedingly patient as always.

"I don't see this as a sacrifice. This is my choice. For the first time in a long time, I'm no longer running away. I'm choosing to be with you."

"Okay, okay. Just think about it a little more. There's no rush for you to come back right away. Enjoy Christmas with your family and friends."

"I won't change my mind, you know. I miss you so much."

"I miss you too. I love you."

Hanging up, I knew that I had to fess up to Mom. I had to tell her what I was planning. There would be no turning back once I told her, no more pretending that I could live in Toronto or San Francisco again. Taking a few months off after the Dotcom meltdown was understandable. Going to Bali to manage a restaurant would derail my career no matter how I dressed it up.

Was this the right thing to do? I could easily pick up the phone, call Drew and get my career back on track. Continue to ascend up the corporate ladder. Adi would become that imagined dream, something that happened in another life. Something my parents never had to know about.

These thoughts were driving me crazy. I couldn't get away from myself.

My decision became easier the next day when I went to Holt Renfrew with Nate and Rachel. Going shopping was unintentional; we were on our way to a family dinner, and the warmest way there, avoiding the wind tunnels of Bloor and Bay Streets, was to cut underground through Holts. Upon entering the beautiful shop, Rachel was overjoyed to see that many items were already marked down in anticipation of Boxing Day. It being 5:00 p.m. on Christmas Eve, we were the only customers around.

We wandered the store and I found myself facing racks and racks of coats topped with an elegant sale sign – thirty-five percent off or more. Oh no, not here again, where I'd dropped a lot of cash on that pale blue shearling that I'd only worn twice. Come to think of it, I had no idea where it was… I made a mental note to check Mom's closet.

Rachel rushed towards the fur coats and threw one on. "Oh, this is so soft and warm, perfect for this insane weather. I miss Singapore so much. I hate winter."

"Yeah, I hate the winter too. My skin is cracking and bleeding. It's so dry, no matter how much cream I put on."

Nate looked over at his wife, now the mother of his baby girl, while sifting through the minks. "How about this one, Rachel?" he asked, holding up a sporty brown mink.

"How much is it?" I asked.

"A few thousand, a great deal with the sale," said Nate in all seriousness.

"Yeah, what a steal," I said, trying not to sound too sarcastic.

I'd never spent money as conspicuously as my friends. But in the past, I could have if I'd wanted to. If I chose Bali, I could never walk into Holts and just drop a few thousand again. Would that really be okay with me? Would I really be okay to be poor?

The job at Pala covered all my expenses and if I didn't spend a cent, I could save about ten thousand dollars a year. Was that realistic? Was that enough?

I'd always questioned the pursuit of money. I'd even said on many occasions to friends, "Isn't enough, *enough?*" Wasn't that why we had that word?

When I left *The Star* five years previously, I'd jumped without a safety net. And things worked out fine. Now four years later, could I leap even further? Knowing me better than anyone else at the time, Drew mentioned that I might want to explore something in non-profit.

That had never crossed my mind. "Why would you say that? I don't know anything about that sector."

"You're passionate about social inequalities like the challenges women face in the workplace, and you fight hardest when it's for the underdog. For the outliers."

I'd been groomed at business school to work for money, for my own security. Mom agreed that money was necessary, but she also taught that all the money in the world was meaningless without happiness and good health.

In my favourite course in business school, Organizational Behaviour, three of my best friends and I, all in serious relationships, had written a detailed report about dual-career relationships. In our youth and optimism, we'd tackled life challenges by outsourcing problems and making fictional compromises with our future spouses. For instance, if our child was sick at school, I was in a board meeting, and my surgeon husband was in the middle of an operation, we'd call one of our parents to pick up the child from school.

Our wise professor, Mitch Rothstein, had given us a good mark, but he'd also given us advice that stayed with me: "Your report contains sound strategies and good compromises, but it's not reality. I don't expect you to understand yet. I want to share my experience with you. In my twenty-year marriage, one or the other partner had to sacrifice, not compromise, something significant to keep the relationship. For example, if one of you receive the job offer of a lifetime in another country, would the other be willing to give up their career at that moment, or perhaps even forever, to support the other?"

Professor Mitch drilled on about the importance of balance. He knew that the overwhelming majority of the biz graduates were vying for the highest paying jobs as consultants or bankers. He'd encouraged us to think about what would really matter at the end of our lives. Did we really want to be tied for decades to a career with impossible hours? Would it be the millions made or the moments spent with children – whether it be nursing them back to health or cheering them on at their first dance recital or hockey game – that we'd truly treasure?

I'd always treated each day as if I was on holiday. I'd stop to smell the roses even when walking around my hometown, chasing adventure after adventure to increase my FAPs score. Moving to San Francisco, and onwards to Hong Kong and Tokyo, and finally ending up in Bali was a continuous arch.

I had to keep going…to experience the whole rainbow and collect as many FAPs as life would offer. Sure, there might be a pot of gold at the end, but for me, that wasn't the goal. I wanted my life to be full of colour, the entire spectrum, all the hues.

On Christmas Day, I finally mustered up the courage to tell Mom that I was going back to Bali. It wasn't asking for permission. It was a statement.

I explained that Brenda had given me the chance to live in Bali without any cost, and that I could still save a bit, but most importantly, Bali was where I'd found happiness and good health. My back and shoulder problems had disappeared under Adi's care and my notoriously dry skin no longer flaked off like a snake. The only lingering pain was my mysterious stomach spasm that came and went. I'd reported my stomach issue to the doctors in Toronto or Hong Kong every time I had a checkup, and they blamed stomach bugs picked up from my travels. But the stabbing pain wasn't persistent, so I didn't give it too much thought. On the outside – as I was eager to point out to Mom – I was glowing.

Despite my earnest delivery of the facts, Mom immediately caught on. "Is there something else going on here?"

I hesitated, breathing in, "Okay, yes, I met a guy named Adi. This is the first time that I've been truly happy since Vern."

"I knew it. I knew that something was making you want to go to Bali. How long has this been going on?"

"I met Adi over a year ago, on my first trip to Bali when you came later."

"Oh my God, it's all my fault. I come a few days late, and you get taken." Mom moaned, holding her head in her hands as if the world would end. "This must be Black Magic. How did this happen in a few days?"

I was alarmed that Mom had blurted out the words "Black Magic." I'd never heard the term until Suryani said it to me in Bali, just a month prior, and now it seemed that everyone around me thought I was undeniably cursed. Sure, we Chinese had our superstitions, but it was always about not upsetting the ancestral spirits, nothing shrouded in evil.

After a collecting my wits and deciding to ignore the mention of Black Magic, I scoffed, "Mom, stop being so dramatic. I've spent most of the year in Bali getting to know him. Adi works at Le Meridien. A gorgeous 5-star resort. He has an excellent job."

Mom pointed at me accusingly and said, "You trust people too easily. You never see their bad side until they hurt you. You don't even know anyone else in Bali. How is this safe?"

I was momentarily taken aback again. How did Mom seem to know everything when I hadn't let out a peep about my travels or my worries?

"I know that you're always worried about me, but you've raised me up to be strong. I'm not staying in some strange place. I'm living at the beautiful guesthouse where my bosses, Brenda and Gede, live with their six children. I stayed there for over three months. It's totally safe. In a way, I'm following your steps, but the other way around." I went for the comparison, trying to lighten up the conversation.

"I came here to Canada to give myself and my children a better life. Now you go backwards," Mom replied, shaking her head.

"I'm not going backwards, Mom. You've been to Bali. Can't you see how much I love it there?"

"I don't know. Does your dad know about this?" Mom asked, looking hopeful that she wouldn't be the bad cop.

"It doesn't matter what Dad thinks. He doesn't really care," I replied in a huff, my eyebrows creasing with resentment.

"I think he cares. He just doesn't know how to show you."

"Whatever, Mom. This isn't about Dad. It's about my happiness and my life. This is what I want. Sure, maybe things won't work out. But that is for me to find out."

Her shoulders drooped in resignation and she conceded, "Okay, okay, I know that I can never change your mind once you have an idea. You go. I'll always be here. I'll always be home when you need me."

"I love you, Mom." I hugged her tight, knowing it was her love and support that gave me this confidence to step off the edge, again and again.

43

BALI, JANUARY 2002

This time when I went back to Bali, I didn't bring my golf clubs. I no longer had baggage space to spare nor a budget to golf. This was my new reality.

I whispered a thought to Professor Mitch: *You had no idea that my sacrifice would be golf, did you?*

Two bellboys lifted my massive suitcases over the cobblestone and down a steep flight of stairs to a set of adjoining family rooms, situated on the ground floor with an expansive terrace facing an enclosed private garden.

Kicking off my sneakers and slipping off my socks, I tread barefoot on the cool marble through the carved wooden doors to inspect my new home. The master bedroom had a lovely four-poster bed with a sheer mosquito net draping from the posts. I walked further into a spacious bathroom with an open-air shower fringed by tropical foliage. The other bedroom off the shared terrace had two oversized twin beds and their own bathroom – perfect for future visits from family and friends.

Brenda came by with her youngest son, Eka, to welcome me. "Are you comfortable here?"

"Yes, I love these rooms. Thank you, Brenda." I said, punctuating my sentence with my nervous giggle.

Her four-year-old was pulling Brenda and whispered loudly, "Why is her laugh so funny? She sounds like a goat." His innocent question made me laugh even more.

"Eka, that's not polite," Brenda admonished.

"It's okay, Brenda. Kids always tell the absolute truth." I bent down to Eka and agreed, "Yes, it is funny, isn't it?"

"I'm happy to have you back. Get settled in and take a few days to get over jet lag. It's low season now. No rush."

I nodded back, "I've never been here in January so let's see how I survive rainy season."

"Have a good rest, and we'll catch up soon."

After a well-needed shower, I waited impatiently for Adi to arrive. I distracted myself by unpacking both suitcases. I no longer had to jump on a plane every week. I could finally settle in properly. Standing up with a big smile, I stretched and let out a contented sigh.

"Ah, sounds like you're home." Adi smiled as he peeked his head into the room.

"Adi!" I ran to kiss and hug him. "Yes, now I'm home."

"Thank you for coming back. I'm glad you made this decision," Adi said, cupping my face in his hands and kissing me back hard.

Catching my breath again, I replied, "It wasn't easy, but I couldn't imagine my life without you. My mom thinks you've done some serious magic to lure me back."

"Rainbow magic." He grinned.

"Yes, rainbow magic." I laughed as I pulled him down onto the bed.

The next few days were a blur as my body adapted to the new time zone. In the sweltering humidity of tropical Bali, I shed the dry skin of Toronto's harsh winter and the final layers of my old self. I felt like a newborn, with soft dewy skin that glowed.

I knew that it wasn't just the weather. Adi loved to caress my hands – whether it was our dinner to arrive or while in bed chatting until all hours. His gestures were quietly moving. They weren't loud pronouncements of romantic love; instead, these small whisperings spoke directly to my soul. I'd finally found my candle. Ours was a slow-burning flame that fed off our passion.

When Adi was at work, I'd catch myself daydreaming, staring out at the view at Pala or lying in bed with an open book that remained unread. Was I living in paradise on earth, an angel gliding in and out of a dream?

Enrobed in a pastel blue chiffon wrap top, a hand-stamped batik silk sarong and beaded sandals, I smiled back at my luminous reflection in the mirror. Concerned friends had advised me not to throw my Armanis away. To always have a backup plan. I prayed that I'd never again don the detested stockings, painful high heels, and constricting pencil skirts of my previous life. If my friends could see me now, they might understand my desire to burn the suits.

Working at Pala suited my personality. I fed off the energy of excited tourists, basked in the gentle calm of my Balinese team, and savoured the nourishing food while spending every day surrounded by nature, far from the confines of an overly-air-conditioned or stuffy office. I inhaled the seductive scents of the tropical foliage, breathing deeply and freely.

I started each day in search of Brenda and often found her huddled with the supervisor in the brightly lit sewing building. The seamstresses bent over old cast iron machines gossiping like a pen of hens. I fingered the colourful pieces of cotton, hand woven in east Bali, that might become crisp bed linens or a custom-made fuchsia dress for Brenda.

After the sojourn in the sewing room, we'd peek into the attached bakery, where smiling Balinese ladies kneaded the daily bread and dusted warm cinnamon rolls with powdered sugar. Made, the Pala driver, would pile the baked goods and the creamy coconut crème brûlées into the back of the van while Brenda and I hopped in for our third activity before 7:00 a.m. – yoga at Pala.

In 2001, Ubud was already gaining its reputation as a yoga and wellness centre with six-week yoga teaching programs building momentum. Brenda hired a young yoga teacher, a fellow Australian named Jesse who'd just completed her certification.

We climbed down the steep stairs to the lowest level of Pala, where the rising sun peeked out from behind the spectacular valley. A beautiful blond with emerald eyes, Jesse hailed from Byron Bay, an epicenter for artists and hippies. She taught us a gentle yoga called Vinyasa. Her lilting Australian accent encouraged us to move as our bodies allowed. There was no pressure. No competition.

Wincing at the sound of Adi cracking his neck and knuckles, I said, "Honey, why don't you join me for yoga class at Pala?"

"I already know how to do yoga. I learned from my guru, Ratu Aji."

"You never told me you had a 'guru,'" I said making air quotes with my hands.

"You never asked," teased Adi. This was his go-to answer whenever I discovered something new about him or Bali.

"Very funny. Tell me about your guru…what's his name again?"

"Ratu Aji. He's a respected spiritual leader in my village. I was one of his students when I was younger," Adi said

"A spiritual group? What did you do?"

"We meditated, did some yoga and learned how to protect ourselves." Adi's words were slow and deliberate.

"Protect yourself? You mean like martial arts?" I asked

"No, from Black Magic."

"Ha! So you know way more than you've told me," I said as I shoved him in the shoulder.

"Look. I was serious. The less you know, the better. Trust me," Adi responded, standing firm.

I sulked, "Fine. Then you'll have to come to yoga with me, and you can't pretend you don't know how. I love the yoga teacher, Jesse. She may not be some Balinese spiritual 'guru,' but she's amazing."

Adi looked resigned. "Okay, okay. Let's see."

I adjusted the signs that Suryani had printed for me – "Sunrise yoga at Pala" – hoping the class would entice more guests to have breakfast afterwards at the restaurant.

Adi bravely joined our class of five as the only man. He rolled out a mat at the back and I took a spot beside him. Despite his reservations, Adi shone in the class. He bent, twisted and stretched in ways that resembled a pretzel.

After the class, Jesse and her sister Judy beckoned us over to the lovely sofas where both of them sat cross-legged, backs straight as rods, bringing avocado slices on toast up to their mouths while looking as graceful as dancers. I thought this pose should be called "Delicate Bird Eating."

That evening, Adi fed me *nasi jingo*, a snack-sized portion of rice with a few shreds of chicken, a small wedge of hard-boiled egg and chili tomato sambal, all wrapped in a banana leaf. This tasted best when Adi mixed the perfect balance of rice, chicken and spicy sambal with his magical fingers. As he presented me with the food, he suddenly sat up, adjusting his body to sit crossed legged on the edge of the bed, and popped a morsel into my open mouth. I almost spat out the bite from laughing too hard.

44

My cousin Darren and his girlfriend, Miche, were going to be the first to use my spare bedroom in February.

Darren was actually a generation above me; his grandmother had been my great-grandfather's first wife. However, being the same age as me, I called him "cousin" to avoid this complicated explanation. He and my younger brother, Ken, had become close drinking buddies when Ken moved to San Francisco. Both were dynamic, charismatic, and heaps of fun to party with. I rarely drank or partied, but our shared loved of food and travel bonded me to Darren too.

Unemployed at the time like most of the Bay area in the dust of the Dotcom collapse, Darren and Miche planned to spend three weeks in Bali.

Miche embodied understated chic. She'd created a comfy home out of the tiniest condo in Hong Kong. Their industrial loft in San Francisco was my dream home – minimalist, modern and functional. I was a little nervous that Miche and Darren wouldn't be comfortable away from their luxurious loft, but my concerns were unfounded.

Miche was enchanted upon arrival, and her wonder gave me new insights about my surroundings. She crouched down to take abstract photos of the way the cobblestones were laid into the ground, gathered varying shades of frangipani flowers and lined them up on the marble table, and fingered the light muslin cotton that draped her bed.

"You're living a dream, Frances. I'm so happy for you!"

"I know, right? I feel so lucky. I can't wait until you meet Adi. He ran out to get lunch. I told him that you two were super adventurous and love spicy food, so he went early to line up for Ibu Oka's *babi guling*."

"Babi guling? What's that, Fran?" Darren asked, lying back in the daybed.

"It's the most delicious roast pig. It's the only thing that this place sells. Ibu Oka's is a total hole-in-the-wall where you have to sit on the floor to eat. Only the locals eat there."

"That sounds like my kind of place. Let's go," said Darren.

"The pig arrives around 11:30 a.m. and sells out early. Adi thought it'd be better to get takeaway so he's already there lining up. This way you can eat comfortably here, sitting on proper chairs."

"Adi's so thoughtful. Sounds like a keeper," said Miche, looking up from her camera. "I can report that tidbit back to your mom."

"What, you're not spying on me, are you?" I asked, my voice wavering a little.

"Never, Fran. I'm sure Adi will pass all the tests," Miche teased, winking at me.

"Tests?"

"Miche is just pulling your leg. We're here to relax, not investigate Adi," Darren said just as Adi came around the corner.

"Adi! We were just talking about you," I said taking the bulging bag of food from him.

"Sorry the food took so long. There was a long line," he explained while carefully unbundling the parcels of rice wrapped in banana leaves. Adi spread out the first leaf in front of Miche, being careful so that none of the rice fell out. My stomach growled as the delicious aromas of roast meat and spices wafted towards me.

"Oh my God, this looks amazing!" Miche said, grabbing her camera again to take a shot and slapping Darren's hand out of the way as he tried to sneak a bite.

"Darren, don't worry. I have yours here. Are you okay to eat with your hands?" Adi reassured Darren as he pushed a banana leaf piled high with food over to my cousin.

"Man, I'm starving. I could shove this whole thing down in one go. Thanks so much, Adi."

"My pleasure. Frances told me how you two love local street food. This is the best there is in Bali."

With his mouth stuffed with rice, Darren nodded and smiled, giving me a thumbs up while nodding in Adi's direction. I took that as a stamp of approval from the first family member to meet Adi. As I carefully scooped up one mouthful after another with my right hand, the way Adi had patiently taught me, I realized that Darren and Miche were the very first from my "old life" to enter into my new reality.

Within a few minutes, Adi had already scored some big points. This was way easier than I thought. There wasn't any awkwardness. Adi seemed to fit right in. Then again, Darren and Miche were two of the least pretentious people I knew. Of course they liked Adi. He'd fed them one of the best meals in Bali on arrival. What was there not to like?

I became their official tour guide. Miche wanted to see as much of Bali as possible during their three weeks, while Darren was happy to just sit back, eat babi guling daily and hit the bars in Seminyak at night.

Suryani arranged a local driver to take us to Besakih Temple, the mother temple of Bali. After Tanah Lot, all other temples would have a hard time impressing me. Tanah Lot Temple represented a magnet that had drawn me to Bali and into Adi's arms.

We were the only car in the entire temple parking lot. Our driver, Anus (yes, that's really his name) told us to walk uphill about a kilometre to get to the temple entrance. Little shops selling sarongs, small wood carvings and cold soft drinks lined the small road leading up to Besakih. There were no shoppers besides us. I'd lent sarongs to Darren and Miche, so we were appropriately dressed. We climbed up some very steep stairs, as if ascending to the heavens, and passed under a gate carved entirely from black volcanic stone. Looking back through the gate, we could see the rest of the temple laid out before us. I had to admit, the view was mind-blowing. All of Bali stretched out in front of me. Besakih wasn't a temple floating in the ocean, but it definitely earned its position as "Mother Temple."

Darren and Miche reignited my entrepreneurial spark – we talked endlessly about different business ideas. Every day they joined me for lunch at Pala and we'd continue talking late into the night on our shared terrace.

Bali was a hub of creative artistry, especially in the villages that surrounded Ubud. Mas village bred clans of woodcarvers. Celuk village brandished silversmiths by the dozens, making intricate handmade jewelry along with fierce Balinese daggers called *keris*. Painters ranging from traditional Balinese to the young artists' movement thrived in the villages of Lotunduh and Penestanan. Adi further expanded the possibilities when he took us to a ceramics factory and the handicrafts village of Tegalalang.

Together, we'd design an upmarket line of homewares, all handmade in Bali. Adi suggested the name, *Taksu*, which translated as a combination of balance, harmony and spirit. I thought it was perfect!

Having worked at an architectural firm in San Francisco, Miche had close ties with interior designers in the region. She would host events in their loft, showcasing our Taksu homewares in an authentic setting. We'd sell custom orders directly, avoiding costly retail outlets and protecting our unique designs.

On their last night, Darren rented a car and drove us down to Seminyak to celebrate the start of our new venture at La Lucciola, followed by dancing under the stars at KuDeTa. Darren was in his element, being more of a vampire than the roosters that Adi and I were.

The drive back to Ubud after midnight was utterly different than the drive down. There were hardly any lights, but Darren drove as if he was racing along Highway 101. Adi and I were too terrified to speak.

Miche repeatedly hissed, "Slow down, Darren," and was repeatedly ignored.

I tightened my grip on Adi as we flew across a crossroad that Darren didn't see. The car suddenly plummeted downward before coming to an abrupt stop, slamming us back into our seats. Darren had driven off the end of the paved road, hurtling the car into the rice fields.

Silence.

Adi finally whispered, "Darren, you missed the crossroad. We could have killed someone."

Despite the trauma of that near-miss, we forged ahead on our Taksu homewares with Darren and Miche. Months later, our first massive shipment set sail from Bali to San Francisco. Unexpectedly, Miche had to move back to Seoul and Darren followed immediately. They'd become a fixture in our lives as they moved even closer to Singapore. Taksu homewares ended before it really started. However, Taksu would rise from the ashes like a phoenix, reshaping itself time and time again in our lives.

✸

Sitting side-saddle on the back of Adi's bike with my right arm wrapped around his waist, we zoomed up the hill past Darren and Miche. Adi and I had zipped out to pick up a last-minute meal of babi guling for them before they set off for the airport.

Miche later divulged that my mom had indeed sent her out to Bali with a mission to find out about "this Adi person" who'd stolen her daughter.

When she saw me with my head thrown back, laughing on the back of Adi's red scooter, her first thought was, "That's the guy Frances is going to marry."

I wished she'd captured that moment on her camera, but it doesn't matter; that image is forever etched in my memory. I had indeed upgraded from my Audi to my Adi.

45

*M*y heart wanted to jump for joy and my stomach wanted to throw up. I was on my way to Adi's family compound for his *Otonon* (or *Oton* for short), his Balinese birthday, where I'd meet his parents for the first time.

Adi had extended the invitation to me a week earlier. He explained, "It's a special ceremony for my four brothers."

"Aren't you the only son?" I asked, wrinkling my forehead in confusion.

"I'm talking about my spiritual brothers. They stand by me all the time, protecting me," answered Adi.

"Oh, of course, your 'spiritual brothers,'" I said, shaking my head. "Please explain."

"Sorry, darling. I forgot that you don't know. Every Balinese is born with four spiritual brothers. They protect me for all my life. On my Otonan, I give them offerings and special things to eat."

"Isn't your birthday on April 5th, which isn't until Friday?"

"My Balinese birthday comes every 210 days or every thirty Balinese weeks. This time, my Oton falls on April 4th. It's a different calendar than the Western calendar."

"You get two birthdays?"

"Yes. But Otonon is what Balinese celebrate. It's much more important. Many Balinese don't even know their real birthday. Only their Oton."

"How do you celebrate?"

"You'll see. I'm going to cook for you."

"And your spiritual brothers, apparently."

"Ah, you understand."

Adi went on to explain that April 2002 was a very special year; Adi's Oton fell on April 4th and his birthday was on April 5th. This would be the closest convergence of the Balinese and Western calendars for Adi. One's Otonon only happens on one's actual birthdate.

Adi, after going to the market at 4:00 a.m. and cooking for hours, had still driven up to Ubud to pick me up. Turning off the main road of Kerobokan village, we zoomed down a laneway too narrow to fit a car. Most Balinese homes hid down these laneways, ancestral family homes that existed centuries before cars and motorbikes.

Adi hadn't told me much about his parents. Only that his older brother had been killed when he was four years old.

Two decades ago, Jalan Kerobokan had been a dirt road. Hardly anyone owned a motorbike, let alone a car. A pharmaceutical salesman driving his company's car hadn't seen the little boy on the side of the road. Wayan was killed instantly. Adi had been a baby in his grandmother's arms as she bought tofu on the other side of the street.

The entire community rushed to their family compound and removed all dangerous items for fear that Adi's parents would harm themselves. Adi's father worked an hour away by bicycle in construction. Without phones or cars in those days, the Banjar waited at the house to give him this terrible news.

When someone dies in your Banjar, you drop everything and go to their compound immediately. Your Banjar stays with you at night, every night, until the cremation. Your Banjar supports you in sadness and happiness – every life ceremony. In this tragic situation, even the salesperson moved in for two weeks; it was the opposite of a hit and run.

I was apprehensive. This had happened a long time ago, but if it were me who'd lost a child, I'm not sure how I'd go on.

As I stepped through the simple wooden gate, Adi rushed over to grab a tray from the terrace floor and excitedly brought it over to me and asked me to try his *sate*. I took one and bit into it. The flavours exploded in my mouth – spicy, succulent minced pork tasting of coconut smoke.

"Oh my God! That is insanely delicious!" I gushed as I reached out for another.

"Eat more! I made a lot for you." Adi's smile was wide with pride and generosity.

Adi always refused to eat the sate at local warungs, turning up his nose and saying, "Mine are so much better."

I'd just reach over and eat the rejected sate myself while teasing him, "You're being a bit arrogant, aren't you?"

He'd adamantly say, "Seriously, you wouldn't eat that if you tried mine." I had laughed at his puffed out chest and thought how unusual it was for Adi to boast when he was usually so humble.

Now as I took sate after sate, cleaning off each bamboo skewer in one bite, I knew I was ruined for all other sate. Around my tenth one, I looked behind Adi to see his parents, sitting on the terrace, staring at me.

Oh my God, I thought, *I've been inhaling these sate, and I haven't even said hello to his parents*. My face turned beet red.

Adi bringing me home was him announcing that we were considering marriage. You didn't bring a girl home unless you were *seriously* serious about her. His parents probably thought, "Oh my God! This is the one he wants to marry?" as I stood just inside the gate, wolfing down enough sate to feed ten polite Balinese people.

"Adi, shouldn't you introduce me to your parents?" I asked as I quickly gulped down the last morsel of sate.

"Oh yes, sorry, I forgot. Everyone knows everyone here."

Adi turned to his mom, "*Me, ini* Frances." Adi turned back to me, "Frances, this is my mother. You can call her 'Ibu.'"

I bowed my head, smiled and said, "Ibu."

Ibu glowered at me and I almost fainted. I looked from Adi to her. He was the spitting image of his mom. He had her face and body shape, except that Adi was always smiling. Adi's mom must hate me on sight, I thought as I shrunk back. Thankfully, Adi's father propped me back up with his friendliness.

Adi's father stood up with a wide grin and crinkled eyes and extended his hand in welcome. "*Selamat datang*, Frances."

"This is my father. You can call him 'Bapak.'"

I stepped forward and took Bapak's hand, rough with callouses, and shook it firmly, smiling back, "Hello, Bapak."

"*Duduk, duduk,*" he replied, pointing to the terrace.

"*Nanti, Pak,*" Adi said back to his dad. "Let me show you around first."

"I'd love that," I stammered, recovering from the horror of my eating frenzy.

Adi pointed to a half-finished building behind us, to the right of the gate. "That's my dining room and kitchen. It's not yet finished. I had to stop because of 9/11. I didn't have enough money to continue."

I walked over to the grey cement building that Adi and his father had built.

Adi said, "You can step around the well."

I looked down and saw a large cement cylinder with a metal covering. "This is a well? Cool! I've never seen a well before."

I followed Adi into the dining room, which was huge, measuring 6 metres by 4 metres; it was the biggest dining room I'd ever seen. Two of the walls facing the inside of the compound were unfinished low walls with cement posts every few metres.

"This is a dining room? I thought that Balinese people don't eat together. They just eat on the terrace or on a step, right?"

"Working at the hotel, I watched tourists eat together, laughing and talking. I like that idea. So I designed this as a dining room."

"You're amazing, Adi. I love how you're willing to adopt ideas that you like. That you don't just do what everyone else does."

He looked at me curiously, as if he'd never thought like that before. "See how the walls are only halfway? That's for the windows. A bedroom wouldn't have big windows all the way around."

"Yes, I see what you have in mind." I said as I admired the sunlit space that Adi had built.

"When tourists come back, I'll have money to finish the room. I'll get wooden windows and doors." Adi proudly extended his hand. "And I need to get a dining table."

"Honey, you're not going to believe this, but I have this massive dining room table. In fact, I have two."

"What? What dining table? Where is it? In Hong Kong?"

"No, it's in Ubud. It's a long story, but I bought them last year. I just couldn't help myself. I didn't have a dining room where these could fit. I didn't even have a home. I figured I'd ship them to wherever I ended up." I scratched my head, wondering at what I had been thinking back then.

"I don't understand. You bought dining tables without a dining room? When you didn't have a home? Why didn't you tell me?" Adi looked at me, completely baffled.

"I don't know. It was before we'd become serious. I didn't want you to think that I was the type of person who spent a few thousand dollars without a thought, but it seems like I took 'impulse buying' to a new level that day. Amazingly, my tables seemed to know there was a dining room waiting for them." Looking around, I was astounded that I actually owned the tables that would fill this vast room.

You may be thinking this is just incredible coincidence, and you're right – there's no logical Western explanation for this. I had the dining tables and Adi had the dining room. But imagine this: Most Balinese rooms measure 3 metres by 3 metres, while Adi's dining room was almost obscenely massive at 6 metres x 4 metres. Most dining tables measure about 2 metres x 1 metres, but both of my tables were 4 metres long. I'd need a loft space to accommodate them, or in this case, Adi's empty dining room. Pure luck and coincidence, right?

But Adi and I believed in fate. We needed each other to complete our individual visions, and these were simply the pieces falling into place, set there by some higher power. I was home.

46

My suite of rooms had been upgraded to the top floor of Stardust Cottages, giving me privacy and a view of the rice fields. At night, I'd read on the terrace while looking out for the headlights of Adi's motorbike as he bumped along the dark road.

My extra guest room attracted many to visit and stay with me, old friends as well as new acquaintances.

Elaine, one of my fabulous four girlfriends from business school, her fiancé Brad, and our mutual friend Karl were coming to dive. These would be my first friends from Toronto to meet Adi.

As one of my closest friends, and my roommate for two years during business school, Elaine had been there for my entire relationship with Vern. Back at university, she'd had a similarly passionate relationship with her then boyfriend, and like me, she'd experienced heartbreak. We were both on the other side of that pain now, but it had taken me a lot longer to get there.

Living in Toronto after graduation, Elaine and Karl had been main fixtures in my life, along with Grace, Nate, Keitha and Crystal. It was a time of freedom. We shared a love of art, food, music and nature – these six friends had helped me heal by forcing me to live.

In the first year after breaking up with Vern, I must have attended twenty concerts: 10,000 Maniacs, Jann Arden, Sarah McLachlan, REM, Blue Rodeo, Cowboy Junkies, Roxy Music, and Sade. We'd find ourselves playing round after round of pool at Rivoli Bar or getting gelato past midnight as we strolled along the quaint streets of Little Italy. One by one, we moved away from Toronto, scattering around the world. Now I was the one who lived furthest away.

I worried that Adi would be excluded from our conversations, whether because of language or the topics we talked about, or his past being so different from ours.

Ironically, it wasn't Adi who didn't fit in. It was me. I'd never been interested in their conversations of world politics or sports, but I used to at least feign interest. Perhaps before, I'd consider looking up the names of famous people they talked about to broaden my own knowledge. Now I couldn't be bothered. I had nothing to prove to anyone anymore.

What I did still have in common with Elaine and Karl was our wide range of taste in food; we could chow down on street side satay or dine in the poshest places. Adi and I accompanied my friends out east to Candidasa. They dove each day while we made food runs to our favourite local fish, sate warung, bringing back heaping bundles for Elaine, Brad and Karl. They were always ravenous after diving. It was the best meal that they'd have in Bali.

On our last evening with them, we headed up to Amankila, the fourth hotel at Aman Group, a cluster of super-high-end resorts created by Adrian Zecha.

I'd been dying to check this place out, having seen numerous photos of its unique architecture in my design books. Amankila was Sanskrit for 'a peaceful hill'. Driving up and up, we had the most spectacular view of the valley below – unending rice fields as far as the eye could see. The property consisted of long, narrow, connected white stone bridges leading from the highest villas on the hill down towards the ocean. This maze of interconnecting bridges was an ingenious design.

We alighted at the lobby – an understated corridor that led to modern white stone steps. In front of us, the infamous three-level swimming pool cascaded down the hill.

We'd come for sunset cocktails at the bar. Seeing the astronomical prices – one drink was equivalent to the entire lunch for three that we'd brought back, Adi and I opted out. I could have splurged on a couple of drinks, but I no longer felt compelled to do things just to fit in with my friends. True freedom.

At the same time, Pala was a constant source of new friendships – ones that crossed into new realms.

I sympathized with a young Singaporean lady who had a bad case of Bali belly and longed for something soupy which we didn't have on our menu. I hopped into the kitchen and quickly concocted a simple chicken broth with vegetables and vermicelli noodles. Grateful for my kindness, the Singaporean couple, Chisen and Sera, who owed an atypical Bauhaus-inspired villa perched high above the Petanu River, embraced me and Adi into their circle. The unique location of their villa, just a few minutes outside of Ubud, would inspire Adi and my seven-year search for the perfect piece of land. Ironically, the search for our land which began at their villa would end there also. .

Another fateful friendship would be meeting Janet, Angela and Kristina who lived in Toronto and NYC and were staying at Stardust Cottages. They sought me out at Pala upon hearing that I also hailed from Toronto. Being strong, independent businesswomen, they were fascinated with my real-life fantasy island romance.

Janet introduced me to Anne Dee who'd bring all of us, including Adi, to a remote, dry village called Tianyar, three hours away in Northeast Bali, behind Mount Agung. We walked around speechless as we witnessed the extreme poverty of these people who lived in mud huts, with the closest water source 4 kilometres away. Anne Dee had been giving vitamins and powdered milk to this impoverished village. Now, she stepped up and started raising funds to pipe in government water. When we got home that night, I worshipped the shower that rained down on me, something I'd taken for granted all my life. I could wash away the dust and grime, but the images of the crumbling homes held up by bamboo, remained fixed in my memory.

All these friendships were a magical meeting of the minds: Janet would be the catalyst for our return from Toronto, Anne Dee's villa would become my refuge from Black Magic, and this glimpse of another side of Bali would beckon us again during the Covid-19 pandemic, to give back to Bali and to feed the poor.

47

When you live far away from loved ones, phone calls are both cherished and feared. When I heard my stepmother Fong Fong at the other end of the line, I knew it had to be bad news. She'd never once called me before.

My Cantonese did not include words like "stroke," but I understood that Dad had had a stroke. She begged me to go to Hong Kong immediately. Dad was in the hospital and didn't want to go on. He wouldn't or couldn't move. She said that he needed to see me. That I needed to be there. *Why now?* He'd never needed me before.

I already held a plane ticket for a trip the following month, with a three-day stopover in Hong Kong before going back to Canada for my 10th reunion at business school in September. I didn't have extra time off from work, or additional funds for a return ticket from Bali to Hong Kong. I didn't really want to help Dad, distant as he'd been all these years. In spite of all this, I walked into the nearest travel agency and booked the next flight out.

Dropping everything for your family was the norm in Bali, so both Brenda and Adi understood immediately. No questions asked. Adi helped me pack for a week and hoped that I could return with good news.

Seeing Dad in the hospital bed made me realize that he was human after all. He was asleep, his face paler than usual. Dad's severe manic depression dictated our relationship. Growing up, I never knew what face he'd show. Mostly, he was devoid of emotion. He sometimes smiled when he teased

Ken or me. Other times, without any warning, his face suddenly went grey with rage simmering just below the surface, making you want to run. We tiptoed softly around Dad, always fearing the worst. Now he just looked frail and vulnerable. And I wanted him to get better.

When he woke, he gave me a tentative smile. I automatically smiled back. One side of his face drooped down a bit.

"Hi Dad, I'm here, and I'm going to help you."

"Thank you…for coming." His eyes misted over as he realized that I was really there.

"Of course, Dad."

Looking around, he seemed hesitant and then embarrassed when he said, "I need to go to the washroom."

"Can you walk?" My eyebrows wrinkled with worry.

"I need help," said Dad as he looked down at his body, all dignity gone.

"Okay, I can help you." I moved his legs around so that they hung off the edge of the bed.

I bent down so that he could lean on me as I held his IV drip. We slowly shuffled to the washroom. It was only ten steps away, but it took a lot of effort. I had to stand, holding him while he did his business.

The following day, the doctor showed me Dad's X-rays where more than fifty percent of his brain showed up as ominous-looking black patches. The doctor said that Dad was lucky to be alive, that Fong Fong's fast reaction getting him to the hospital had saved him. However, Dad needed to start moving. That's why Fong Fong had asked me to come. Dad hadn't wanted to get out of bed. She was shocked that he'd asked me to help him to the washroom. Okay, I had a mission now. Get Dad to walk.

I coaxed Dad into the hallway with him leaning against me. We took slow steps. One, two, three. I laughed, trying to get him to smile. He grimaced, but he kept going.

"Come on, Dad. Let's just get to the canteen. It's only a few steps more. We can eat breakfast together."

"They won't let me eat rice. They say I have diabetes."

"It's okay, Dad. You always said that I lived to eat while you ate to live. Now you just need to eat to live."

Dad looked totally exhausted from the twenty or so steps, but I was so proud of him. A hospital worker came by with a tray. It didn't look appetizing at all.

"What is that?"

"It's congee made from oatmeal."

"Is it sweet?"

"No, it's flavoured with chicken broth. It's okay. You're right; I am eating to live."

Dad was sleeping when Fong Fong and an Armani-attired woman entered the room. They motioned for me to step out into the hallway with them so Dad could rest.

"Do you remember me, Frances?" asked the glamorous woman.

"Uh, no. I'm sorry, do I know you?"

"I'm Monica. I lived at your dad's house on Davisville when I went to university. He's like a godfather to me."

"Oh, okay," I replied simply, but I was thinking, *Wow, how people transform.* I remembered a mousy Chinese girl with nerdy glasses.

"We're taking you to a *cha chaan teng*; it's around the corner in Happy Valley. They have the best *nai cha* and buttered buns."

"Sure, as long as it's quick. I want to be here when Dad wakes up."

Over my steaming cup of creamy sweet tea, I watched Fong Fong and Monica gossip. They didn't seem to have a care in the world for Dad. Monica filled me in that she was in banking and married to a super-rich guy from Brunei.

"So your guy in Bali, is he a super-rich Indonesian too?"

"No, he's not," I replied, finding her questions intrusive and downright tacky.

"So what does he do for a living?"

"He's a spa therapist at Le Meridien."

"Ah, so he's hot."

I rarely disliked people, but when I did, there was no going back. Monica, I did not like. I hastily stuffed the rest of the sweet bun into my mouth and chased it down with the milky tea. With my mouth still full, I mumbled that I'd better get going to check on Dad, leaving more than my share of bills on the table. I'd only just started being comfortable talking about Adi to my family; he wasn't going to be the topic of conversation with someone I hardly knew.

As soon as I left the air-conditioned café, the August humidity enveloped me as if I'd entered a sauna fully clothed. I tried hurrying back to the hospital, but my feet dragged in the heat.

Dad was sitting in the chair by the window when I walked in. I sat down across from him, wiping the sweat away from my forehead.

"Where were you?" asked Dad.

"Fong Fong and that woman, Monica, took me out for nai cha."

With a knowing look, Dad nodded slowly, "Ah, nai cha... Remember before when we used to meet at Tsui Wah for afternoon tea?"

"Yes, Dad, I remember. You were the one who first took me there when I'd just moved to Hong Kong. It was a loud and dirty, and I didn't wanted to order anything. Now I love that place. We'll go there when you're better, okay?"

"I don't know if I can work anymore. The doctor said that I have to avoid stress."

"It's okay, don't worry about that now. Just get stronger first."

"So you saw Monica. You know, she's an investment banker. She makes a lot of money."

"Yes, she told me," I replied, rolling my eyes. "She's not exactly humble, is she?"

"She can be proud. She came from nothing, and she's very successful. She chose a rich husband."

"That's great if money is what makes her happy."

"I didn't say that, but you need money to be safe. Who is this Adi that Mom tells me about?"

Hesitating, I looked at him and said, "Dad, I think I've found my candle."

Seven years after Dad had assured me that my candle was waiting for me, Dad gave me a rare smile and patted me on my hand, "I'm glad. I can't wait to meet him."

Lying in bed, Adi and I faced each other on our sides. Adi brushed a few strands of hair away from my face, leaned forward and kissed me. I'd just told him about my dad's firecracker and candle analogy. Adi's eyes shone from within, a bright steady flame that licked his deep brown eyes and stilled my heart.

"A candle. Hmm, time to ask the *Pemangku* for a good date then."

"A good date?" my eyebrows arched.

"Yes, a good date to get married."

"Why do we have to ask a… what did you say? A Pe Man Coo? What's that?"

"A Pemangku is a priest. They determine the best days to get married on the Balinese calendar."

"Shouldn't this be based on things like when the wedding venue is available and when my family have time to come to Bali?"

"Wedding venue? Darling, the wedding will be at my family compound. Remember, you're marrying into my village."

"Yes, I get that I'll live in your village after we're married, but I didn't know that we had to get married in your family compound. What about my family and friends from overseas?"

"Well, they can come too, of course; I mean, a few more people won't make much difference when the whole village is coming."

"The *whole* village?"

Adi scratched his chin, "Well, we can try to cut it down to just my Banjar and family."

"And how many people would that be?" I asked, a bit panicked about what his answer would be.

"Um, let me think…" Adi looked up to the ceiling as if he was counting in his head. "Anywhere between 400 to 500 people."

"WHAT??" I sat up. "What do you mean? How do we fit that many people into your compound? I mean, your place is spacious, but 500 people is a lot of people."

"They don't come all at once. It's staggered."

"How about the wedding reception? I've always envisioned an intimate sit-down dinner of my closest family and friends, maybe a hundred people tops," I said dreamily.

Adi looked hesitantly at me, searching for words to explain. "Darling, a Balinese wedding is different. It's not really about the meal. It's about ceremony. Of course, we'll feed everyone, but it'll be all day long, like a buffet."

"Buffet?" To a Chinese person born and bred in the food haven of Toronto, the word "buffet" connoted questionable quality lukewarm food in ugly stainless steel warming trays. I squeaked again, "Buffet?"

"That's how we feed four to five hundred people," Adi answered logically.

Exasperated, I snapped back, "Yes, I just didn't know that we had to invite the whole village and feed them! And I HATE buffets!"

Adi looked taken aback, not knowing how to respond.

I put my head in my hands, "Sorry, I don't mean to freak out. Let me take this in. It's just not what I expected."

Adi took my hands into his, rubbing them, which calmed my nerves. He waited until I'd sorted things out in my own head.

"Okay, I get it. There are Balinese traditions that we must follow. I'll be happy as long as I can plan another separate dinner for my family and friends too. I'll need your help to get prepared. Not only for the wedding but for life as your wife. It's kinda sinking in that this is a big deal."

"Of course, we can do anything you want outside of the main ceremonies. I understand that your family and friends will want to spend time with you after coming all the way to Bali."

I hugged him tightly. "Thank you, sweetheart. You're right; this is going to be even better than I imagined. Now I get to plan two wedding parties, not just one!"

"So what month are you thinking of? I need to give the Pemangku a range."

"Well, it's August now. Usually, people need to know a year in advance."

"WHAT?" Now it was Adi's turn to be shocked. "What do you mean a year in advance? I don't know if we can get a date that far away. Usually, you get the date one month, maybe two before the wedding."

"That's not going to work. My family and friends need to ask for vacation time off and they need to plan to come to Bali. I think the earliest we could do it would be May or June of next year."

"Okay, okay, let me see what I can do."

With joking in my eyes, I said, "I'm sorry that marrying me is so complicated. Are you sure you wouldn't prefer a Balinese girl instead?"

"You're right. It could be easier. But I'm not looking for easy. I'm your candle, right?" he said, pushing me down onto the bed and holding my head up to his face. "And you're my everything."

Adi and his parents went to the Pemangku with the first-ever request for a wedding date nine months away. Thankfully, the Pemangku was understanding and gave a few options for May 2003. One was May 5th which we thought was exceptionally auspicious – "5-5-5."

The calendar flipped into September when vacationing families departed Bali. Then it was time for me to fly back to Canada for my 10th alumnae reunion at Western Ivey Business School, with a quick stopover in Hong Kong.

Adi suggested that I choose an engagement ring in Hong Kong so I'd have something to show my mom when I got back to Toronto. Balinese people did not exchange rings, so I was very touched that Adi understood the significance of rings in Western culture.

I'd always had a difficult relationship with my dad. I'd only become slightly less guarded and comfortable around him when I lived in Hong Kong and he was happiest with Fong Fong, and his stroke had drawn us closer. I was actually excited to see my dad on this trip. I even decided to stay in their tiny apartment, sleeping on the tiny makeshift bed, to spend more time with him.

But first, I needed to call to check if that would be okay. I rarely called anyone from Bali as calls were crazy expensive, so I had to keep it short.

"Hi Dad, can I stay with you when I come to Hong Kong on the 17th?"

"Yeah, you can stay here, but we're leaving on the 18th for a short cruise to Singapore."

"What? I told you that I was coming from the 17th for four days."

"Fong Fong thought it would be good for me to get away. To relax."

Why do they need to relax? I thought. *Fong Fong doesn't work, and Dad's been recuperating from his stroke at home.* But I hid my skepticism and said, "Oh, okay, that's fine. I'll stay with Kai Ma when you leave."

"I'm going to Bali too."

Taken aback, I said, "What? I didn't know you were coming to Bali. When?"

"The last week of September."

I looked at the phone in disbelief, pausing before answering. "But Dad, you can't come then. I'll be in Toronto. I told you that. Can't you come when I get back?"

Dad answered angrily, "I didn't plan this. Monica booked this for us. It's when she has time off work."

"But…but Dad, you've never been here before. I want to show you around. For you to meet Adi."

"Monica booked us in Adi's hotel. Le Meridien, right? We'll meet him."

"I don't know if Adi will be comfortable meeting you without me."

"Don't worry, we'll just meet him for a meal."

"Okay, Dad. I'll see you in a week."

I clicked off my phone and looked up to see Adi gazing at me with so much tenderness and concern. "Are you okay, darling?"

Sinking to the floor where Adi was sitting against the bed, I slumped against his oversized shoulder and let my sadness seep out.

Sniffling and wiping tears from my face, I berated myself, "I thought me rushing to Hong Kong last month meant something to my dad. That he wanted to see me, but he doesn't care. It's still just about what he wants. I'm so stupid. I wasted my time off work. I wasted hundreds of dollars on that last-minute flight. Yet he treats me like crap. Why did I even bother to be a good daughter?"

"Because that's who you are. You did the right thing. We don't get to choose our parents. But we chose each other, and I'll never let you down. I promise." Adi held me close and stroked my hair.

I sank into him, curling my body into his. Adi was my future.

When I saw him this time, Dad was a much weaker version of himself. He walked with a slight limp, as if he'd had one too many to drink. We were at a mall in Kowloon, the other side of Hong Kong that I'd only visited twice. Dad and Fong Fong's small cruise ship departed from Kowloon harbour.

With time to spare, Fong Fong pulled me into a flashy jewelry shop to help me find an engagement ring. Peering through the glass case, I stared at hundreds of rings of different cuts and designs. Fong Fong kept pointing to oversized rocks. None of the styles spoke to me; I found them too big and a bit repulsive. Adi had given me enough of a budget to get one of these, but they didn't suit me.

"Let's go. These aren't what I'm looking for," I remarked as I turned to leave.

Suddenly, Fong Fong squealed in excitement, hopping up and down on her 4-inch platform heels. I looked over her shoulder to see what the excitement was about as a salesperson pulled out an obscenely large "F" pendant covered in diamonds.

Like a sly kitten, she rubbed her cheek against Dad's shoulder saying she'd been looking for ages for an "F" pendant. She held the flamboyant necklace to her chest.

"How much is it?" asked Dad, looking at the diamond initial brandishing on Fong Fong's bare skin.

"It's only forty-thousand!" replied Fong Fong, fluttering her fake eyelashes at Dad, saying it like forty-thousand Hong Kong dollars was only fifty American dollars, not the five-thousand dollars it actually cost.

I coughed in shock. That was more than the budget for my engagement ring, which was a once-in-a-lifetime purchase, not a spur-of-the-moment impulse buy. I turned to Dad, expecting him to tell her that they hadn't intended to buy anything, especially as he was no longer working because of his weak condition. And remind her why we were in the shop in the first place – to get Frances an engagement ring.

"Get it if you want." Dad smiled, looking as happy as a clam.

Fong Fong clapped in delight, hugging Dad while reaching for his wallet.

My mouth dropped in disgust. My heart hurt. Who was this man? Dad had never in his life bought flowers or even a birthday card for my mom, let alone jewelry. My mother had bought herself jewelry when she started bringing in more income than Dad. Growing up, I'd believed he was incapable of showing us love or giving us gifts because he'd grown up poor. He'd said that luxuries were a frivolous waste of money. I believed him to be a depressed person who we could not cheer up. Now, I could see it wasn't him; it was us. We were the family that he was unwilling to love. He was capable of love. Just not of loving us.

Kai Ma could always read my mood. "What's wrong?"

"Dad and Fong Fong. I thought I'd be at peace with Dad when he finally found his own happiness. But I can't stomach how Dad spoils her rotten. He was so stingy to Mom. Whenever I go out with them, Dad tells me to pay for their meal and never lets Fong Fong pay for anything."

"Oh, Wah-Wah. It's because you and your mom are so strong. He can't handle strong women."

"We had to be strong to survive. I think Fong Fong is actually a lot stronger and quite a bit smarter than she lets on. She knows exactly how to play Dad."

"Nevermind them. Let me take you to one of my favourite jewellers. I'm sure your ring is there."

Kai Ma led me along the heavily polluted Stanley Street where the *siu baa* (minibuses) bumped along the busy one-lane road, beeping pedestrians out of the way. My elegant godmother, jarringly out of place amongst the office workers getting off work, didn't notice as she led me into a nondescript, older building. Down a narrow hall of offices and tiny shops, she pulled open an old-fashioned glass door set in wood frame, setting off a tiny bell. The air-conditioning rushed out.

An elderly Cantonese man, tall and slightly bent over, greeted my godmother warmly, "*Ah Lor-Tai, nai ho ma?*"

"*Ho, ho.* This is my *kai neui* and she needs an engagement ring," Kai Ma said, gesturing to me, her goddaughter.

"Congratulations," the man said, shaking my hand. "What are you looking for?"

"Well, I'm not exactly sure…my husband-to-be said maybe something with three diamonds." I still couldn't call Adi my fiancé; the word just got stuck in my throat. Adi was so much more than just my fiancé.

"Three diamonds. I have something that you might like."

He reached into the window and put a ring on a dark navy velvet tray. It was a delicate three-diamond ring with two smaller diamonds flanking the centre stone, set in a unique band. It was love at first sight. I carefully lifted the ring out of the tray and slipped it onto my fourth finger; it fit perfectly. As I turned my hand this way and that, the centre diamond threw off glittering sparks.

My godmother commented right away that the diamond had an unusual fire.

"Yes, the diamond's cut is exceptional. It's an 'Ideal Brilliant' cut with more symmetry and even cuts than you typically find. This gives the diamond 'fire,' as your kai ma called it."

I was nervous, "How much is this?"

"Well, since you're Lor-Tai's kai neui, we'll give you a special price. Your kai ma is one of my most loyal customers; she's been buying from me for over thirty years. Don't worry, we'll take good care of you."

I walked out of the store with the ring on my finger. The jeweller was also going to custom make our wedding bands – one of white gold to match the band of my engagement ring and the other a thick band of platinum for Adi. My godmother would bring them with her to our wedding. I couldn't wait to show Adi the final bill for our wedding rings – the cost of our three rings was less than the budget he'd set for my one engagement ring.

Driving to my old university town of London, Ontario, I enjoyed the last vestiges of summer. Autumn was my favourite time of the year. The maple trees started their transformation into golds, burnt orange, cranberry and cocoa.

For our five-year reunion in 1997, I'd stayed at the most charming Victorian inn, just a bit south of downtown London. That weekend had gone by in a blur, not giving us enough time to catch up properly. This time for the tenth reunion, I'd booked the entire inn for my classmates – many were bringing spouses and babies – so we could enjoy breakfasts together and lounge in the communal living rooms, in addition to catching up during our reunion events.

My hands sweated when they were usually cold and dry. Some of my best biz school buddies – Keitha, Crystal, Elaine and Nate – were gathered in the living room. Avoiding them, I rushed upstairs to drop my bags off and gather my courage to announce my engagement to Adi. I suspected they thought my time in Bali with Adi was just an extended sabbatical from real life, a crazy Frances thing to do before I got back on track. Not a lifetime commitment.

As I hesitantly made my way back downstairs on the thickly carpeted stairs, I passed Tom, Keitha's husband.

He hugged me in greeting and immediately noticed my ring. "Hey! What's this?" he said, lifting my left hand up to take a closer look.

Blushing, I giggled, "I'm engaged to Adi."

"Congratulations, Fran!" He pulled me into the living room to Keitha, who was cradling their firstborn, Parker. "Look at this, Keitha. Fran's engaged!"

Everyone stopped chatting. I watched as their faces registered the shock. None of them could imagine that our wedding was already in the works.

Keitha jumped off the couch, handed Parker over to Tom and gave me a tight squeeze. "I'm so happy for you, Fran!"

Crystal and Rachel both looked up from the other sofa, held down by their own babies, and extended their congratulations too. Nate came to kiss me on my cheek and wish me the best, and Elaine bounced up to hug me.

"Do you have a date? Where are you going to do it?" Keitha asked, always the super organized one.

"Yes, we're planning for May 5th, 2003, in Bali." I smiled back, remembering her and Tom's beautiful church wedding followed by the reception at the Four Seasons. "It's going to be at Adi's family compound. A little different than the Four Seasons, eh?"

"Wow, Fran! I had no idea when I was in Bali with you in June. I wish I'd known; I'm not sure that we can make it back to Bali since I'll be doing my master's degree and Brad's working," said Elaine.

I tried to hide my disappointment, which probably showed on my face anyways. "It's okay, I know it'll be hard for all of you to get to Bali."

I'd attended all of their weddings. Keitha and Tom's in Toronto, Crystal and Ted's in Carmel, and Nate and Rachel's in Singapore. I was grateful in particular for that last wedding, for the role it played in my meeting Adi. I was sad, but I got the message: travelling to Bali for my wedding wouldn't be a priority. I'd arrived too late in the wedding game. They were already on to the next phase in life.

The best part of my trip home was receiving Mom's support to marry Adi.

It wasn't easy for her as everything about my decision represented unknown risks, but she'd always encouraged me to live my life as I wished. To not let anything get in the way of my dreams. However, she'd never, *ever* thought I'd forge this entirely new path.

She spun a globe to the other side of the world to point out the tiny island of Bali to her friends. I was to marry into a completely different culture. Indonesia was patriarchal; I'd belong to Adi's family. Mom feared this more than anything. She knew my fiercely independent character. She trusted that I would be polite and respectful, but she could not see me kowtowing to anyone if push came to shove on critical matters.

Mom decided that she'd spend Christmas and New Year's in Bali. This way, she would have some time to get to know Adi and meet his parents. What could I say? Mom had every right to come; she had my best interests at heart. And I was confident that Adi could handle anything Mom threw at him.

Meanwhile, back in Bali, Adi was in the hot seat. Dad, Fong Fong, Monica and her husband had checked into the villas, the top category of accommodations at Le Meridien Golf and Spa Resort.

Of course, I grumbled, "Only the best for his precious Fong Fong."

Dad had left a message at the spa requesting Adi's presence for dinner at their villa.

I called Adi to see how it went. "Hi honey, good that you're still taking my calls. I was afraid my dad scared you away. How was it?"

"It was okay, I guess. I've never been in that situation before."

"Were all four of them there?"

"Yes, that was..." Adi paused and found the word, "awkward."

"I'm sorry, honey, that I wasn't there. I feel so badly for you to have to meet my dad on your own."

"I handled it okay. He asked how I was going to support you."

"What did you say?"

"Just the truth. I have a good job at the hotel, a house, and I can take care of you. Not the same as in Hong Kong or Canada. But I can support you here in Bali."

"And what did he say?"

"He just nodded and said, 'That's good. You seem like an honest guy. I think Frances will be happy.'"

"Well, that's a relief. Do you have to see them again?"

"I don't think so. They're going sightseeing today. They leave tomorrow."

On the way back to Bali, I stopped over for one night in Hong Kong, staying at my dad's. He gave me his approval of Adi in person. "Adi, *ho lo sut*." He was genuine and humble, Dad said. "I only met him briefly, but he has an open, kind face. I can see why he's your candle."

*P*art of my compensation package for my work at Pala included the use of one of Brenda's cars. Even though I'd arrived in January, I'd never driven the car and likely never would since I didn't know how to drive manual.

I'd survived driving on the other side of the road in Melbourne but driving in Bali was a whole different level of insanity. Motorbikes weaved between each other and dodged cars in a complicated dance known only to the locals. I'd seen more than one Balinese girl shoot out of a laneway without stopping or looking at all and drive directly into oncoming traffic, causing all the other motorbikes to swerve violently to avoid her.

Adi had obtained his car driver's license while I'd been away so we could finally go on longer trips around the island.

It was a Sunday in October, and we were in the seaside town of Sanur to celebrate my birthday.

Four times in the past two months on Jalan Ngurah Rai, going to the airport and back, I'd passed a sign that read, "All-You-Can-Eat Dim Sum for 99,000 Rupiah." Authentic Chinese food didn't exist in the Bali of 2002. Warungs sold what they claimed to be "Chinese" food, heavily Indonesianized versions of *chow fan* and *chow mein*, somewhat like Americanized Chinese food of neon red sweet and sour sauce.

Despite knowing that the "All-You-Can-Eat Dim Sum" buffet wouldn't be anything close to the real deal, I still loved watching Adi pop *har gow* and *siu mai* into his mouth. His favourite dim sum turned out to be *fung zaau* (spicy braised chicken feet) – Adi was game to try anything. His unquenchable sense of curiosity and playfulness drew me closer to him as he raced neck and neck with me for the most FAPs collected.

Adi sang along to a romantic Balinese ballad by his favourite band, Michael Learns to Rock on the radio. With perfect pitch, his voice wrapped around my body like an embrace.

The news came on, and Adi went pale, breathing in, "Oh no."

I turned to face him, "Are you okay? What's wrong?"

Adi pulled the car over to the side and stopped on the side of the road. "Frances, there was a bomb in Kuta last night."

"What? Oh my God. When? I don't understand."

"It was at a bar called Paddy's. It was bad, hundreds injured and dead."

My first thought was, *What's going to happen to our wedding?* We were only eight months away. I'd already asked my family and friends to save the date. I shook my head and decided it was out of my control.

The rest of the day was a blur. We joined an emergency gathering of Ubudian expats at Ary's Warung. In epic Ubud form, the meeting started with us standing in a circle holding hands while an eccentric artist recited a poem scratched out on the back of a menu.

Once we broke apart, everyone started out shouting questions: How could Ubud businesses help the victims? Who could volunteer at Sanglah Hospital? Who could raise funds for food and hospital supplies? Frustrated with the ensuing mayhem, I tapped on my chair and asked if we could all be quiet for a moment. Everyone stared back. I was still considered an outsider as I rarely mingled with the expats. Nonetheless, I forged ahead.

"Um, maybe we can get a bit more organized. Perhaps, we break out into smaller teams? One for each area that needs help?"

A long-term Canadian expat Petra stepped beside me and put her hands on my shoulders, smiled and agreed, "Yes, that's an excellent idea."

That's how I joined Petra on the volunteer media team. Our mission was to tell real stories on the ground from Bali to counter the international narrative. The media frenzy had blown up the bomb story into an epic saga, scaring off even the bravest tourists. Bali had taken a whole year to recover from 9/11. Overnight, the island emptied out again.

Mom called in a total panic, imploring me to return home. She'd seen horrific scenes of the bomb site on TV. Her phone was ringing off the hook with concerned (and nosey) friends.

"Mom, Bali is one of the safest places in the world – the police don't even have guns. The media aren't fair. When 9/11 happened, they didn't warn people not to go to New York. People understood that a terrorist attack could happen anywhere. It's not the place that created this. I'm so angry that the media is destroying the lives of so many innocent Balinese people who rely on tourism to make a living. It's insane."

"Okay, okay, calm down. You're right. The Balinese didn't do anything wrong. We need to support Bali now. I'm still coming in December. I'll let everyone know that you're fine. I'm relieved that you're safe. I love you."

There was a massive outpouring of love and generosity in the immediate aftermath – local restaurants and hotels sent food and volunteers to the hospital. As November approached, the island remained empty. Hotels asked their staff to take unpaid leave; half the team worked one month and then rotated with the other half of the staff the next month.

One of my waitresses, with her eyes wide with fear, asked if something awful would happen on November 13th. I looked at her in confusion and then realized her uncanny logic: 9/11 World Trade Centre, 10/12 Bali, 11/13.… I hugged her and tried to reassure her that we were safe.

The Balinese are some of the most peaceful people in the world – a tiny Hindu island in the middle of the world's largest Muslim archipelago. I'd been in the States when 9/11 happened. A year later, I was in Bali after the terrorist bomb. The remarkable difference was how each community reacted. Americans had retaliated immediately, destroying an entire country to unearth the criminals. Bali retreated within.

Every Balinese person I spoke to asked the same question: "How could we have prevented this? What did we do to anger the Gods?"

Then, "We need to look at ourselves and change our behaviour. We need to be able to protect tourists better."

Lying in bed with the mosquito net closed around us like a cocoon, I asked Adi, "Why do the Balinese feel that they're to blame? I don't understand. It was terrorists."

Adi thought and slowly replied, "Some believe that we've forgotten our traditions and values, that we've veered too much towards Western culture, especially Kuta."

I'd avoided Kuta since my only visit there in May 2001. The energy in Kuta pulsed with darkness and greed, in stark contrast to the light I felt in Ubud.

"Do you think this too?" I asked, leaning into him.

"Bali has changed. There's more money here. It depends on how people use it. Many people now have electricity and water. We need these things to live. In that way, tourism has helped us."

"What about the culture?"

"Young people buy TVs, motorbikes and cellphones. We need motorbikes to get to work. But young people still learn Balinese dance, gamelan music, kite-making, and Ogoh Ogoh. So our culture is very strong."

"Yes, I loved watching you play gamelan at your uncle's temple. I can't believe how much you guys practice. You're right; I can't think of anywhere in the world where teenagers sit beside older men practicing gamelan night after night to perform at temple ceremonies. Bali is truly magical. We need the rest of the world to know it's safe here."

"Let's hope the biggest cleansing ceremony ever will restore balance. We'll purify every home too."

"When is that again?"

"November 15th."

On that day, I sat cross-legged beside Suryani, among thousands of Balinese, on the main road of Kuta, just south of the bomb site.

The energy changed when the first chimes of the *Pedanda* bell rang out. The nervous chatter of the crowds faded away. An eerie calmness enveloped us. The wind swept down the road, rustling the flowers in our canang and threatened to extinguish our lit incense. The same wind lifted the hair on my arms as we raised our hands in prayer. Tears rolled slowly down my face. I begged God to give comfort to those who were taken so violently, to those still recovering from the attacks and to their families.

Peace descended.

*A*fter the bomb, despair set in. Pala had ten times more staff than customers. Adi guided me back into the light. He gave me the perfect projects to occupy my restless mind – our wedding invitations and outfits.

We'd gone to great lengths in the past, handwriting thirty maps and guides for Yosh and Marie's wedding, so Adi was ready for whatever idea I would throw at him. Or so he thought.

During our trip to East Bali, Adi and I had visited the double-ikat village of Tenganan where I discovered the *lontar*, a traditional religious scroll of Sanskrit symbols inscribed by hand on palm leaves. As I held the lontar up to the light, the individual leaves, threaded together and dropped down like a scroll, revealing ancient words of wisdom.

The lontar was inspiration for our wedding – Balinese and timeless. Adi naively agreed to my idea, envisioning paper invitations printed in the style of the lontar.

As I leafed through the sample invitations at a printing shop, I shook my head and said, "This is not what I imagined. We need the invitations to be real lontar."

Adi opened his eyes wide and coughed, "You want us to make two hundred invitations out of palm leaves, strung together?"

"Yes, do you know a traditional printer? One who can print on palm leaves?" I asked.

"Print on palm leaves?" Adi scratched his head, probably wondering, if this was just the process for the invitation, what was the rest of the marriage going to be?

This is how we embarked on our epic wedding invite saga.

Petra created an utterly unique design to be silk-screened onto seven leaves; the romantic words of Rumi led into the details of our wedding events. On the back of the leaves was a hand-drawn image of Saraswati, Goddess of the Arts and Learning, my favourite goddess. We would bind the separate leaves together with string, insert a matching map of Adi's family compound and gently slide the whole package into a custom pocket envelope enclosed with twine. This smaller envelope and the outer envelope had the image of Rama and Sita embracing with our names, Adi and Frances, underneath. Petra even had the foresight to design thank you cards with the same theme.

Now that we had the design, we had to execute the production – all done by hand, primarily Adi's and mine.

The printer who did the work for Adi's spa tested a few palm leaves using silkscreen. The finished "lontar" leaf shimmered with a brushed antique finish. We high-fived each other, thinking we'd gotten over the biggest hurdle in our invitation marathon. Wrong. The printer insisted that we get the palm leaves. Adi nodded grimly, understanding what this meant more than I did.

After that, every day that Adi and I had off together, we'd travel around the island from market to market looking for palm leaves. The challenge – okay, *one* of the challenges – we faced was that we could only use the largest palm leaves in the heart of a bunch. All the other leaves were too small.

I now understood the reason why the printer refused to supply the leaves. The task of finding leaves alone took us weeks.

The printer had the difficult job of cutting each leaf to size and then carefully screen printing each one. Each leaf was printed once on the front with the correct part of the invitation words. Once dried, the artist printed the corresponding part of the Saraswati image on the flipside. In addition to the English version for my family and friends, we printed fifty Indonesian versions for Adi's closest family and friends.

Adi and I had the final job of stringing the pieces together so that the image of Saraswati fit back together like a jigsaw puzzle. Seven leaves bound together completed one invitation, which unfurled like a scroll once opened.

I hand-wrote the addresses for one hundred and fifty invitations on the bigger outer envelope, which protected the smaller envelope that contained each lontar. From there, I piled them carefully into oversized FedEx boxes – about one hundred to Mom in Toronto, another thirty to Kai Ma in Hong Kong and the rest to Ken in San Francisco.

Adi and I devoted each evening in November and part of December to bind each wedding invitation. Sitting at the marble table on our terrace, I bent to pick up some leaves that the cool breeze had blown off the table where piles of printed leaves, string, Chinese coins, envelopes, and twine lay waiting to be assembled.

I paused to stare at Adi, who was painstakingly pushing the string through yet another palm leaf and tying it on the top with one of the antique Chinese coins. Seeing that I'd stopped, Adi asked, "What are you looking at?"

"You. You're my best friend. I don't know anyone else in the world who would've done this with me. I love you."

Adi took us to Klungkung village, thirty minutes east of Ubud, where Balinese wove ceremonial *songket*. We stepped out of the glaring sunshine into the dusty market, squinting to see piles of folded songket next to stalls with bolts of hand-spun cotton in a rainbow of colours. A wry-looking seller threw open one of the songket to display the silver threading through the thick fabric. I fingered it and shook my head; I'd die of heatstroke if I was wrapped in heavy weaving on my wedding day.

Adi looked at my frowning face with concern. "You don't like it, do you?"

"No, it's not my style. I can't imagine us dressing up in shiny gold and white sarongs with the massive crowns, either. I would look like a stuffed sausage."

"I have my songket from my Toothfiling ceremony. It's a deep blue and purple one. Not so flashy. Maybe we use that?"

"I don't think so, the songket is just too heavy, it must weigh 25 kilograms," I said, reaching for some of the colorful cotton "All's not wasted; I love this handwoven cotton. Let's buy a few metres and have Suaji's staff make boxes for our wedding thank you gift."

"We have to give thank you gifts?" asked Adi. "To all four hundred guests?"

"No silly, not for the Balinese wedding, for the Chinese Tea Ceremony and dinner reception at Pala. It's 120 boxes in total. We can put our Taksu candle holders and little candles in them." I thought aloud as I sorted bolts of the colourful cotton – cherry red striped through with lighter pinks, teal streaked with dark navy and a bright orange mixed in with rusty brown – how pretty and unique these fabric boxes would look at each place setting.

Knowing it was futile to dissuade me from any creative idea, Adi sighed and asked the seller to cut four metres of each for the boxes.

Back in the car, I turned to Adi, "Would it be possible for us to wear understated outfits? How about a lace kebaya for me and a jacket like the ones you wear for the gamelan? I have the two sarongs from the Bali Arts Festival that I haven't worn yet."

Being an avid gamelan player, Adi had taken me to Denpasar to watch the spectacular dance performances accompanied by the best gamelan orchestras at the Bali Arts Festival the previous June. Besides the performing arts, traditional batik and weavings were displayed and sold in one of the arts buildings. We happened upon two exquisite, hand-painted, silk batik sarongs. In 2002, hand-painted batik was already a dying art form. Batik of this quality took a year to create.

The sarong was of exceptional skill and talent. Using hot wax, the artist had painted an intricate scene of fluttering butterflies, swooping birds and blooming flowers onto the cream silk. The silk then had been dyed several times – once for the deep navy blue lines, again for the rich coffee brown, and a third time to give it a glowing golden hue. This would be my wedding sarong.

The other sarong was an abstract pattern resembling a Japanese kimono, a rich cranberry red on cream silk. I'd inadvertently bought the ideal sarong for our Chinese Tea Ceremony. Red was the colour worn by Chinese brides.

Pausing to carefully form his words, Adi replied, "That would be more comfortable. It'll be a long day. Yes, let's do that. Why not? We're already mixing Balinese with Canadian." Nodding his head, he agreed. "I like simple. Not looking like peacocks."

The following day, we searched up and down Jalan Suluwesi in the main city of Denpasar for lace fabric to make a kebaya to go with my sarong.

Although there were at least fifty shops, they carried the same inventory: itchy synthetic lace with bold patterns in bright hues such as fuchsia or royal blue.

"I think we have to go to Alta Moda. It's the shop where Brenda buys her soft cotton lace. I think it's on the expensive side, but a kebaya only needs a couple of metres," I said, grateful that I wasn't spending thousands of dollars on a traditional white wedding gown.

Adi put his arm around me, "Let's go now. I'm sure we'll find something there."

I'd never been inside Alta Moda, a fabric shop with glittering ball gowns and tuxedos in their display window. An aggressive salesperson accosted us with a measuring tape thrown over his shoulder. Surprisingly, we were not judged as "window shoppers." The salesperson led us to the designer French lace section deep in the shop. The bolts of lace raced from the floor to the ceiling in an octagon-shaped room with a low, octagonal sofa. Adi seated himself, ready for hours of indecision.

Not knowing if I had to bargain, I kept my face neutral as I said, "I'm looking for very soft cotton lace, in a light cream colour. Nothing in white."

The salesperson immediately started pulling down bolts of the delicate lace from the cream section. He unravelled bolt after bolt in dramatic fashion, naming each one after a fashion designer – this one is Christian Dior, this one Versace – laying some over the plush sofa where Adi was seated.

The salesperson draped some lace over my left shoulder and another design over my right. I felt like a princess, or Julia Roberts in "Pretty Woman." Wow, these guys are good. Even if you didn't want anything, you'd feel compelled to have five ballgowns made. Adi grinned as he saw how much I enjoyed the royal treatment. I rarely shopped in Bali. Nothing fit me, as I towered over the typical Balinese woman. My wedding kebaya would be custom-made, sure to fit like a glove.

I selected a Chantilly lace with a delicate scallop to edge the hem and sleeves of my finished kebaya. The salesperson cut a bit of rich brown silk for the camisole to wear underneath.

Adi piped up, "How about the other events? The ceremony before the wedding, the Young Generation reception and the Chinese tea ceremony?"

"I need that many outfits? I hadn't budgeted for so many." My forehead wrinkled with worry. "You're right, but I can't spend what we just did for that piece of lace."

Grinning widely, knowing he could sell at least another three pieces of lace, the salesperson directed us to another area, "These fabrics are less expensive, and we have a few pieces from the ends of bolts that are fifty percent off."

"Okay, I'll look through these end bits. Adi, why don't you head over to the suit fabrics and pick out what you need for your jacket."

5 1

$\mathcal{M}$om was coming to Bali to meet Adi for the first time. But first, I was meeting her for a week in Bangkok before we flew back to Bali together for the Christmas holidays.

My eyes nearly popped out of my sockets. Mom, Dad and Fong Fong stood together outside Bangkok immigration – an unlikely place for Mom to meet Fong Fong, Dad's much younger new wife, for the first time.

Fong Fong, hanging onto Dad's arm, wore a glittery top with a hot pink feather boa draped around her neck and black vinyl skinny pants tucked into 5-inch knee-high boots. On the other side of Dad, Mom looked regal in a black pant suit with an understated, elegant blouse.

Feigning enthusiasm, Mom smiled and said, "Frances, your dad wanted to pick you up so we could all go to dinner together." She patted me on the shoulder, which in Chinese culture translated to a full-blown hug.

"Ummm, great. Thanks, Dad, for coming all the way out to the airport."

Dad nodded in my direction while Fong Fong preened, shaking out her boa and fluttering her fake lashes. He'd aged considerably, limping slowly as we walked out to where the car and driver waited. Dad had suffered another minor stroke. Thankfully, Fong Fong had recognized the symptoms immediately and rushed him to the hospital, where he'd received medicine right away, minimizing the effects. However, this had put an end to Dad's career, forcing him into early retirement.

The conversation in the car and during dinner focused on what had suddenly become a neutral topic – Adi and me. We sat in a funky new restaurant owned by friends of my godparents. The chef had prepared a special menu, bringing out one surprise after another. One dish that stood out was a tiny suckling pig, the skin paper-thin and the pork succulent and tender.

Fong Fong slapped Dad's hand away as he reached for another bite, "You can't eat that. It's too much fat."

Dad's hand retreated, as if he were a little boy being admonished by his mother. Mom raised her eyebrows and looked at me. I was equally shocked that Dad didn't react in rage.

Mom changed the focus, "Frances, I delivered the invitations, one by one, to your aunties and uncles."

"Thanks Mom, I didn't expect you to go house to house." I squeezed her hand as she remained stoic and brave, sitting in front of Dad and his second wife.

"Of course, your invitation was so beautiful and too delicate. I couldn't just put it in the mail. Everyone opened it right away. My friends were amazed that you and Adi made them by yourselves. And that you sent them all the way from Bali." Mom beamed with pride.

Mom and I left Bangkok for a short and unplanned jaunt to Cambodia before we would fly back together to Bali for Christmas. Neither of us had planned to go to Cambodia. While Mom had been examining the new watch along with the leather sandals that I'd bought for Adi's wedding gifts, I was trying to book a trip for us to Laos.

The travel agent shook her head, "You can't go to Laos. You need a week to get the tourist visa from the consulate."

Frustrated with myself for not planning better and wondering a bit how I let this happen, I asked, "Do you have anywhere else we can go, departing tomorrow?"

The agent clicked away on his computer for options and suggested, "How about Angkor Wat in Cambodia? You can get a visa on arrival. We have a four-day package including flights, transfers and a four-star hotel."

Uncharacteristically, I turned to Mom, "What do you think? Do you want to go to Cambodia?"

Mom looked at me a little more closely. "Just go to Cambodia? But...you always plan everything. To the last detail. You like to research the best places to stay and eat. I mean, you've been to Laos…and that's where you wanted to bring me. Why are we booking at the last minute?"

I took in Mom's words. "Sorry Mom, I've just been too busy with the wedding plans. Can we go with the flow? When else would we travel to Cambodia?"

"I'd never planned to go there, but why not? Let's go," agreed Mom.

That's how we found ourselves in Siem Reap a day later. A young Cambodian named Thom who looked no more than eighteen years old had our names on a sign and led us to a brand new Toyota Camry. Leaning back into the buttery soft leather seats, to me it felt as luxurious as a Mercedes. Funny how my perspective had shifted. Previously, I snubbed my nose at "boring" family cars, but now the Camry felt indulgent compared to sitting on the back of Adi's motorbike.

As we bumped along the dusty road from the airport, Thom convinced us to hire him for the next three days to tour Angkor Wat. Then he suddenly announced, "Here's your hotel, Royal Cambodian. It's very new, only opened last year."

A gold plaque announcing the hotel name in a cursive font shone against a nondescript cement structure that resembled a '70s office building. I apparently hadn't paid any attention to the Bangkok travel agent when booking. I adamantly avoided hotels that included "royal," "majestic" or "palace" in its name. Any property adding these descriptors often lacked character and rarely had regal decorations or any sense of history that these names implied. As predicted, the hotel, while sparkling clean, had scant decorations. The walls were painted in a dull color, the floor laid with shiny white ceramic squares. Our room revealed two utilitarian beds and a simple washroom with a stand-up shower.

My lack of planning showed as more cracks appeared. The front desk receptionist shook her head and said, "Siem Reap no bank machine. No ATM."

Not fussed, I asked, "Okay, where's the closest bank to withdraw cash on our credit cards?"

She looked at her watch and said, "Bank already close. Monday is holiday. Bank open Tuesday." She held up four fingers to indicate the days.

Looking a bit panicked, Mom flipped through her wallet and found two hundred dollars cash and some Thai Baht. I had another sixty dollars. The cost of the car, driver and our day passes to the temples totalled two hundred dollars. My hope to pay for the day passes by credit card was dashed as I handed over our precious cash at the entrance of Angkor Wat.

Not daring to look at Mom, I cringed, expecting her anger and criticism.

Instead, Mom looked at my anxious face and calmly said, "Don't worry, worse comes to worst, we can eat all our meals at the hotel. We can pay with a credit card. I never expected that we'd be in Cambodia without enough money. This is an adventure for sure." We both broke into laughter.

Our guide Thom was clever, taking us in the opposite direction of the tour buses. Each temple we visited had a scattering of tourists or was completely empty. My favourite temple was outside of the main complex, about 35 kilometres away. Looking up at the fairy tale-like structure, I imagined skilled artisans gently tapping away at the soft pink sandstone to create the exquisite tapestry of intricate sculptures, capturing the ultimate devotion in a timeless temple called Banteay Srei.

Ironically, our lack of funds helped us see the temples at the best times of sunrise and sunset. And we sheltered out of the noontime heat in the cool aircon of our room. The food, like the hotel, was not impressive, consisting of bland curries watered down for tourists.

We joined a local boat tour, paid through the hotel, of a floating village just outside of Siem Reap. The extreme poverty of people living in bamboo shacks tore at my heart, reminding me of hardship I'd seen in Tianyar, the small village in Northeast Bali, a side of paradise most tourists never see.

Other travellers recommended FCC, the French Correspondent Club, housed in a former governor's mansion. There, Mom and I tasted our first and only Khmer food. Mom enjoyed fish *amok*, redolent of lemongrass with spicy chilli tamed by fresh coconut milk. I savoured my beef *lok-lak*, a stir-fry rich with oyster and tomato sauce. We sat on the terrace of the colonial gem, feeling the cool nighttime breeze on our last night in Cambodia.

There was never a quiet time to see the most famous temple, Angkor Wat, so we saved it for the end. Mom, exhausted from our temple tour on steroids, stayed in the cool comfort of the car.

Straining my neck to look up at the massive structure, I crossed the long walkway suspended over a moat containing hundreds of lotus flowers. A lady had fallen to her death while descending the temple steps years before and her husband had installed a new stairway with a railing at the temple's rear to prevent future tragedies. Even with the new stairway coming down, there was no way that I'd attempt to climb the old stone steps leading up; they were worn down, some to only a few centimetres in depth, impossible to get even a toehold. I remained frozen at the bottom of the looming temple watching as barefooted saffron-robed monks flew up the ancient steps.

As one of the monks approached, I stepped forward and asked, "How do you do that? How do you climb that and come back down without falling?"

He smiled back at me and responded, "Do you believe in God?"

Arriving in Bali from Bangkok, Mom and I were greeted by Adi with a handwritten sign. He looked as sweet as always. I couldn't see how Mom could not like him.

He'd driven Pala's white van to pick us up, anticipating a lot of luggage. I worried for him; he looked so tiny as he unloaded our oversized suitcases from the baggage cart into the big van. Could he even see over the high dashboard? Nonetheless, every action of Adi's showed so much care and thoughtfulness. I could feel his nervousness as he deftly maneuvered the van out of the parking lot.

Mom was uncharacteristically quiet, saying that she understood that Adi had to concentrate as he wasn't used to the big van or the busy roads of south Bali. I appreciated her thoughtfulness too.

Suryani welcomed Mom as if she was the queen visiting, giving her a chilled glass of hibiscus tea that became pink with a squeeze of lime. Adi hovered behind Mom as she climbed the steep stairs to our suites on the third floor, ready to steady her if needed.

Mom exclaimed, "How beautiful, how beautiful!" over and over as she took in the carved wooden doors, her marble bathroom, and the colourful cushions as she sat down on the day bed on our shared terrace.

I breathed in, smiling. "I'm so glad you like it. Now you can picture exactly where I am when I call you."

"Yes, it's so peaceful here. I can see why you chose Bali." She motioned to Adi to sit down too. "The invitations that you and Frances made were so unique. All my friends were amazed by your talent."

"Thanks, Mom."

My eyes opened wide as I didn't expect Adi to call her "Mom" in the first few hours of meeting her. I sucked in my breath, not knowing how Mom would respond. Adi knew that it was custoPala in Chinese to call her "Auntie Bessie" out of respect, but he also knew that proper names were a landmine in our family and in Chinese culture, where you never call an elder by their first name. My brother's wife had inadvertently called Mom by her first name when they became engaged, which is perfectly polite in Western cultures. Mom had immediately asked her to call her "Auntie Bessie" – a more familiar term, but one that wasn't common for Westerners. Even after marriage, my sister-in-law still couldn't bring herself to address her mother-in-law as Mom or even Auntie Bessie. There was often just a pregnant pause as Patricia looked at her uncertainly, not knowing what to call her.

I guess Adi decided to just go for it and jump right to the heart of the matter. I'm marrying your daughter, so you'll be my mom too.

"Yes, yes, I like you calling me 'Mom,'" smiled Mom, patting his shoulder, which Adi and I both knew translated as a big bear hug in our non-demonstrative Asian culture.

Adi looked at me knowingly as if he'd won the lottery. I grinned at him, thinking, *I'm marrying a sage who knew how to be a saint when necessary.*

Mom came to work every day with me at Pala. She was the perfect partner for my upcoming Christmas feast, a somewhat risky menu for my Balinese kitchen staff.

I'd sold out both lunch seatings. The expats rejoiced when they saw the flyers for roast turkey, something unheard of in Ubud in 2002. I'd sourced the turkey months in advance, making sure to get other essential ingredients such as frozen cranberries.

My cooks swooned when they saw the turkey. Relative to the rest of the world, Balinese and their chickens were tiny in size. A 13-kilogram turkey looked completely foreign and freaked out my team. Even my waitresses, bar staff and cashiers crammed into the kitchen to get a glimpse of the monstrous bird. Mom couldn't stop laughing at their reactions.

I'd never made cranberry sauce before; neither had Mom, who also detested the goopy, cloyingly sweet concoction. This was the age before Google, so Mom and I decided to wing it. We tested a small batch by cooking the frozen cranberries with some of our homemade pineapple jam and a splash of Cointreau at the end.

I asked Mom to taste it first, scared that we'd made a mess before we'd even started. "Well? What do you think?"

"It's delicious. I don't usually like cranberry sauce, but I could eat a whole bowl of this!"

"Yeah! Let's call this Bessie and Frances's Cranberry Pineapple Cointreau Compote!"

On Christmas, we crowded into the kitchen at sunrise to stuff the turkey, which barely fit into the oven, and help prepare the rest of the elaborate meal. My kitchen team cranked out the sides. Guests arrived for the first seating at 11:30 a.m.

We pulled out the turkey a few hours later and I held my breath as Mom cut into it. It was perfectly roasted, with the juices running clear. Mom and I actually hugged each other in relief!

Mom dutifully took on the job of head turkey carver. My team and I raced to plate; we piled generous portions of the succulent meat beside our fluffy mashed potato, sautéed vegetables and a cute little banana leaf dish of our signature cranberry compote. Our Christmas lunch was a smashing success. Years later, Mom and I still giggle when we remember the faces of my Balinese team meeting a turkey for the first time.

Christmas and New Year's are usually Bali's peak seasons. However, terrorism now trumped tourism. The events of 9/11 had scared off travellers, but the October bomb thwarted any chance of recovery, driving the island into further economic decline. Due to the lack of tourists, Adi and I turned our attention to a potentially more explosive situation – the meeting of the future in-laws.

We were gathered at a long wooden table facing the ocean at Bela, the local seafood warung in Jimbaran. Everyone, including me, was oddly silent. Among my mom, Adi's parents, Adi and I, there wasn't a single common language. Adi had to translate between his parents and Mom and me, and the words were not forthcoming. Bapak and Ibu rarely ate out, and certainly not at a beach café in Jimbaran with the mother of their future daughter-in-law. Their discomfort was palpable.

If Mom's first meeting with Fong Fong could be described as lukewarm, her first meeting with Ibu was glacial. We faced the last bright rays of the sunset at Jimbaran Beach as well as the stone glare of Adi's mother. Even the warm smiles of Bapak and Adi couldn't thaw the ice.

Mom muttered under her breath in Cantonese, "Let's go pick the seafood."

I sprang from my seat. Adi rose and followed me after encouraging his parents to enjoy the view.

Mom continued in Cantonese, asking why Adi's mother was so unfriendly. With my limited Chinese vocabulary, I didn't have the words "depressed" or "uncomfortable," so I whispered that we'd talk about it later, looking pointedly at the back of Adi's head. Mom nodded and continued towards the back of the warung.

Made, the spice maker and my moped driver, still manned the tables. He grinned as we ignored the printed menu and dove into the fish tanks with our hands. Mom selected several live crabs trying to claw their way out of the tanks while I picked through jumbo prawns, sniffing and squeezing each one, tossing only the freshest ones onto the antique scale, and Adi felt the firmness of a glistening red snapper while peeking under its gills to check for freshness.

Ibu finally smiled when the drinks and food arrived at our table. All of the seafood had been expertly grilled with spicy tomato sambal and served with blanched *kangkung* (morning glory) and steaming white rice. I immediately heaped rice, crab, fish and prawns onto Ibu and Bapak's plates, serving them first. Mom smiled her approval.

Food always united families. I grinned when Adi's parents happily dug into the food. My shoulders finally relaxed when Mom became too preoccupied with tackling the crab to pay attention to Ibu's facial expressions. Her focus pivoted back to the meal, begging me to try some of the crab that she'd carefully picked out of the shell.

"No, Mom, I don't like crab. It's totally not worth the effort. It's like diet food. You spend more energy trying to get the meat than what you eat. You actually lose weight eating crab. You should eat these instead." I effortlessly plucked another succulent prawn from its shell and popped the whole thing into my mouth.

"Darling, this crab is really good. Tender and sweet. Try some," Adi insisted as he gave me a precious pile of meat that he'd spent the last ten minutes prying out of the shell.

Not to be outdone, Mom shoved a small pile of crabmeat onto my plate too.

"Mom, you know what? You know that saying, 'Marry someone like your father.' I'm marrying my mother!" I giggled as Adi reached up and brushed yet another smear of sambal from my chin. "See what I mean?"

We couldn't get back to the privacy of Mom's room fast enough; Mom, an extreme extrovert, had admirably held her opinions throughout the meal and the drive back to Ubud.

Mom sat down on the daybed and started with, "Frances, have you thought about what marrying Adi means?"

"Of course!" I snapped back. "I'm not a child, Mom."

"Don't talk back to me. I'm just telling you things that you need to know. If your mom doesn't tell you, who will? You'll live with Adi's parents. In the same house. You can't even live with me, your own mother," Mom countered and strengthened her argument. "You're very independent. Used to getting things your way."

Trying to hold it together and calm down, I replied, "I know Mom, but I'll learn to deal with it. Adi says that his mom is like that with everyone. It's not personal. I don't know. Maybe she's never gotten over Wayan's death."

"That was a long time ago right? Like over twenty years?" Mom asked.

"Yes, but do you ever get over your first child dying? I can't judge her, Mom. Please just trust me. I'll figure it out. Adi promises to always protect me."

Thankfully, I had other human shields for the rest of the time Mom was in Bali, so we no longer had to bring up Adi's mom again.

After spending Christmas in Singapore, Nate, Rachel and their four-month-old, Mindy, came to Bali to bask in the sun for a week before heading back to the minus-forty Celsius windchill of frigid Toronto. Rachel moaned of her exhaustion from the long-haul travel and not having Nate around due to his punishing hours at work. Nate's stress simmered just under the skin; his lips pursed and forehead wrinkled as he changed yet another wet diaper.

Mom and I moved with them to the 5-star luxury of Le Meridien. We were all happier. Adi pampered me every day at the spa where we'd first met fifteen months earlier. Adi also arranged two of the best masseuses (no Puji in sight) for Nate for his daily four-hands indulgence. Genuine smiles appeared across his face as he wondered if he could export Sri and Wardani to Canada.

In their private plunge pool, Nate bounced Mindy as she gurgled in delight. Nate laughed unrestrained. New parenting was a phase not to be endured but experienced. I tucked this away for my future self. Parenting moments were snatches of time, ephemeral at best – FAPs collected when you weren't expecting them. My heart also softened for Ibu. Losing a child must be the worst experience for a parent. To have moments like this violently torn away from you forever, it must be unbearable.

"Honey, why are you so exhausted? There are hardly any tourists on the island," I asked as I nestled into the crook between Adi's oversized shoulder and muscular chest.

"The golfers booked massages that required strong pressure, so I ended up working back-to-back for all eight hours. They're here for the tournament."

"What tournament?"

"It's not a big deal; I mean, Tiger Woods isn't playing. Only the number two guy." Adi yawned sleepily.

I sat up, switching on the bedside lamp. "You mean Ernie Els is playing at Nirwana?"

"Yeah, yeah. That's his name. I think the other guy is called Nick something."

"Nick Faldo?" I squeaked incredulously.

"That sounds familiar."

"Oh my God! Why are they here? Can we go? What time does it start? Does it cost anything to watch?" Out tumbled my questions.

Adi squinted at me. "I thought we were sleeping in tomorrow. It starts around 8:00, but it's Sunday, my day off. You want me to go to work? To watch these guys hit a ball?"

Shoving him excitedly, I exclaimed, "Yes, of course! You won't be working; we'll be watching Ernie Els LIVE! I can't even believe it. This is epic, like once-in-a-lifetime epic. So why are they here again?"

"It's a charity event in support of Bali. Our occupancy is less than fifteen percent. The layoffs are starting this month." Adi's eyebrows creased in worry.

"Business has dropped right off for Pala too. Brenda said that they'll only be able to keep me until our wedding."

Panic crossed Adi's face, "If you stop working there, what'll we do? There are no jobs in Bali."

"There's always my backup plan," I hesitantly divulged.

"Backup plan? What backup plan?" Adi sat up, rubbing his eyes.

"I think that if I call Drew, my old boss at *The Toronto Star*, I can get a job. Not what I want to do, but it's the easiest way for us to save money and come back to Bali when things are better."

"You mean we'd move to Canada? What would I do?"

Creasing my eyebrows, I wondered aloud, "I have no idea how immigration works. I guess we'll need to start looking into it, but my bigger concern is your parents. Don't we have to live with them once we're married? I mean, we're the only ones taking care of them, right? And what about all the Banjar duties?"

"As I'm the only son, my dad can take over my Banjar responsibilities for me whenever I can't do it. It's like he's my backup, and my mom is yours. If we live in Canada, they would take the duties for us. It's never happened before, but I guess we don't have a choice."

"But would your parents agree to this? I can't imagine they would allow you to leave Bali."

"Well, let's hope that doesn't happen and that tourists come back soon. But if they don't, you'll have to call Drew." Adi put his head back down, closing his eyes as sleep overcame him again.

In the seriousness of our conversation, I'd forgotten why I'd turned the lights again back on. *Ah, the golf tournament – Ernie Els, Nick Faldo. There's no way that I'd miss that. I better let Adi sleep since I'm going to wake him early tomorrow.*

I'd been away from golf for almost a year now. It was a luxury that I could no longer justify, especially when saving up for our wedding. Despite working at Le Meridien for five years, watching the tournament was Adi's first time on the golf course.

My mouth gaped open as we walked over to the first hole, where there were only a handful of spectators. Usually, in the tournaments that I'd attended in Canada, such as the Bell Canadian Open or the one at Nicklaus North in Whistler, there were hundreds if not thousands watching. So much so that I'd never actually seen any professionals hit, only seeing the backs of other spectators, maybe ten people deep.

Now, I was standing here while four golf legends: Ernie Els, Nick Faldo, Vijay Singh and Justin Rose bantered back and forth as if they were alone on the course. I shook my head in disbelief. If I stepped a bit closer, I could actually touch Ernie as he prepared to tee off. There wasn't any need for a referee to call silence. The twenty or so of us, including the four golfers and their caddies, were already hushed in anticipation.

Ernie stepped up to his ball, settled into his stance and swung. His ball sailed past the coconut trees and landed perfectly on the fairway. So this was how this course was meant to be played – golf in its highest form.

We walked behind the players a respectable distance away – for the entire eighteen holes – observing every shot of each player. Us spectators even laughed along as the golfers joked and teased each other for a missed putt that didn't matter. We could hear their entire conversation. It was surreal.

Adi whispered in my ear with a wide grin on his face, "Darling, you are so cute. I've never seen you like this. You're actually bouncing as we walk on the grass."

I looked down at my running shoes. Yes, I did feel like I was walking on clouds. I was blissfully happy.

I squeezed Adi's hand tighter and pulled him in for a quick hug. "Thank you so much for bringing me here. This feels like a dream."

When Adi and I reminisce about that day, I get a dreamy look on my face and repeat for the thousandth time, "I saw Ernie hit over and over again. I still can't believe it."

Adi wisely replied, "This is how God works, darling. Everyone was worried about Bali having no tourists because of the bomb. Yet because of the bomb, your favourite golfers came to support Bali. And you were one of the lucky ones who got to watch them."

Eleven days later, in the middle of greeting two customers at Pala, an excruciating pain made me gasp for air. One of the ladies settled me back onto the wooden bench, where I promptly fainted. Thankfully, the two ladies were nurses and immediately positioned me on my side as my body went into shock.

My strongest cooks and bartenders, all men, picked me up, piled me into the van and took me back to Stardust Cottages. A doctor rushed over but couldn't determine anything wrong and prescribed me iron pills for low blood pressure. My head cook stood by, shaking his head in great remorse and apologized for making my food too spicy.

Suryani shook her head, tutting that it better not be Black Magic again. When I laughed out loud in nervousness, my insides felt like they were going to rip apart.

For over two years, I'd been having mysterious stomach pains that doctors in Toronto, Hong Kong and Bali had not yet properly diagnosed. Not one doctor had given me a clear reason for the sharp, debilitating stabbing in my lower right stomach that would suddenly come on without warning and disappear minutes or hours later.

Adi had taken me to BIMC, an international clinic of so-called "expat experts" whenever I keeled over in pain, but often my symptoms dissipated by the time we made the arduous one-hour drive from Ubud to BIMC. The prim doctors, with their lilting Scottish accents, prescribed useless painkillers and of course, the requisite iron pills for every "female" problem.

These doctors' visits had curtailed our precious downtime, needed for our various wedding tasks. Adi and I had to become even more resourceful and efficient, tying my doctor's appointments to my kebaya fittings, both on Jalan Ngurah Rai. Whenever my pains abated, I prayed that I was miraculously cured of the unknown ailment. However, things had become worse as we crept closer to our wedding date.

The following morning, Adi took me to Sanglah, the biggest public hospital on the island, where specialist doctors must contribute a daily shift before going to their private practices. Everything about Sanglah horrified me. Instead of gleaming ceramic tiles smelling of antiseptic, I nervously avoided smeared blood dotted here and there on the floors of the crowded open-air corridors.

"Adi," I whimpered. "Isn't there anywhere else we can go?"

"I'm sorry, darling, but this is the only hospital with the complete equipment to check out what's wrong with your stomach." Squeezing my hand in encouragement, Adi pressed on through the sticky, foul-smelling patients waiting at Emergency.

A nurse took my blood and urine samples while a radiologist led me into a freezing room for X-rays. Lying in a flimsy green robe, I felt totally exposed as an attending doctor looked at my charts.

He pointed to a small blob on the X-ray and calmly stated, "Your appendix here is inflamed. I recommend that we remove it immediately before it bursts."

"What?" I paled and grabbed onto Adi's hand, stammering, "You...you can determine this by looking at an X-ray?"

"Well, it's not one-hundred percent conclusive. I wish we could do an ultrasound, but our machine is broken," the doctor said with a shrug.

"Broken? Maybe we'll go to a private clinic and get the ultrasound first." I was already pulling my capris back on under the robe.

"Well, I wouldn't wait. If the appendix bursts, it can be fatal."

"Okay, I understand. I'm going to get changed and we'll settle the bill. We'll come back as soon as possible," I said, while thinking there was no way in hell that I was ever coming back here again.

The bill was outrageously expensive, but I handed over my credit card and paid, knowing that Pala covered my medical costs. I reached for my blood tests and the X-rays, but the nurse shook her head and haughtily said, "These belong to the hospital."

"I just paid a ridiculous amount of money for these tests, so they're mine. The hospital has no use for them. I do. Please can you help me out here?" I begged.

"Sorry," she said, giving me a smug and condescending grin as she turned to gouge the next patient.

"Sorry, my ass," I mumbled under my breath as I swiped the entire file off the counter, sending all the other files flying. I grabbed Adi's hand and ran out the door. We both rushed to the car, which Adi had parked on the street, and jumped in. A security guard caught up by the time Adi started the engine. Knowing the guard had no weapons, Adi smirked at him and gave him a wave as the car shot off.

"I hate people like them, abusing the tiny bit of power they think they have," I complained as we drove, and then I burst out laughing. "Did you see her face? She was in complete shock. And all those papers flew off the counter! It was like out of a movie."

"I can't believe we just did that, but that nurse didn't give you a choice." Adi shook his head as he focused on the road. "I'm going to take you to Mas Clinic. It's the closest one in Ubud. Let's pray that they have an ultrasound machine. It is common for pregnant women, right?"

"I hope so, but if Sanglah doesn't have a working one, that's kinda scary."

We were at the reception of the clinic in Mas, which to my relief looked a thousand times cleaner than Sanglah.

Adi turned back to me, "Well, the good news is that they have a brand-new ultrasound machine."

"And the bad news is?"

"The only person that knows how to use it works on Tuesday nights."

"You mean Tuesday, as in four days from now?"

"Yes." Adi looked defeated. "I'll take you back to Pala so you can check in and tell the staff that you're okay. Let me think about our next options."

Back at Pala, an American couple who'd dined with us the day before was back for afternoon tea. They waved me over and immediately noticed how pale I looked.

"Are you okay? I think you better sit down," the husband, Sam, said, motioning.

"Oh. Thank you. Yes, it's been pretty crazy. I fainted yesterday, and the doctor at the main hospital says that I need an appendix operation. So I'm kind of freaking out. I can't tell my mom, or else she'll have me flown out to Singapore."

"The doctor told you that you need your appendix out? This is serious. Do you know what happens if it bursts?"

Shaking my head, I prayed that wouldn't happen.

My eyes grew bigger as Sam continued, "Well, I do. My appendix burst a few years ago, and it was the most excruciating pain I've ever experienced. Even talking about it makes me cringe. The toxins from a burst appendix go into your bloodstream, essentially poisoning other organs. I spent more than a month recovering in hospital, and the cost was insane."

"If my fiancé were here right now, he'd say that you're a 'Sign from God.' How is it that the first person I talk to after going to two hospitals today has direct experience of a burst appendix? Thank you so much." I grabbed his hand in appreciation.

"No problem, but you better get to a hospital fast. Don't let that burst. I can't imagine what the hospitals are like here."

"Yeah, believe me, you don't want to know." I shivered as images of smeared blood and dirty beds came back to me unbidden.

After I relayed Sam's warnings and Suryani's other concerns about Black Magic, Adi said, "I'm taking you to Kakek Kuta. We should check the spiritual side too."

"Agh! Do we have to?" I cringed thinking about the visits to his family's Balinese Balian (healer), whom we called Kakek Kuta. I'd experienced his harrowing healing practices on my weak left ankle, which I'd broken at age eleven and had never healed properly.

Going to a Balian's house is the opposite of going to the doctor. In place of a pristine, clean doctor's office, you enter a family compound. Kakek Kuta's home hid behind a small entryway wedged between two shops selling handicrafts on one side and flip-flops on the other. Several generations lived, huddled together, in a warren of rooms edging the compound, surrounding a small open courtyard and a low terrace – layered with years of grime and dirt – where Kakek Kuta healed his patients. Kakek Kuta examined each patient to determine if the cause of the illness was medical or magic. From there, he'd try to cure the patient of the ailment. He might prescribe a traditional herbal tonic or extract a deadly curse. That was the last place I wanted to go.

We made a detour to Dr. Oka, the doctor in charge at Le Meridien. Adi needed a doctor's certificate to excuse himself from work. When he explained that he needed two days off work to take me to the hospital, Dr. Oka asked to see my charts, including the X-ray.

The second Dr. Oka glanced at the X-ray, he agreed that my appendix looked inflamed. He suspected that I had chronic appendicitis, which is very difficult to diagnose as the pain comes and goes, sometimes over a matter of months or years.

"Yes, yes! That's me!" I exclaimed, relieved that a competent doctor finally diagnosed me correctly. Dr. Oka referred me to an obstetrician-gynecologist in Denpasar who would definitely have an ultrasound machine. This doctor could confirm if I needed the operation. From there, he wanted me to go directly to Prima Medica, a private hospital.

Another Godsend. Adi took us to the OB/GYN clinic, dismissing the idea of Kakek Kuta, to my great relief. We waited for over an hour to finally get into the office only to find a junior doctor standing in for his boss that evening.

Adi spent considerable time explaining what we needed.

Adi turned to me with despair set in his eyes, "Darling, stay calm while I tell you what the problem is, okay? He can't do the ultrasound on the right stomach as he's an OB/GYN doctor, not a specialist for the appendix."

I whispered back in fear, "You're kidding me, right?"

"No, I'm not." Distress crossed his face.

I breathed in and smiled at the doctor, ignoring the strong urge to flip his desk over and do the ultrasound myself. "Okay, please ask him to do the ultrasound anyways. He can scan my entire stomach and just tell us if that area looks inflamed. We won't hold him to it. Or he can just swipe the ultrasound over that area and print it out. We don't need him to diagnose me."

Adi leaned in earnestly, and with his gentle coaxing, the doctor gave me the ultrasound which confirmed the worst.

If I was going to die under a knife a few short months before my wedding, there was one more thing to do; I insisted that we get a good Chinese meal before checking into the hospital. Adi shook his head as he watched me inhale greasy plates of stir-fried beef and sweet and sour pork ribs while wolfing down the rice with my chopsticks.

Adi and I both exhaled a sigh of relief as I climbed into the bed in my pristine room at Prima Medica, a brand-new private hospital. Adi's parents and Suaji sat in the comfortable sofas, glancing at me anxiously. Oddly, I wasn't scared. I felt like I'd checked into a 5-star resort.

I hadn't called my mom; if something happened to me during the operation, I figured that her worrying wouldn't help. As I pondered my decision, Ibu brought out canang offerings and incense. Adi explained that they'd do special prayers at the hospital temple shrines to ensure a safe operation. Ah, better to have faith than fear.

The next morning at 5:00 a.m., Adi shook me awake and helped me onto the gurney. He squeezed my hand tightly as they wheeled me to the operating table while Bapak followed. Ibu had rushed off to give the offerings. I'd never seen two faces more fearful than Adi and Bapak's as the double doors swung closed on them.

"Water…water please," I whispered, my voice not able to scratch out the words. After what felt like an eternity, a nurse noticed that I was indeed alive and in need of water.

A steady stream of visitors drifted in and out of my room including

Brenda, my Pala staff and Suryani and her boyfriend, Edu. Mom was beside herself when I called and told her the good news that my ailing appendix was now in a glass jar beside my hospital bed. She didn't find me funny at all. She only calmed down when I told her that I found the best Chinese food in all of Bali. Where? In the hospital!

53

$\mathcal{A}$di drove like a snail, maneuvering carefully around deep potholes or piles of stone on the road back to Ubud. I sighed in relief as we pulled into the parking lot of Stardust Cottages and then screamed as Adi slammed the door and shook the car.

"Oh my God, I'm so sorry, darling. Are you okay?" Adi rushed around the car and opened my door ever so gently now, steadying me as I got out.

"I don't know whether to laugh or cry. You tried so hard to keep the car from shaking during the entire two-hour drive and then you slam the door after being so careful. I can't laugh or cry. Or this cut across my stomach will hurt even more."

I shuffled slowly up to our suites trying to maintain an even keel. There I found a letter from Brenda saying that she could no longer afford me and would cover only a portion of the expensive appendix operation. Now that really hurt.

Adi looked panicked as I read the letter to him, "Darling, without your job here, I don't think we can stay in Bali. There just aren't any jobs here. I think you have to call Drew."

Calling Drew renewed my faith that years of hard work were valued and not easily forgotten. In that one call, he told me that I could come back, not as a director, but he guaranteed me a managerial position and told me to start packing for Toronto.

After talking to Drew, I found Brenda in her office. I sat down and said that I would've expected her to come talk to me, not leave a letter under my door. Her face dropped in embarrassment. Here was a wildly successful women, ten years my senior, who hadn't had the courage to face me. Before I moved out, she came to give me a wedding gift of the white linens trimmed with navy from her sewing room. She wouldn't be coming to my wedding after all, as she'd decided to head home to Brisbane for a few months.

A few days later, I found myself homeless but welcomed into my future husband's home on February 27th – two months and six days before our wedding. Once the shock of being tossed out of Stardust Cottages, a place that I'd considered home for the previous two years, wore off, I turned my thoughts to my future with Adi.

Adi took all this in stride. I guess that everything we did was unconventional, so why not have the bride move in before marriage? I'm not sure his parents felt the same, but I didn't understand Balinese. Even if they complained day and night about me, I would be none the wiser.

The new dining room was our temporary bedroom. As a local construction worker and carpenter who built homes in the village, Adi's dad had installed intricately carved wooden frames, windows and a sturdy door to the dining room just days before my arrival. Adi draped sheets over the windows to guard our privacy.

Typical of most Balinese family compounds, each building was built as needed and as funds allowed. The buildings wrapped around an open central courtyard paved with interlocking cement tiles. Every family temple must be in the holiest corner of the compound, which is determined by the direction facing Mount Agung, the most sacred place in Bali. For most of Bali, this was the northeast corner of a compound. In northern villages such as Lovina, the family temple was situated in the southwest corner.

As Adi's father was the head of the family, Bapak and Ibu's building sat beside the family temple. The most easterly room was the *Kamar Suci* (prayer room) where Ibu's Goddess had a shrine. Ibu was *Pemangku Dalem* (the Queen), a highly revered position in the village temple. The adjoining room was their bedroom, and their private sitting room spanned the front of these two smaller rooms.

Outside Bapak and Ibu's rooms, a sizable terrace paved with orange-brown ceramic stretched in front of two bedrooms that Adi's parents rented out called *kos* – small rooms which tourism workers lived in to be close to their workplace.

The two westerly rooms that were now Adi's rooms were initially built as *kos* rooms. Adi moved there as a teenager when the southerly rooms built by his grandfather decades earlier started crumbling and were no longer safe. These rooms, barely standing, were used for storage with a small *bale* area reserved for ceremonies such as our upcoming wedding.

Throughout the compound, cracked paint bubbled up on the walls because of the humidity and torrential tropical rains. No matter how many times Adi's dad stripped and repainted, water would eventually creep up and ruin the walls. To counter this, we left the new cement walls of the dining room and kitchen unfinished. We reasoned that without any paint, there wouldn't be any to peel.

Adi hired our neighbours to build a new stone gate to replace the small wooden gate that had been around since his grandfather's time, to mark our new beginning. Adi selected Kerobokan stone, a hard charcoal stone flecked with black and quarried from the river where he'd splashed and climbed tropical trees to snatch ripe mangoes or guava. I was rather critical of the finished gate, as the craftsmen had not followed Adi's instructions (a pervasive problem here).

Adi wrung his hands in frustration, "Darling, it can't be fixed. I don't think anyone actually notices except us."

"But we're the ones who will live with this gate for generations!" I wailed, failing to understand how distressed Adi already was with my disappointed pout.

"I'm so sorry. I don't know what to say. I tried my hardest, but we've been so busy that I haven't had time to sit here and watch the workers."

When I looked at Adi's sad face, I snapped back from my fantasy of perfection. What was wrong with me? Of course, Adi didn't want mistakes. I had to let go of my absurd expectations. I gathered him into a big bear hug and apologized for my overreaction.

Balinese compounds don't have built-in closets, so we needed to buy a new wardrobe to house my stuff. Adi and I found a large mahogany wardrobe selling well below its value because of the lack of tourists. I felt guilty for spending money we didn't have, but Adi countered that the wardrobe was an investment, one that would stay in our family for generations.

Sorting and organizing my belongings into the wardrobe was a slow and comforting process that helped me assess my situation calmly. I had no desire to move back to Toronto, but this might be a Godsend for the beginning of our marriage. At Jasmine, we'd been surrounded by staff and friends. Here in Adi's compound, we were surrounded by his parents and neighbours.

I'd already found one nosy neighbour rifling through my underwear (hence the urgent need for the wardrobe) and another had inhaled a special box of chocolates that Mom had given me for Christmas. Adi wasn't exaggerating when he told me that everyone in our village knew everything about everyone. I was quickly accepted into Adi's community because of my open face and constant laughter. My laugh, which had marked me as different and distinct most of my life, was now a magnet; people would holler greetings to me at the morning market and wave to me as Adi and I sped off on his motorbike to the beach.

The only nut I couldn't crack was Ibu; she rarely smiled. I'd bounce out of bed, greeting Bapak and Ibu with a chorus of *Selamat Pagi* (good mornings). While Bapak would chime *pagi* back, Ibu would just grunt. I wasn't sure what to make of this, but Adi encouraged me to just be who I am.

Maybe this move to Toronto would be a perfect solution; I could just be who I was without judgement, and Adi would experience my hometown and get to know my family and friends. Adi had never been outside of Bali. Things could be a lot worse than landing a lucrative job with just one phone call. I'd been gone for five years, but I'd be returning to *The Star*, a place of comfort and camaraderie. I reminded myself, *Consider this a "Sign from God" that you're truly blessed.* We'd hunker down for five years, enough time to have kids within the free Canadian medical system and stash away our earnings in dollars, and then move back to Bali when tourism recovered.

This was just a temporary detour from life in Bali, a new beginning for both of us: the great Canadian adventure.

Our wedding preparations took on a fevered pitch as we entered March, only two months away from our wedding. But this didn't stop the cycle of Balinese ceremonies.

Adi and I joined a handful of expat friends at La Lucciola on Petitenget Beach to witness the incredible Melasti Day ceremonies. Thousands of Balinese descended on the beach on this day. Women, men and children walked 7 kilometres in the scorching sun alongside chariots carrying the God statues, with the walking gamelan band's energetic music pulling them forward.

The energy on the beach was electric. Pemangku faced the ocean ringing holy brass bells while chanting mantras over piles of offerings arranged on top of bamboo mats laid out over the beach. Studded across a kilometre of the white sand beach were large chariots – painted crimson, black and golds – holding the statues of the temple Gods. These chariots stood proudly behind the priests performing the symbolic cleansing ceremonies for the Gods before the Balinese New Year, three days later.

From time to time, we'd hear screams as a Pemangku, dressed from top to toe in white, rushed towards the sea in a trance with others pulling him back from the crashing waves. Lumpia and sate sellers added to the din of noise as they peddled their spicy snacks. Balinese ladies covered their heads with colourful scarves and huddled together under the few palm trees to shield themselves from the noontime sun.

I memorized the scene, knowing that Adi and I would ache for this when we lived in Toronto. Nothing else compared to life in Bali.

The next event leading up to the Balinese New Year was the Ogoh Ogoh parade. The young generation leapt about, adrenaline running high as the teenage boys hoisted the Ogoh Ogoh onto their shoulders while the younger boys carried their miniature Ogoh Ogoh ahead of the gigantic monster. I joined the smattering of teenage girls to walk beside Adi as he played in the *reong* (the gamelan marching band). I didn't care that I was at least a decade older than the teenagers in the parade. I revelled in the glow of the fire torches, flickering in the blackness of the dark moon, lighting the way for the Ogoh Ogoh.

Imagine Halloween on steroids, where twenty of these giant monsters marched along the darkened streets with their own gamelan band, ending up at the main crossroad for a final duel, with one Ogoh Ogoh winning the village competition. Our Banjar was exceptionally ambitious with one of the best gamelan groups in Bali, playing a unique rhythmic song written by the head of our gamelan. Every time the gamelan hit the chorus, we'd all sing and yelp right along.

Two years earlier on the day tour with Robert, I'd collected photos of Ogoh Ogoh to rack up my FAPs. I realized at this moment that I'd forgotten to keep track of FAPs for many months. As I looked around at the radiant faces celebrating together, I raised my torch in victory, acknowledging that my whole life had magically transformed into one continuous adventure!

If you peeked into our compound the following day, you'd never know it was Nyepi Day, also known as Silent Day, where no movement, fire, fun or work was allowed.

Family members and our closest neighbours had snuck down our laneway before sunrise and now sat silently on our terrace, surrounded by hundreds of coconut leaves, bamboo skewers, and pieces of offerings ready to be assembled. Their hands moved like lighting, a flurry of non-stop activity as some women expertly cut into the coconut leaves while others stitched them together with bamboo sticks, as thin as needles.

My future mother-in-law was clever, recruiting a large team of offering makers for our wedding on Nyepi – a day they'd otherwise be at home sleeping.

It's extremely unusual for Balinese to marry outside of their culture. Moving into Adi's family compound before our wedding was unheard of. Because of our unique circumstances, I experienced the makings of a Balinese wedding firsthand. All Balinese weddings are held at the groom's family compound, not in a temple or a church. Since my "family compound" (a.k.a. Mom's condo) was in Toronto, Ibu decided to incorporate the bridal part into the groom's part of the ceremonies – the first time this had ever been done in Kerobokan, if not all of Bali.

Foreigners rarely got a glimpse of the inner workings of a real Balinese ceremony and suddenly, I was smack dab in the heart of this magical culture.

5 4

*A*di and I were so engrossed with wedding tasks that we paid little attention to the emergence of a new coronavirus. By early April, SARS hit Hong Kong, Singapore, Taipei and Toronto.

One friend after another emailed to say they had to cancel their trip to Bali. My brother Ken feared flying with my baby niece, Maia, who was only seven months old. I agreed with him immediately, not wanting to risk their health. Bertram, one of my best friends from biz school, and his wife Alexandra had booked two weeks off their banking jobs in New York for our wedding. With the onset of SARS, they didn't have an additional two weeks to quarantine upon arrival back to the States. Other friends in Toronto and the U.S. faced the same dilemma. Cancellations poured in.

I sank deeper and deeper into depression, spending days huddled in the dining room cum bedroom. Adi and Bapak had broken down the wall separating Adi's two rooms to make one long room, measuring 7 metres by 2.5 metres, to become our new bedroom, but Bapak was still busy installing ceramic tiles.

My heart fell into my stomach the moment I heard Grace's voice over the phone. "I'm so sorry, Fran. I'm actually in Queenstown with the girls. I meant to call you earlier, but I was still hopeful that I'd come even if Jonathan and the girls couldn't."

"It's okay, Grace. I understand, but why are you in New Zealand?"

"I had no idea how bad SARS was. A few days ago, Jonathan went into the office, and they split the entire team into two. They figure if half of the team gets taken out by SARS, the other half can still keep the company alive," Grace said, stumbling over her words as she told me the story. "That very day, they moved half of every department to another location in remote Hong Kong. When his office did this, Jonathan put me and the girls on a plane to New Zealand that very evening!"

"Oh my God! This is insane. I'm so glad that you're safe."

"Well, actually, there's another reason why I might've not been able to come even without SARS looming over us… I'm pregnant."

"WHAT!!" I screamed, "That's amazing! I'm so happy for you. How are you feeling?"

After getting off the phone with Grace, my excitement evaporated, and I collapsed in Adi's arms.

"Honey," I hiccupped through tears, "Grace can't come."

"Darling, I know this looks really bad right now, but…God gave us SARS for a reason."

That knocked my tears aside right away. "What are you talking about? How can you think that anything good is happening here? Ken probably can't come, my biz school friends can't make it, Kai Ma and her entire contingent from Hong Kong have cancelled, Grace is in NEW ZEALAND. And the worst thing is that SARS is in all the cities where my family and friends live: Toronto, Hong Kong and Singapore. And even worse, if people could come, Hong Kong, Singapore and Taipei are the only cities that they can transfer through to get to Bali from North America. This is unbelievable. What good reason is there for this to be happening to me?" I shouted, my hands gesturing uncontrollably as I raged on.

"Think about it. Our overseas guest list was 120 people. Now it's about twenty, right? We can move our Chinese tea ceremony from Pala to Begawan Giri. I'm pretty sure that we can afford it now."

"WHAT?" I screamed again, this time drawing my future parents-in-law into the dining room to see what all the yelling was about. "Begawan Giri… You mean it? We could have the tea ceremony and dinner there?" I shouted as I sat back down on the bed in disbelief.

"I don't see why not. It's your dream wedding place. Let's do it."

"Oh my God, you're the most amazing person in the world. And so smart. I would never have thought of this idea."

"You might've if you had stayed calm." Adi's eyes twinkled as he lifted my chin to kiss me.

"Well, that's why I'm marrying you. You're my calm."

Adi and I zoomed up to Begawan Giri that very day. I had spent endless hours crafting the dinner reception menu for Pala, so I launched into specific details that usually took months to decide on. The executive chef held his hand up to stop my barrage to ask who the event was for; he'd gotten accustomed to having me arrange events for other guests.

He threw his head back in laughter when I replied, "This is for Adi and me!"

We galloped to the finish line. Each Sunday, women from our village descended onto our terrace, covering the entire 3 metres by 5 metres with palm leaves, rice cakes, sugarcane, dried coconut, and an assortment of mysterious items that they'd transform into hundreds of wedding offerings.

I hopped around with my camera attempting to document each offering from beginning to end, but it was nearly impossible – the women's hands worked too quickly to follow. I planned to make a scrapbook that I could study on my own. There wasn't a step-by-step process; they just knew what to do. How I was ever to learn skills that everyone else had picked up as children? I figured that if I recorded everything, I'd have a head start on my life as a Balinese wife.

I soon learned that the only way to learn was to sit on the terrace and follow along. I was slow, but making offerings was similar to wrapping dumplings, which I'd done since I was four years old. There was a lot of laughing at my mistakes, especially when I blamed the bamboo stick for breaking. However, my heart swelled as neighbour after neighbour bent over my hands and helped adjust my technique – or lack thereof!

Men contributed at night. You'd find our neighbours sprawled out on the floor doing various tasks: a few wielded sharp knives to cut and carve bamboo into thousands of Balinese sate skewers, others tore palm leaves from their stalks and wove them together into a crisscross pattern of mats, and several others erected posts and a roof structure around our compound. The woven mats covered the temporary roof structure and would shelter us from the sun. With our wedding in May – the start of Bali's dry season – rain was not expected.

These two months living in a real Balinese compound revealed a whole new world to me. I couldn't believe that our neighbours and our Banjar devoted so many days and nights in the preceding months to help us. I'd learned from my Pala staff that all their days off were spent preparing for and participating in ceremonies, but I'd never understood why. Now I'd experienced what "it takes a village" meant. How I would be forever tied to this community when Adi and I returned from Canada. I felt like the luckiest person in the world.

55

THE WEDDING

’d adhered to the tradition of not seeing the groom the night before our wedding. My family stayed with me at Le Meridien Resort where I had first met Adi – that significant encounter that had led me to this moment.

The navy and gold silk sarong had been hand painted with hot wax and dyed to create a sumptuous masterpiece of tiny brushstrokes. I wrapped the sarong around my waist, tying it in the traditional way for a Balinese bride, displaying the fluttering butterflies and lively peacocks. I slipped on my custom tailored dark brown silk camisole, which would set off the delicate patterns of my kebaya. Being careful not to tear the fragile French lace, I inched my arms into my wedding kebaya. It fit like a second skin.

Mom opened the safety box and retrieved several soft velvet and silk pouches as well as a long rectangular box. She flipped open the cover of the box vertically to reveal a set of rather gaudy jewels. My first instinct was to reject the necklace immediately, but Mom was quicker. She'd already placed the necklace on my neck and turned me towards the full-length mirror. Mom looked hesitant as I gazed critically at my reflection.

The extravagant necklace transformed me into a royal Balinese bride, and strangely I exclaimed, "This matches perfectly. Thanks, Mom."

Exuberant, Mom clipped on the matching earrings before I changed my mind.

Mom unwrapped a selection of rings that she'd prepared for our Chinese tea ceremony. Our Chinese tea ceremony should have been held before the wedding but was now to be held five days later at Begawan Giri to accommodate everyone's travel schedules.

Firstly, Mom lent me her ring – it was my "something borrowed" – and I slid the South Sea pearl onto the third finger of my right hand. Mom then gave me the ring that Kai Ma had given her to pass to me, a spectacular, rectangular cut emerald. I slid it onto my fourth finger, as Mom and Kai Ma should always be side by side. My father gave me a protective jade ring from my paternal grandmother, which I wore on the third finger of my left hand, beside my engagement ring. Weighed down in family jewels, I carried my family's love and traditions that would go with me into my marriage.

Floating into the hotel's lobby, goosebumps ran up my arm as I took one last look at Tanah Lot Temple as a single woman. This was the exact view that had welcomed me to Bali less than three years earlier, on October 6th, 2000. Today was May 5th, 2003. The widest smile spread across my face as I stepped towards my destiny that was Adi. A calmness descended with a deep knowing that I was blessed by all the Gods and Goddesses of Bali.

As we neared Adi's family compound, tall *penjor* – celebratory offerings made of towering bamboo, palm leaves and strands of rice – waved to me in greeting. Adi, with the help of his young generation, had transformed the entrance overnight. A printed sign reading "Om Swastyastu" stretched across our laneway, hanging off the *penjor*.

Our narrow laneway was crowded with tables piled high with colourful Balinese cakes teetering on *wanci*, traditional Balinese offering trays carved from wood. Adi's aunts greeted guests lined up for the cold sodas, already dripping with condensation at 8:00 a.m.!

I ducked under the stone gate to find hundreds of guests sitting on plastic chairs that covered every available space. Adi rushed over to take my hand and pulled me towards him. My heart beat a little faster as I looked into his kind eyes. Despite being slightly crushed by so many guests and the underlying buzz of chatter, we were suspended in our little bubble of bliss as we grinned at each other. It felt like the most natural thing to be with Adi.

I looked closely at Adi's face and noticed dark circles under his eyes.

My eyebrows drew together as I asked, "Why are you so tired?"

"We finished the decorations at 5:00 a.m. I was up all night, I wanted everything to be perfect," Adi said proudly as he looked around.

I hugged him again. I couldn't believe that he hadn't slept the night before our wedding while I'd slept like a log in a luxurious hotel room.

Behind the throngs of villagers, I could see my friends Greg, Vanessa, Sharon, Crystal, Janet Z. and Judy, sitting together on the rented red and blue plastic seats, facing our family temple. I hopped over and embraced them in crushing hugs. They gingerly hugged me back so as not to mess up my outfit and hair, but I couldn't care less; having my loved ones here in Bali was what really mattered. Mom, Dad, Fong Fong, Andrew, Ken, Patricia, baby Maia, Darren and Miche arrived shortly afterwards and wove through the crowd toward us. Somehow this tiny contingent of my family and friends had overcome all the obstacles – the distance, the Bali bomb, even the risk of SARS – to witness my wedding.

The Balinese treated foreign guests with such respect, giving them the best of whatever they had. In this case, it was the newer plastic seats under the shade of a roof of crisscrossed woven coconut leaves that the neighbours had spent a month making for us. My friends sat in relative comfort with the best view of our wedding ceremonies. I felt slightly uneasy looking at my Balinese Banjar community leaning against posts and sitting on any available step, mopping sweat off their foreheads.

Adi led my family and friends into our family temple. Everything had a mystical sheen; hundreds of Balinese wedding offerings laid out on bamboo mats on the temple floor. Looking around at the pale pink patina of our family shrines, I felt the presence of our ancestors smiling down at the unfolding scene.

Adi's grandfather, Kakek, would lead most of our wedding ceremony while the Pemangku who'd chosen our auspicious date would perform the final ceremonies. I bowed my head and smiled back at his wide grin. We communicated with smiles. I felt nervous as I didn't speak high or even low Balinese, which was how the ceremony would be conducted.

Adi rubbed my wrinkled brow and reassured me, "Just follow me, darling."

I looked into his eyes and knew that I would follow him anywhere. Adi indicated that we had to sit on the bamboo mat beside Kakek. Nervously, I inched my way down and sat with my legs tucked under my knees and my buttocks resting on top of my heels. This was the polite and expected way for a Balinese woman to sit during ceremonies. As a man, Adi could sit cross-legged. How unfair!

My eyebrows drew together in concentration. My body tensed as I wasn't sure how long I could actually sit in this position. One of our neighbours kindly held a Balinese umbrella to shade me.

Older Balinese ladies rushed about, placing burning incense here and there on top of the many offerings laid out in front of us. Kakek lifted his holy bronze bell, rang it three times and the ceremony commenced. Standing near our ancestral shrine facing us, my family and friends stopped chatting. Meanwhile, the Balinese contingent babbled on as though nothing was happening!

Adi guided me through the ceremony. We wafted the incense smoke towards ourselves and then waved the smoke away. We dipped our hands into little bowls of water mixed with crushed leaves. When this was done, Adi gently pulled me up. I hopped up and down to awaken my numb legs.

I'm sure there is an official name for the next part of our ceremony, but for all intents and purposes it could be called "the part to embarrass the bride and make everyone laugh." Adi instructed me to walk around another set of offerings three times, and then sit on the coconut.

"What? Why? No, really? There's no way I can sit on that coconut in this get-up."

Adi pleaded to me with his eyes, "Please try. It's just part of the ceremony. I'll hold on to you. Don't worry."

Adi often failed to warn me of such things. I couldn't blame him, as they were just part of his culture, what he had grown up with. I guess he hadn't stopped to think how odd this would be from my perspective.

I drew in my breath and painted on a frosty smile as I squatted, teetered on the coconut and then kicked it behind me. Everyone cheered as though I'd kicked a winning goal. Our photographer, Pak Agung, was beside himself. He'd taken thousands of photos at hundreds of weddings at The Ritz Carlton, but this was a first! He'd captured a Canadian becoming Balinese.

With my silly grin back on again (for real), we proceeded to a tiny laneway just outside our gate. To my astonishment, I had to kneel again in the most uncomfortable position on a thin bamboo mat covering the uneven rubble and concrete pathway in the staggering heat. Adi's relatives hovered above and behind me, making the small laneway even more claustrophobic and sauna-like. How would my fragile silk sarong survive the day?

As I started to sway, Adi reached for my wedding handkerchief embroidered with love knots. Gazing at me tenderly, Adi wiped droplets of sweat off my brow and from under my eyes. This became my most cherished wedding photo – Pak Agung captured our devotion to each other in one shot.

Adi directed us to our bedroom for the next portion of the ceremony, filling me with panic. Would everyone join us in our most private space? These were our neighbours, people I'd live beside for the rest of my life. Was our bedroom even presentable? Steps away from our bedroom, I surrendered to whatever would happen next. It was clearly out of my control.

Stepping into the cool darkness of our room with the ceiling fan whirling above was a nice reprieve from the heat and crowd outside. Thankfully, only Kakek, Nenek (Adi's grandmother), Bapak, Ibu and Pak Agung, the photographer, joined us for this intimate ceremony. Hundreds of offerings that didn't smell the best were piled high on our bed. We sat gingerly on two plastic stools at the end of our bed, facing the bed and the offerings, while Kakek performed the ceremony beside us. My body relaxed, knowing that I didn't have to sit on the floor here.

Kakek rang the bronze bell to start the ceremony, chanting sacred mantras while continuing to ring the bell in his left hand. Like an early morning songbird, the chime cut above the chatter of the guests in our courtyard. A feeling of total peace enveloped me. We were going to build our life here, on top of all the history of Adi's family. In the room where Adi grew up, we would grow our family. With Adi beside me, his grandfather on his other side, his grandmother at the head of the bed and his parents standing behind us, I knew that I was home.

Next, we pulled my parents back into the family temple to give the bridal offerings. Usually at this point, our entire Banjar would proceed to the bride's home, usually within the same village or sometimes an hour or two away by motorbike, but certainly not overseas to Canada. Ibu had modified the ceremony and laid out the necessary bridal offerings on a table to present to my family's Gods and ancestors with my parents and us as witnesses. As the ceremony began, a handful of raindrops fell from the sky.

Adi's best buddies slapped him on the back, "You're so lucky man, I can't believe you got rain!"

While couples hope to avoid a downpour at all costs by employing rain stoppers – priests who hold off the rain – a sprinkle is most auspicious, as if God was blessing us directly with holy water.

We sat down on our terrace where a trio of *rindik* players had added a lively melody to the increasingly loud buzz of our wedding guests. Village leaders ringed around us and Adi's dad and my mom witnessed as we signed our official wedding documents. Suddenly, there was silence behind us.

Adi pulled me up quickly, "The king is here."

"King? What king?" I whispered back.

"The king of Kerobokan. Sometimes he attends important weddings. Even though I gave him one of our invitations, I wasn't really expecting him to come."

"Ah, okay," I responded, gently pulling my kebaya down and adjusting my sarong.

My cheeks were sore from smiling so widely. Added to that, the overwhelming number of warm bodies huddled so closely together in every inch of Adi's family compound made it feel like a sauna, but I had to make my husband proud. The king was here!

I followed Adi's movements as he took the king's hand and bowed to him and then to the queen. They'd brought with them an entourage of Brahmans, the highest clan in the Balinese caste system, with names like Ida Bagus and Ida Ayu.

My eyes shot open when one distinguished man addressed me in English, "What is your name?"

Adi quickly whispered, "That's Ratu Aji, my guru. Say, 'Ratu Aji, my name is Frances.'"

I quickly caught on, "Nice to meet you, Ratu Aji. My name is Frances."

"So, you like Bali? Since you marry De Adi here." Ratu Aji smirked as he tipped his chin to Adi.

"Yes, I love Bali!" I answered excitedly, a bit surprised that he called Adi by his nickname, De Adi, short for Made Adi.

"What do you like about it?"

"I love Adi of course. And then, there's the delicious food, the ceremonies. All of it."

"You like food? Do you cook?"

"Yes, I love to cook."

"What can you cook?"

"Um. Chinese, Italian, Thai," I said, thinking back to my cooking course in Chiang Mai.

"I like Thai. You cook Thai for me, okay?"

"Now?"

He roared back with a hearty laugh, "No, not now. You are busy with your wedding. Next time."

"Okay. I promise I'll cook you Thai food one day."

Little did I know that seven years later, Ratu Aji would hold me to my promise.

Hours later, after all the ceremonies had ended and the guests had gone, the villagers were back to their compounds and my family back to the resort, my friend Sharon had stayed to chat.

Sharon commented, "Sweetie, the moment I walked through that gate, I could feel the love."

"Ah, the gate. Well, it's not exactly what Adi had planned. He built the gate and planted that mango tree to mark the beginning of our life together," I said, pointing to the lush green tree in the middle of our courtyard.

"Massive gestures of love," Sharon said, nodding her head in approval.

Sheepishly I admitted, "Actually, I freaked out when I first saw it. The gate is supposed to be about half a metre higher, above the roof of the dining room, not crashing into it."

As we looked up together at the solid stone gate, Sharon admonished me in her frank New Yorker drawl. "Honey, Adi's intention is pure and full of love. That is a gate of love. I hope you can see that."

"Wow, I love that – 'Gate of Love.' Yes, Sharon, you're right, of course. My family, Adi's family, our dearest friends and his village all passed under it on our wedding day…and the gate will guard us for generations. Thanks, Sharon. I have to go find my husband to thank him for his brilliance!"

When I'd moved in two months earlier, my long wood tables, bought so long ago and stored in Gusti's wood warehouse for over a year, moved in too. Ten unfortunate neighbours had hauled each table down our laneway. When the men finally got them into the dining room, the tables fit perfectly, as if we had custom ordered them for the room.

Each table had been pushed to one side of our dining room to serve as huge buffet tables for our four hundred wedding guests. The remains of the wedding feast, laid out on platters, were now on the floor being shared by the guys as they chugged back Bintang beer.

Adi and his best buddies from Le Meridian sprawled out on our dining room floor, laughing boisterously. My heart filled with happiness seeing the pride and joy in Adi's eyes. He was enjoying the first dinner party with his best friends in the dining room that he'd built.

"What's so funny, guys?" I asked.

"Adi's won the all-time Top Employee Award at Le Meridien!" shouted out Wayan, one of the bartenders at the resort.

Looking at him suspiciously wondering if I needed to slow down the consumption of Bintang, I questioned, "Really? How did that happen? Adi stopped working over two months ago in preparation for our wedding and our move to Canada."

"They're teasing me, darling." Adi bumped Wayan in the shoulder.

Wiping the smile off his face, Wayan continued, "No really, Adi has won, hands down. Let me explain. When we all started at Le Meridien five years ago, we had extensive guest training. Our GM drilled it into us every day for a year. It was like a mantra. 'Your job is to turn a complainer into a happy guest, and a happy guest into a repeat guest.'"

"Okay, so how does this have anything to do with Adi?" I asked, slightly fearing the answer as the guys smirked back.

"Adi takes the prize because he turned a complainer into a happy guest. A happy guest into a repeat guest. And a repeat guest into a WIFE!"

I fussed around Adi like he was a newborn. We'd just spent four carefree days in Singapore and we were ready to depart for our respective destinations.

Nervously, I flipped the florescent orange tag around his neck saying, "First Time Flyer" so that it could be visibly seen. Adi was flying on his own from Singapore to Toronto with a four-hour stopover in Hong Kong, where I imagined I'd lose him forever if he didn't get to the right gate – there were over one hundred gates in Hong Kong's massive airport compared to Bali's ten.

Adi's solo flight situation had transpired because I was flying directly from Singapore to San Francisco. Being a foreigner in Bali, I always had to hold a return ticket off the island which was the ticket currently in my hand. Adi had to fly to Canada, as it was too difficult to obtain a U.S. travel visa for an Indonesian.

Adi shook his head when I asked him to doublecheck his travel belt for the umpteenth time. He patiently recounted the Singaporean dollars, Hong Kong dollars, U.S. dollars and Canadian dollars that I deemed necessary if something went wrong in transit. Adi even recited Kai Ma's and Grace's Hong Kong phone numbers by heart to reassure me. We'd had two and a half months to prepare for this. I looked at Adi who was calmly observing the coming and goings of those in the Changi airport. I realized that I was the one who wasn't ready to go.

✻

Our first few months as a married couple had flown by in whirlwind of activity. Our wedding, unintentionally and intentionally, continued for months after our official May 5th date.

"Darling, what's all the noise?" I asked, rubbing my sleepy eyes, pushing aside the mosquito net that wrapped around our bed.

Adi peeked out the small window and jumped back. He said in a panicked voice, "Hurry, get dressed, there's a hundred women in our courtyard carrying wedding gifts."

"What?" I shrieked as I leapt out of bed looking around for something appropriate. "Why are they here now? Don't they know our wedding was yesterday?"

"Oh yeah, I forgot. They must be from Banjar Gede. They had a wedding in their own banjar yesterday so they must have decided to come today instead."

"They can do that?" I shook my head as I wrapped myself in a sarong and quickly pulled on a lace kebaya. "Honey, you really need to prepare me better for life as your wife."

"I like how you say that. Please forgive me, my wife," Adi said, grinning as he pecked me on the lips and pulled open the door to greet our unexpected guests.

That evening, Ken and Patricia came earlier to join a reception at our family compound where we'd be formally accepted into the Banjar as a married couple. When Patricia peeked into our storage room, she was shocked to see hundreds of colourfully wrapped boxes stacked from floor to ceiling across the entire span of the wall.

"Are those your wedding presents?" Patricia asked in awe. "Why haven't you opened them?"

"Oh yeah, those. Why don't you go ahead, open one," I generously offered.

"I can't open your wedding presents," she replied, her eyebrows reaching up in wonder.

"No, seriously, you can open them. You'll see."

"Umm, okay." Patricia carefully peeled off the wrapping of one box and found six simple glasses, "Oh, these are nice."

"Now, open another one."

Patricia opened a similar sized box and found another set of six glasses but with a slightly different design. A third box revealed an etched glass bowl. The fourth, another six glasses of yet another pattern.

"There are probably six hundred glasses, fifty different sized bowls and a few sets of teacups stacked against that wall, in a variety of styles. None matching," I said with a sigh.

Patricia burst out laughing knowing how particular I was about, well, everything.

I was ready in my "join the Banjar" kebaya and sarong, but we wouldn't be taking on the village duties; we were moving to Canada instead. Back in February, Adi had spent countless nights explaining to his parents that there weren't any suitable jobs in Bali and moving to Toronto would only be for a maximum of five years. Bapak and Ibu understood, but having their only child leave was especially heartbreaking.

Sadly, the need for Balinese going overseas to earn money was becoming more and more common. Many worked on cruise ships to make ten times what they could in Bali. While we'd much prefer to stay in Bali, Adi and I agreed that this short-term sacrifice would give us the savings needed to start again when Bali recovered.

Our wedding festivities continued at Begawan Giri Estate where we held our Chinese tea ceremony. During the planning meeting, I'd asked for the Tea Lounge which overlooked the spectacular view of jungle and expansive gardens. The hotel would only permit our ceremony to be set up in the coconut grove because the Tea Lounge was reserved for staying guests. I'd conceded instead of complaining (who had I become?) Either I'd miraculously transformed into an acquiescent Balinese person, or I didn't want to wake from my wedding dream where Begawan Giri had actually become reality.

Adi and I arrived at the estate with his family and our photographer to do a family photo session before the other guests arrived. The set-up in the coconut grove looked a bit odd; the white banquet chairs stood out starkly against their lush green surroundings. To my utter delight, half an hour before the ceremony began, a large raindrop fell on my arm. Another blessing of holy water! The outdoor tea ceremony would be simply impossible with the rain. And so, the ceremony moved to the Tea Lounge which was the ideal place for our tea ceremony.

After the ceremony, we moved to the Kudus House, which perfectly fit our small group of guests of twenty-two dear friends and family. It was a lovely evening full of laughter and the most succulent Babi Guling we had ever eaten. Even Janet Z., who would become a top restaurateur and "Top Chef Canada" TV show judge, rated our wedding feast as the best she'd ever had. She gushed on about having two pieces of my dream wedding cake – a light chiffon sponge filled with wild strawberries and Chantilly cream. I'd been adamant that my cake was to be enjoyed right away, not preserved in inedible fondant.

Because of the ongoing SARS situation, my family scored a luxury stay at the Dusun Villas for under a hundred dollars a night for a three-bedroom pool villa. Yes, that's right. A honeymoon with my family; my nearest and dearest people.

Oddly, on our last night at the Dusun, my body broke out in hives and I turned red as a lobster. My left ear, the same one that I'd injured learning to dive, felt like it was being stabbed repeatedly by a thousand tiny needles. Dr. Oka came to the villa and gave me an injection to reduce the inflation of my hives and lessen the pain in my ear.

Adi's eyebrows were creased as he rubbed my arms gently, "Darling, how do you feel?"

"It's extremely itchy. I want to scratch my skin off. It feels like tiny worms crawling underneath the skin," I whined as tears smarted in my eyes. "And my head feels like it'll split open because of this ear pain."

"Hmm. I hope this isn't something from the wedding," Adi said.

"What do you mean, that was over a week ago? I'm sure it's an allergic reaction to the fish I ate at lunch," I said, closing my eyes as the medicine relaxed my body.

"Sure. Sure. We had our balian, Kakek Kuta protect our family compound for our wedding ceremonies, but he's not as powerful as he used to be," answered Adi.

"What do you mean? You think it's Black Magic?" I asked. I was perplexed as Adi remained secretive about Black Magic, never going into the specifics of how, or even what, it was.

"I hope not...but you never know. Don't worry. We'll have Kakek Kuta heal you before we leave." Adi pressed behind my left ear, comforting me with his touch and his words.

I kissed Adi hard when I left him at the check-in counter at Singapore Airlines. I turned back to memorize his outfit as I ran to catch my flight to San Francisco.

Our real honeymoon and time alone as newlyweds had started in Singapore a few days earlier. Adi's first flight ever took two and a half hours, but he said that it felt like five minutes – as if we flew up, and then right back down again. With the agonizing pain in my ear, it felt like the longest flight ever. Despite my discomfort, it was thrilling for me to witness Adi's first time flying. To pay homage to where our love story began, we chose to stay at Le Meridien on Orchard Road.

Twenty hours later, I was relieved to hear Adi's voice calling from Toronto. We'd reunite there as soon as I finished up in San Francisco.

His first experiences in Canada took him for a loop. Mom had picked him up from the airport at night. Adi was immediately confused as his watch showed 9:30 p.m., but the sun was bright.

"Mom, what time is it?" Adi asked thinking he didn't adjust his watch properly.

Mom replied, "It's nine thirty."

"Then why is the sun still out? In Bali, the sun sets around 6:30."

Mom laughed. "Of course, you're not used to this. The sun sets late in the summer here."

When they got to Mom's condo downtown, Adi's ears popped all the way up the elevator to the eleventh floor. Mom pulled Adi over to see the view from her balcony and didn't understand why he shook like a leaf and hung close to the wall. Only when Adi was back inside to safety would he explain to Mom that he'd never been in any building taller than a coconut tree.

The earache persisted so I consulted an ENT specialist when I arrived in Toronto a few days later. The ENT specialist performed weeks of tests on my ears but couldn't find anything medically wrong. From there, I'd spend years going to doctors and balians in Bali without finding a cure. It took me becoming a Pemangku, a temple priestess, and having Barong's power to ward off the Black Magic.

Mom threw a dinner reception for the friends and family in Toronto who hadn't been able to fly to Bali due to SARS. She'd planned to host the gathering in her brand-new condominium's party room. We'd even printed an additional palm leaf that matched our original wedding invitation to give to our Toronto guests. But when we arrived in July, the party room wasn't completed yet. This ended up being another Godsend!

Our Toronto reception ironically ended up at Four Seasons, where many of my business school friends had held theirs. To my delight, we scored the private dining room at Truffles, Four Seasons' Signature restaurant, not the generic ballroom. Usually, this would have been well-above the budget for our fifty guests. However, because of SARS, the top-tiered restaurants across the city, such as Truffles, offered significantly discounted 'Summerlicious' menus to lure diners back out. And they'd agreed to extend the special for our dinner reception!

It was the never-ending wedding celebration that I'd described growing up to Mom – one party after another, all in different settings and even in different countries.

Our final wedding 'event' was held at Toronto City Hall, where we had a civil ceremony to finalize our Canadian marriage papers. We were now officially husband and wife, in Bali and in Canada.

With everything in place, I was ready to show Adi my world. I imagined years of joy and adventure in Toronto, but I would be wrong.

SIGN UP FOR PRIESTESS POSTCARDS

Thank you for reading my first memoir, TRESNA, Gate of Love. I hope you'll join me on the rest of my journey in the series, Chronicles of a Balinese Priestess.

I would be very grateful if you can write a review so more people can learn about my book.

Please review this book at:

Amazon

Barnes and Noble

Chapter/Indigo

Goodreads

Please sign up for my monthly postcards from Bali where you'll get inside peeks of real-life as a Balinese priestess at Frances Tse Ardika.

To thank you for your review and signing up for my monthly priestess postcards, you'll receive our online wedding album from 5-5-5!

BLESSINGS AND GRATITUDE

LOVE is what TRESNA means. This book was built on the love of so many...

My biggest cheerleader has always been my mom, Bessie. She walked over to Grace Hospital and pushed me out in the early wee hours of October 10th, 1969. And then, thirty-one years later, she missed her flight to Bali so I'd finally meet my soulmate, Adi on October 10th, 2000. And now, I'm birthing my first memoir TRESNA, Gate of Love on October 10th, 2021. Thank you, Mom! I love you.

If you're meeting Adi in these pages for the first time, you may think I've exaggerated his character. But in real-life, he's so much more than the sum of my 4Cs, he's my E. *Titiang tresna tekan bli, Adi.*

Thank you, my darling daughter, Santi for being the best bookworm ever – some of my most cherished moments are of us laughing over words, what they mean, how they sound, and having your dad look at us like we're nuts!

Como, thank you for being my shadow, my protector and my foot warmer.

Dad and Ratu Aji, I see you both everyday when the butterflies flutter around me in Adi's garden. Dad, thank you for teaching me that I needed to find a candle. Ratu Aji, thank you for pushing me to write my books.

Barong, my tiger God. Thank you for everything.

Grace, my best friend, and life-long ally, I've adored you since I was two. Being 'lost together' with you taught me about love and life. Thank you for your massive heart and the ability to always find the right words for me. I love you.

For my dear brother, Andrew who transformed into "A Sign from God!" When I ask him important life-defining questions such as "Would you like mango or rambutan for dessert?" he always has one answer, "Hard to say..." But when asked about my previous cover options, he called me immediately (he NEVER calls me) and wrote multiple very-opinionated emails detailing what I really needed. Thank you, Andrew for speaking up when it really matters. I love you!

Ken, my dearest younger brother whom I've always looked up to, thank you for always being there for me! I love you so much. The Little Wooden Cottage is waiting for you (and Maia and Alex, of course!)

My real-life fairy godmother, Kai Ma, you inspire me to always create, give, look for beauty and what lies deeper. Thank you. The other Little Wooden Cottage is waiting for you, Kai Ye and Dong Dong! I love you all.

For my beta-readers and blurb-beaters: Alysson, Anthea, Judy, Justin, Karoline, and Marnie, I'm so grateful for all your different insights and viewpoints. And thank you, Anthea, my fairy for adding your magic to my website.

I'm truly blessed to find a book team who I'll have for the entire series of Chronicles of a Balinese Priestess. My first draft was completed in ninety days because of my wonderful writing coach, Rachael Herron and an amazing group of newbie women writers who cheered me on. Thank you, Tenyia Lee for your thorough developmental and line-edits. I loved learning more about the craft of writing from you. Thank you, Britanie Wilson for your keen eye and understanding of Canadian verbiage. Thank you, Xavier Comos at Cover Kitchen for dishing up the best covers ever – I can't wait until my readers see how the whole series comes together!

Thank you to all those who've touched my heart and given Bali so much love – family, friends, and clients from Taksu Bali shop, Taksu Bali Travel & Weddings, Tresna Bali Cooking School, and our Little Wooden Cottage who've become our village. You and thousands of donors from all over the world rose up together to support feedbali.com. Thank you. My series will donate 10% of all profits FOREVER to Yayasan Tresna Bali Jaya. Together, we'll protect this magical island, her rich culture, her natural beauty and her kind people.

Om Santi Santi Santi Om.

ABOUT THE AUTHOR

Originally from Canada, Frances Tse Ardika met her future husband on her third day in Bali on October 8, 2000, and in the years that follow, she'd fulfill her destiny as the first foreigner to become a Balinese Pemangku (Temple Priestess).

Prior to settling in Bali, she lived and worked in Hong Kong, London, San Francisco, Tokyo, and Toronto. Together with her husband, Adi, Frances owns Taksu Bali Travel & Weddings, Tresna Bali Cooking School, and two lovely Little Wooden Cottages in Ubud, Bali. When Covid-19 hit Bali in March 2020, they pivoted their businesses to create Feed Bali, which has provided over half a million meals to feed almost 5000 families.

Frances is the proud mum of Santi, her fellow bookworm and Como, her loyal rescue pup. If she's not typing away on her computer, you'll find her baking delectable cream scones or wrapping dumplings with her daughter. Or perhaps walking in Adi's garden with Como at her heels.

She loves sharing her deep knowledge of places to eat, play, pray and stay in Bali with like-minded foodies and travellers. And hopes one day to have the biggest book club in Bali!

If you'd like to receive her monthly postcards from Bali and join our Tresna Bali community, please sign up here www.francestseardika.com.

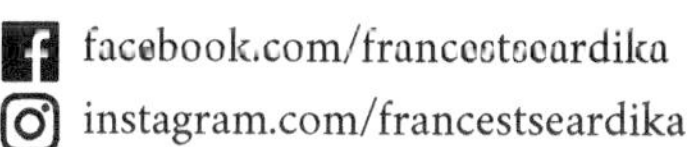